Spiritual

Quest

The Journey of

Self Discovery

Sandy Newell

Acknowledgments

During the wonder-filled process of writing what is contained within there have been many people who have been a part of the journey.

My children you have inspired me to be the best person I can be. It is my wish that the world you look at reflects the qualities of love, peace and happiness. You are the light of my life.

My Earth Angel sisters, your unconditional love and support warms my heart. You have held my hand, watched me fall, picked me up and walked along side me every step of the way. Our circle of five.

Mum whose patience is second to none. Your nurturing, kind nature makes you the most beautiful person. Dad-forever alive in our hearts.

John, whose creative spirit turned notepad pages into something of significance.

Thank you to the mentors and friends who have walked with me through the different stages of my journey, to you I am truly grateful.

I am honoured and humbled by spirit. Thank you for the inspiration and insight that helped form the concepts presented on the pages of this book. By allowing spirit to flow through me I have realised that the desire to live our dream is essentially our purpose calling us to act.

My gratitude goes to those of you who read what is written in these pages. May your journey be in the direction of your dreams.

With Love, Sandy

CONTENTS

Welcome	7
REFLECTIONS	
Abundance	15
Acceptance	24
Balance	38
Believe	48
Bliss	57
Blockage	74
Change	94
Clarity	103
Connection	123
Contemplation	140
Creativity	148
Dream	162
Embrace	171
Empowerment	182
Energy	202
Enlightenment	212
Expression	226
Flow	237
Forgiveness	251
Happiness	264
Harmony	275

Healing	*283*
Hope	305
Imagination	312
Inner Child	321
Inner Sanctuary	347
Inspiration	356
Intention	363
Intuition	*371*
Journal	*380*
Journey	393
Karma	429
Love	443
Miracle	455
Past, Present, Future	466
Perception	*479*
Purpose	489
Reflection	499
Reframe	*507*
Seed Of Light	516
Shadow	*525*
Transformation	*549*
Transition	561
Trust	*573*
Wisdom	590
Energy Centres	600

Spiritual First Aid	647
Letter of Commitment	657
About	*658*
Glossary	660

Disclaimer

The material contained within is not meant as a replacement for medical or psychological assistance. The information contained within is from the writer's perspective. The content is meant for entertainment purposes only. There is no research or clinical trials to back its compilation.

The writer or any associates assume no liabilities of any kind with respect to the accuracy or completeness of the contents. Choosing to implement any of the information provided is the responsibility of those choosing to do so and not of the writer, or any associate.

If there has been a history of trauma or abuse it is recommended that professional assistance be sought before attempting any of that contained within. To do so is at the discretion of the reader.

Copyright © Sandra Lee Stevenson-Newell 2017

This book is copyright. No part of this book can be used or reproduced in any form without written confirmation from the author. For more information please contact www.souldrivenlife.net

First Edited by Jan Shakespeare

Welcome to the amazing journey you are about to embark on. By selecting this book you have awakened to the fact that you are on a spiritual journey. This book will assist you by taking you to where your journey begins. Being the realm of your Inner-Self, it is here that your Essence resides and by connecting with your Essence you will have everything you need to expand and evolve into all you can be.

By unveiling your Inner-Self you will not only gain immense insight into who you are and what you are here to do, but also about life and all it pertains. Such insight branches you laterally and brings to light that you are a multidimensional being. And, that you are Soul, partaking in physical life composed of what is perceived as mind, body and spirit. This trio is often viewed as individual aspects, but in fact are interrelated in every sense of the meaning.

Embracing the wholistic nature of your being facilitates balance and wellbeing, both of which are the precursors of living a fulfilled life.

However, we often get distracted, lose connection

with our inner-selves, and become heavily influenced by external happenings. We find ourselves dealing with the demands of daily life and lose touch with what is really important. The way this is experienced is different for everybody, but those of you reading this get the gist of what I am talking about. Basically we find ourselves stumbling along, rolling from one day to the next, year to year doing the same thing. Our aspirations dull along the way and the likelihood of taking the plunge seems to move further away with each passing year.

The ramifications of this cycle means we under achieve in the creation of what we really want and become slaves to our own grind, all the while feeling unfulfilled. You may wonder if there is more to life and if there is, why haven't you found it. We tend then to settle into a comfort zone thinking aspirations are merely wishes that will never manifest.

Perhaps this sounds like a dismal story, but it is just that, a story. that is being played out by you as the main character. But, here within lies a grand power because as the main character and director of your story, you have the power to edit the story and recreate it in any way you want.

Firstly it is imperative to acknowledge where you see yourself right now at this point in time. Wherever you find yourself is the starting point for the next stage of your journey. It is here that you will explore your thoughts and feelings, which serve an important purpose as when they are acknowledged you will see that everything around you reflects some aspect of yourself. Don't believe this? Delve into this book and see that as perceptions, thoughts and feelings shift so does the world around you.

The birth of new awareness is to see through the eyes of the heart and Soul. When the eyes of the heart and Soul are open we see the miracles in everyday life. This is to live as an enlightened being. That's right you don't have to go running off in search of spiritual enlightenment. Because all that can give you spiritual enlightenment exists within you. Yes, it lives and breathes in you. You only need remember how to harness its qualities.

By picking up this book you hold the reflections, tools and techniques that will help you remember and thus assist your life journey, which is your Spiritual Quest.

There are several ways to use this book. You can read it from front cover to back. You can select a chapter of interest or that is relevant to you now. You can randomly choose a reflection and read. Or you can flip through the pages and stop where you feel you would like to. This is harnessing your own intuitive ability and trusting that you will receive exactly what you require. You have all that you need to take it from here.

May you journey with love in your heart and be guided by the light of your Soul.

Each chapter contains icons representing the following

Reflect

This is a concept developed for personal reflection, where the content is open for interpretation based upon what is required for you, individually. Allow yourself to soften and relax. Open your mind and your heart to receive the gifts contained within.

Create

Create consolidates what has been reflected upon, emphasizing certain key aspects. These are tools and techniques with unique attributes available for personal use. They are quick, accessible; provide instant effect and pearls of wisdom to ponder.

Pledges

Pledges are a declaration of commitment to Self, effective for bypassing conscious scrutiny and to enlighten the unconscious. These can be personalized to your unique requirements or objectives. Audio Pledges are available on the website: www.souldrivenlife.net

Affirmations

Potent, positive reinforcement that engages the mind for beneficial outcome. When said often the unconscious internalizes and accepts the affirmation. Can be used as an instant exchange for non-serving thoughts, or at any time for additional strengthening of purpose or resolve.

Journeys

These Journeys are a delightful way of connecting with your Inner-Self providing insight that facilitates awareness and understanding. They help you build confidence on your path of Self-discovery and enjoy the wonderfully positive effects of feeling more balanced, harmonious and calm.

THE

JOURNEYS

> *It is not by coincidence that those who open their hearts and minds to receive are those who discover exactly what they are looking for and exactly what they need.*

Spiritual Quest

Abundance

Immerse yourself in the abundance that surrounds you

 By tuning into feelings of abundance you create a positive vibration. It is this vibration that attracts to you the what you desire.

Whether you are aware of vibration or not we all have a rate at which we vibrate and it fluctuates in accordance with our thoughts and feelings.

For example have you ever noticed that the day you are feeling 'out of sorts' is the same day you come across people who mirror your feelings. Now consider when you go out feeling great. These are the days you come across people who mirror the same.

This is a reflection of what your vibration is aligning with.

Now you know this, you can become more aware of how what is external to you is a reflection of what is internal. It is this astounding realisation that brings true meaning of you create your reality.

Let us look at the vibration of abundance creating abundance. There is a natural law of the Universe, known as The Law of Attraction, that specifies that what we put out is what you will get back. What we are talking about here is your inner vibration. Superficial projections do not fool this law is is attuned to the vibration of your inner thoughts and feelings.

If the vibration of inner thoughts and feelings are attuned to the frequency of lack then that is what will be returned. Same is true if thoughts and feelings are aligned with the frequency of abundance. Abundance is what we will receive.

CREATING A VIBRATION OF ABUNDANCE THROUGH GRATITUDE

One way of creating a vibration of abundance is through gratitude. Having gratitude creates a vibration to receive as we are appreciating all that we have. Such appreciation creates an opening to receive.

One of the first things to do right now is to grab a piece of paper and write down what you are grateful for. If you are feeling challenged to think of anything to be grateful for think about this. The fact that you are reading this means that higher awareness has awakened within you and that is something to be grateful for.

Looking at nature offers immense appreciation. Each morning the sun blesses us with a new day. The sun invigorates and restores energy. Its radiance is essential for life. That is something to be grateful for. With a little focus or re-focus there are plenty of things to be grateful for.

TECHNIQUE

Practising the art of appreciation and gratitude opens the channels to receive. Be mindful of where you are placing your focus. When it comes to the Law of Attraction there is no differentiation between positive and negative. We get what we focus on. Positive attracts positive and negative attracts negative.

Generating positivity in your life begins with your thoughts. Positive thoughts carry positive energy that will attract like energy. The same is true for negative thoughts. Focusing on what is not wanted sends energy to that very thing and calls it in.

Becoming aware of the energy your thoughts are generating is imperative. When negative thoughts are detected they can be exchanged for positive. The use of visual images is of great assistance, as it keeps the mind positively focused.

So what happens when your visual image is positive and you are thinking positive thoughts but not receiving the desired outcome?

Although aligning what you see, hear and feel with positivity will have a positive impact on your life there may be aspects that reside in your subconscious that have the opposing affect.
These are the underlying beliefs, emotions and the inner-dialogue that opposes the positive intentions.

Underlying beliefs and emotions emit energy and if that energy is negative then negativity will be attracted. This invites the assessment of the beliefs and emotions.

Identifying the beliefs and emotions that undermine your good intentions can be done using tools such as reflection, journaling and meditation. These tools enhance conscious awareness. When consciously aware you are empowered to shift the energetic atmosphere, which will align you more closely with your Abundance vibration.

INFUSE YOUR DAY WITH FEELINGS OF ABUNDANCE

Start your day with gratitude; you have the gift of a new day ripe with opportunity.

Be thankful for the food you eat, taste it and feel it nourishing every cell in your body. If it doesn't nourish you, don't eat it.

Appreciate the water you drink. Water cleanses and hydrates. Feeling drained? Try a fresh glass of water as a remedy. It is instantly gratifying.

Be thankful for your health and maintain it by using a natural, practical approach. If unwell utilize the time to rest and repair. Sickness is the body communicating that something is in need of attention. Attend and be healthy.

Appreciation of what you have right now, no matter how big or small, generates a positive vibration and a positive mindset. Be grateful to be on this Earth with the opportunity to experience life and all it has to offer.

Expand feelings of appreciation of what you have into what you want. Attune your thoughts and feelings with your inherent abundant vibration and watch a radical new way of being evolve.

PLEDGE OF ABUNDANCE

I immerse myself in the Abundance that surrounds me. I attune my thoughts and feelings to the vibration of positivity. I expand feelings of gratitude for all I have right now. Through gratitude and appreciation of what I have. I align my vibration to receive. I accept the abundance that now flows into my life.

SUMMARY

- Expand feelings of appreciation of what you have into what you want.
- Attune your thoughts and feelings with positive vibration.
- Through gratitude and appreciation of what you have you align your vibration to receiving.
- Abundance begins to flow the more open and accepting you become.
- Continued gratitude and appreciation enhances and expands your energy reaching outward to connect with like energy.
- Positivity maintains the flow.
- Life is enriched by the fulfillment of wishes,

hopes and dreams.

ABUNDANCE

I open my arms to receive the abundance entering my life.

Spiritual Quest

Acceptance

Peace is found through the grace of acceptance

 We cannot change what has been done, trying to do so is like trying to push the river in the opposite direction to the way it flows. Lack of acceptance can cause us to become stuck with burdens from long ago.

Accepting what has happened helps the emotional aspects that are attached to loosen their grip. As the emotions loosen their grip and begin to let go, we find ourselves more able to move into a space of acceptance. This is to let go of whatever ties us to an experience, an event, circumstances or a situation.

Letting go gives us the freedom to take back our power and cease feeding our valuable energy to an unworthy cause. Letting go is not about forgetting or not caring, but about releasing the associated inner conflict. Any form of inner turmoil prevents us from finding inner peace.

Being at peace within oneself is to accept all aspects of self. There are many aspects that contribute to our assumed identity. Some we know and some are yet to be unveiled. The way to get to know is to explore the inner realms of self. To do this requires one to be accepting of any aspect that surfaces.

Denying any aspect of self is what distances you from getting to know who you are. Denied aspects do not disappear because we refuse to acknowledge them, they lurk as shadow aspects that negatively influence thoughts and feelings.

You may be unconsciously aware this aspects exists, but denying its existence sends the message that it is unacceptable in some way. This sews the feeling of non-acceptance. This inner conflict interferes with our connection to your Higher Self, which is the most important connection to have.

How do we accept what we deem unacceptable and rekindle connection to our Higher Self? What we deem unacceptable aspects of self are not unacceptable at all, they are misunderstood aspects created through interpretations of our experiences.

These are unfulfilled needs that crave attention. Identifying aspects and uncovering needs require some investigation to facilitate understanding.

Reflecting upon experiences allows you to establish how experiences were interpreted and identify the thoughts, feelings and behaviours that have emerged from this. This insight provides you with an opportunity to see the emotional connections and how these emotions trigger behaviour. Rather than focusing on the behaviour you begin to see the reason for reactions.

Acknowledging yourself in this way enables you to understand and empathize with why you do the things you do. This facilitates self-acceptance.

Self-acceptance also helps us to accept others as we can see how each one of us responds to emotional triggers. This does not mean that we have to accept certain types of behaviour, but it does allow us to accept why people do the things they do.

The behaviour and actions of self and others represents the inner workings of our personal thoughts and emotions. Knowing this lessens the impulse to take things personally and instead focuses on what we can learn from what is experienced.

If something causes sadness we can feel what it is like to be touched by compassion. If we undergo hardship we learn how to be resilient.

While we can have empathy for what others have experienced, it is when we experience things for ourselves that we gain true comprehension.

We learn and grow through experience. Accepting this as part of life and being aware of what manifests on an emotional and physical level enables us to deal with the outcomes of our experiences effectively. When this view is embraced, it become evident that life happens for us.

Looking at the bigger picture of what life presents awakens us to how and what we learn through our experiences. When we do a check of emotions attached to past or current experiences it is important to sit with them and derive meaning.

Experiences are interpreted through your emotions, thus the importance of gaining insight and attending to what you are feeling, how you are feeling and even where in your body you feel.

If we do not process the emotional connection to an experience we risk distorting perspective and stealing from ourselves something of value. Finding the lesson of the experience facilitates wisdom. Through wisdom of past experience we can make choices aligned with what is in our best interest. This is how we steer ourselves forward in positive ways.

Acceptance is not admitting defeat or being dis-empowered, it is finding peace with what we cannot change and choosing to focus on areas we can. Acceptance leads to forgiveness in which we are able to forgive those who have caused discomfort and conflict in our lives. This includes accepting ourselves by understanding the reasons why we do the things we do.

Self-acceptance is to embrace those aspects that are in conflict. This enables us to make choices that are aligned with what we want for ourselves now and for the future. Acceptance is the healing code that empathises with individual aspects and enables them to find solace. Once achieved these aspects no longer thirst for attention and will soften and assimilate to become one with the whole of our being. This enables us to take charge of our lives and live as we choose.

The Gift of Acceptance

Settle into a comfortable position. Take a deep breath in through your nose and then exhale out through your mouth.

Relax on the in breath and on the out breath imagine all tension is being released. Repeat this a few times until feeling calm and relaxed.

You see yourself going on a journey. It is the journey of life. Upon this journey you will encounter many things that will come packaged as experiences. An experience may be an event that occurs or circumstances that you find yourself faced with.

You find yourself at one of your favourite places, this is a place you feel comfortable. You are waiting for a gift to arrive.

Your gift may be presented as an event or a set of circumstance that oppose what you would have hope for. You look at this gift and feel like giving it back to the person delivering it, thinking why would you ever want a gift like that.

Sensing your apprehension the person delivering

the gift puts it down at your feet and disappears.

You now have a choice to continue to think of this gift as an unwanted interference to your life or you can open the gift and see what it contains.

You decide to open the gift and find that within it contains something, maybe more than one thing that you had not expected to find. The gift of your experience has given you more than you could have anticipated.

If what you receive is unpleasant know that you can view the light and shadow aspects of the experience. Today you are choosing to shine the light on the shadow.

There are light and shadow aspects of every experience. But you know that focusing on the shadow aspects will do little to assist your journey. However by turning your attention to what has been gained you can see that the experience has provided you with something of value. Ponder what this is.

How have your experiences contributed to who you are today? Ponder this from a positive perspective. If you find this challenging ask yourself what someone close to you might say about you or if this is difficult ask what your guardian angel would say about you.

It is important to expand perspective on experiences. Different perspectives enhances insight. From this we can uncover the gem. The gem being what was learned or realised from the experience. This instills some positive association to the experience. For example, when I was a teen, I was steering onto an undesirable path. I went jogging one day and was hit by a car. This resulted in years of pain, immobility, emotional turmoil and immense fatigue. I was unable to remain awake for more than half hour at a time, after which I would sleep for hours. If someone had of told me that there was a gem in this experience, I would have thought they were absolutely crazy. However, as it turns out there were many gems in this experience and the gems continue to be uncovered. For example sometime when I feel it is impossible to do something, such as committing to writing a book, I am reminded of all that I endured and overcome in those years.

Emphasizing the positive does not dissolve the negative association, but it does provide choice. From which perspective do you want to see this from? It serves no purpose to hold onto counterproductive emotion, except that it puts a gaping hole in the ability to be happy.

When I talk about negative association this is termed only for identification purposes. Often negative is associated with bad and positive with good. However, as has been expressed hat appears as negative can have positive outcome for example building inner determination and courage.

Acceptance is not always easy, but if the layers of an experience are peeled back then deeper understanding can be obtained. It is through this understanding that acceptance can be derived.

Moving from the physical, mental and emotional aspects of an experience, to how the experience has assisted your growth is to see from a spiritual warrior perspective.

Think about such things as resilience, empathy, compassion, understanding. If an experience is casting a shadow over you and interfering with your ability to find happiness it is because the pearl laying at the core of the experience is yet to be uncovered.

A way to uncover the pearl at the core of an

experience is to think of yourself as an observer of the experience. An alternative perspective is gained when observed through objective, rather than subjective eyes. This is often what is needed before clarity and understanding can be obtained.

To assist any resistance to acceptance start by trying to describe what the resistance looks and/or feels like. Then see this as an aspect of self that is unable to accept. If it is not possible to gain an alternative perspective then do not burden yourself, but rather accept that this is how is if at this point in time.

Recognize that this is not the whole self and that although one aspect may not be able to derive acceptance it doesn't mean that it has to hold you back. Acceptance may arrive in an unexpected way and when least expected.

PLEDGE OF ACCEPTANCE

I accept that there are things I can change and things I cannot. Accepting what I cannot change frees me to focus on that which I can. Release from the past enhances the choices I make in the present. This creates a positive foundation for my future. I know that my way forward is focusing on what I want and making continued progress in that direction. Everyday I do something that contributes to my growth. My continued development sees me positioned exactly where I need to be. I accept the responsibility; I am the driver of my destiny. I choose to focus on what moves me forward in a positive direction.

Let go of all that has caused emotional pain. It may not be easy to do, but it will be most liberating and rewarding. The alternative is holding on, which will only cause inner conflict. Accepting that the only way forward is to let go is like being lifted upon the wings of the angels and carried toward a life of fulfillment.

SUMMARY

- Accepting what you cannot change and changing what you can enables us to let go and shift direction.
- Holding on causes conflict, letting go allows freedom.
- Derive meaning and accept that there is a lesson to every experience.
- This is holding the torch as you travel.
- To be bound to the experience itself is likened to travelling in the dark.
- Acceptance leads to forgiveness in which you are able to forgive all who have caused discomfort and conflict in your life, including yourself.
- Free yourself from the fragments of the past and accept that from this point forward you are free to live as you choose.
- Acceptance will facilitate forgiveness. Forgiveness heals the broken-hearted.

ACCEPTANCE

*I find inner peace
through the grace of acceptance*

Much of what happens in life is unknown; it is how we work with what happens that determines the journey.

Balance

You are a multidimensional being. A Soul utilizing the body as a temple to experience physical life.

Feeling the body, hearing the mind, and connecting with the Soul is the secret to finding and maintaining personal balance and well-being. Ailments of the body, agitation of mind and restlessness of spirit indicate the need for balance. Inner guidance comes as an aid when balance is called for. Answer the call and attend until the natural state of equilibrium is restored. You have discovered the secret language that holds the key to inner balance and well-being.

As multidimensional beings synchronization of the mind, the body and the Soul, which is ultimately one and the same, viewed from different perspectives, is the foundation on which balance is created.

How does one find balance? Finding balance requires assessment of priorities and questioning how much time and energy is dedicated to those priorities.

Priority assessment provides an overview of how

time and energy is distributed. Looking at the priority scale will show that what is thought of as a priority may not be receiving as much attention as assumed.

Work/family balance is an example of how the priority scales can easily tip without detection. Family is often the priority and work is the means to support the financial needs of the family as well as maybe fulfilling certain personal aspirations.

However, often so much time and energy is dedicated to work that it zaps time and energy from the family. Second priority interferes with the main priority. This changes the question from where do your priorities lie to how are your priorities attended to?

Putting time and energy into any one thing to the detriment of all else tips the scales in an unfavourable direction. Once the scales tip there are feelings of stress and dissatisfaction. This is the first indication that there is a need for re-balance.

Appraising where and how time and energy is

being distributed calls for consultation with the inner well-being manager. This aspect will assess the reality of where time and energy is being distributed. This honest appraisal is guided by the Higher Self, which may arrange priorities differently to what is currently adhered to.

The Higher Self will evaluate from soul perspective and deliver an appraisal which places Soul as the number one priority. If the needs of the Soul are being attended to other areas of life will begin to shift in favourable ways. And although it won't always be smooth sailing there will be deeper understanding of what happens and why.

But, who has time to be bothered with Soul stuff when there is a busy world whirling around us? The answer is that natural flow and order is derived from being Soul conscious, thus begins the exploration of the mind, body and spiritual interconnection and how this relates to overall well-being.

At some stage during life, the yearning to find balance will boil up into the consciousness and set one upon the path of Soul awakening. This does not mean meditating morning, noon and night to the detriment of all else. What it does mean is balancing all aspects of life so they work in harmony with each other. This is the emergence of mind/body/soul unity.

Finding balance is to appraise time and energy dedication and redirect as deemed necessary. To help with the appraisal tune into higher aspects of Self to receive wise guidance and counsel. Achieve this by using the breath to bring your focus within. Please note, when higher aspect is used this is not meant in a hierarchical sense, but more as way to describe consciousness.

Conscious use of the breath helps reduce mind chatter and opens communication with the Higher Self. This is where mind, body and soul can merge. Together these three active components of your being will demonstrate how working with one attends to all. An interconnection that will guide what is needed to achieve balance.

Spiritual Quest

TECHNIQUE

It is advantageous to make regular visits to the space where mind, body and soul merge as from it comes a sense of inner-peace which will expand outward and touch every day in many ways.

Take a deep breath in through the nose and exhale out through the mouth. Repeat this a few times and as you do feel your body relax and your mind become calm.

When you have reached a state of calm, your thoughts have settled and you are comfortably focused on your breathing, ask yourself how can I best achieve balance?

Just allow whatever comes to float into your mind without becoming attached or trying to figure out solutions. Allow this process to continue until you feel you have gained enough insight into which areas of your life need attention. Observe intuitively guided solutions.

In a journal or on a piece of paper draw **a circle**.

Take a deep refreshing breath before bringing your focus back to the present. When you have returned to the present moment pick up a pencil.

Firstly you may like to write what was revealed in the mini reflection. Then think about each area of your life.

From the centre of the circle draw lines outward in proportion to the amount of focus given to each area of your life.

- Evaluate the picture. Does it look balanced?
- Is there a proportion of time dedicated to you?
- Are your priorities receiving the attention you think they do?

Shift the lines of your circle to reflect how you would like to see your life balanced. Remember to make room for any projects or hobbies that you would like to do.

Although you may not be able to see a way of doing them at this point in time, by placing them in your circle you are setting an intention and within time you will find yourself fulfilling your desire.

Sit back and take a look at your circle.

What does it reflect?

If you can see imbalance shift your lines and keep adjusting until you see balance emerging.

When you are happy with your Circle Of Balance draw a new circle reflecting your adjustments. Commit to applying at least one of these changes over the coming week.

Revisit your Circle of Balance on a daily basis to ensure you remain on track and are making the adjustments needed to create balance.

This circle is a tool that can help prioritize and balance the essential and non-essential aspects of your life.

PLEDGE OF BALANCE

I balance my life by giving equal attention to what I want to do and what I have to do. I prioritize to ensure I am able to do something for my mind, for my body and for my spirit. I balance work and play, so I get the most out of every day. My balanced approach keeps me goal focused and action oriented. I am actively achieving what I aspire to achieve.

SUMMARY

- Synchronization of all that you are forms the foundation on which balance is created.
- Anchoring self upon the core of your being is the pivotal point of centredness.
- Ailments of the body, agitation of mind and restlessness of spirit indicate the need for balance.
- Inner guidance comes as an aid when

balance is called for.
- Answer the call and attend until the natural state of equilibrium is restored.
- You have discovered the secret language that holds the key to inner balance and well-being.

BALANCE

Through balance I nourish my mind and body. This liberates my Soul and enables me to live a fulfilled life.

Believe

Believe in Yourself

 Belief has the capacity to motivate people to do extraordinary things.

Self-belief contributes enormous power and influence to every aspect of life. You are the one who holds the key to your destiny. Through higher aspects of Self you connect with intuition guidance. Here lies the untainted seed of self-belief. Those which do not contain preconceived ideas about self.

The intuitive Self holds the truth of who you are and knows you are much more than the underdeveloped parts of the mind can conceive.

When we introduce the intellect into the equation we orchestrate a powerful force. Intellect and intuition are phenomenal companions, with the capacity to make anything possible. Believing in oneself ignites the flame of potential. Believe you can and you will.

The same is true when there is a lack of self-belief heard as the, "I can't", mantra that douses creative ability and defuses the energy to fulfill aspirations.

Doubt is a response to things that we are uncertain of, that confront our ability to do something or challenge us to step into unknown territory. Succumbing to doubt is to allow doubtful inner-dialogue to go on unchallenged. This reinforces a low opinion of self which effects emotional well-being, actions, behaviour and causes self-esteem to plummet, resulting in feelings of being inept, worthless, unlovable or whatever else we can drag ourselves down with.

This is a form of self abuse and requires urgent attention to encourage and nurture the esteem into a state of health. First is to contemplate self defeating beliefs and reflect on the impact these beliefs have on thoughts and feelings.

A process that begins by identifying the aspects that are dousing self-belief. Often these aspects are holding on to outdated beliefs that are not even factual but a perception formed at a time when feeling insecure, lonely, conflicted, lost, isolated, rejected and the list goes on.

If not expressed these emotions get stuck and repeat, through inner self talk and negative mantras. The cycle of belief reinforcement continues: belief stimulates emotion, emotion stimulates thought and thought reinforces belief.

Thoughts, emotions and beliefs are intricately connected. Actions and behaviour reflect whether this cycle is pivoting on a positive or negative axis. Negative behaviour will be accepted as normal until awareness dawns and associated repercussions of the behaviour are recognized as being less than satisfactory. It then becomes apparent that change is needed.

This insight provides the awareness needed to exchange dis-empowering beliefs for ones that empower and build self-esteem. To enact such requires the conscious decision to take action and make a firm pledge to weather the storms and accept the challenges encountered along the rambling path of self-discovery.

Ensure to travel with patience and determination as they will make the most reliable and worthwhile companions.

Being aligned with the values of kindness, empathy, gratitude and honesty is to be aligned with the good of all. Anything opposing this serves only to cause internal and external conflict and disharmony.

The need to compare, judge and criticise comes from dis-empowered aspects of self. These aspects are shadowed by their own insecurities, which are then projected onto others without thought or feeling about what it might be like to live the life of that person. The saying "When you point one finger, there are three fingers pointing back to you." is potent, particularly from an energetic perspective, as the negativity generated by this reinforces self-doubt.

The flip side of this is to choose to see positive aspects in others. This facilitates self-belief especially when we contemplate the 'little known truth' that what we see in others exists within ourselves.

Oftentimes we measure ourselves against others, this is destined to cripple even the most robust esteem. Instead find satisfaction in your own achievements because no matter how big or small, the person who needs to recognise them is YOU!! This is the foundation self-belief is built upon.

Exchange Self-doubt for self-belief

Be aware of the presence of doubt and how limiting it is. Transform doubt and limitation into certainty and conviction. This is done by constructing thoughts so they facilitate self-belief. Remain aware of how inner-dialogue is making you feel. If it is dampening your spirits shift it immediately. This can be done by flicking the switch into affirmation mode or envisioning a positive image in your mind.

Continue to redirect thoughts until they follow the direction you want to go. There may be times when you stumble. Keep going and allow the emerging power of self-belief pick you up and carry you further than you thought possible. Stand tall within yourself and remember that if you believe you can, then without doubt you will.

See yourself illuminated in light and say "I believe in me" and persist through thoughts that may try to oppose this mantra. There may be tears as anything blocking you surfaces. The reassurance of the mantra will help them shift perspective. Keep going for a full ten minutes and keep the mantra going in your mind for a day. If negativity or detrimental inner-dialogue arises repeat the mantra " I believe in me".

Crossing the bridge to self belief is liberating. New confidence will emerge and give you the courage to follow your dreams, your passions and to take on things you may have wanted to do, but thought you would not be able to. "I believe in me". Keep this at the forefront of your mind.

The power of this belief empowers you to be the person capable of achieving anything you deem possible and as anything is possible this offers enormous scope.

Read, write, listen to, watch and research material that develops self-awareness. Exchanging old beliefs for new and enhancing what is already known will see the emergence of a renewed sense of self. A self that will strive and achieve the excellence you deserve.

PLEDGE OF BELIEF

I believe in myself wholeheartedly, as I am the one who holds the key to my greatness. I choose to unlock the vision of my true self which is that of my spirit, created in love and light from the ultimate source of energy. I evoke this energy and recognize the dynamic being that I am. I am **me** -with gifts and talents that are unique. Every aspect of me has been created through perception and I can recreate that perception as I choose.

SUMMARY

- Believe in yourself as you are the one who holds the key to your destiny.
- Disengage from imposed beliefs.
- Move beyond obstacles that distort your self-belief, as they serve only to sabotage.
- Believing in yourself holds enormous power and influence.
- Instilling conviction into self-belief is symbolic of spreading your wings to fly.

- Reach through the compromising layers of the intellect and assume the position of empowerment.
- Igniting the potential of belief in self will set you free to soar to heights of great magnitude.

BELIEVE

I see myself as a dynamic being capable of doing all I imagine. I utilize the combined power of my intuition and intellect to create a self-belief of phenomenal power.

Spiritual Quest

Bliss

Bliss is found by aligning thoughts with positivity

Bliss is the natural state of the soul achieved by being present, which enables soul essence to flow through you.

Connecting with the soul is to open the channel that connects heaven and earth. This connection brings peace and harmony to the inner being, which is to experience a state of inner bliss. Achieved by being centered in the present moment where feelings of love, gratitude and joy can be captured and truly appreciated. Being calm and clear allows each moment to flow effortlessly into the next.

Discovering bliss in daily life is to be aware of what is happening right now. It is to be conscious of thoughts and the affect they are having. Precious moments are lost to thoughts that fade back into the past or dissolve into the future. Remain present in the moment of now. Experience everything in the present without being distracted by memories of what has been.

It is easy to get bound to preconceived ideas of the future and forgo the flow of what is occurring in the present. Life can easily become an echo of the past or projection of the future.

Opportunities are lost if the mind is anywhere other than focused on the moment. Spending time with a special person, appreciating the beauty of nature, eating and actually tasting food, feeling water quench thirst and hydrate the body, listening to and hearing music, feeling the warmth of the sun, noticing the cleansing effect of the rain, watching the snow falling, seeing the abundance life offers can only truly be appreciated when viewed in the present moment.

You are where your thoughts are and if they are not aligned with the present moment the pleasure of that moment such as being with that special person or seeing something beautiful passes by and is lost forever.

Being present requires conscious effort. Take a moment to reflect on the thoughts you were just having. Where were they taking you? Were there any associated emotions attached to the thoughts? Did they have positive or negative association?

If these questions are asked at various times during the day it becomes evident that a large proportion of time is spent thinking about the past or fast forwarding to the future. Time spent in a swirl of unproductive thoughts distracts from truly appreciating the moment that is here right now.

Being in the moment is to acknowledge feelings that are pleasurable and also those that are unpleasant. The ability to feel is something of significant value. Naturally we want to immerse ourselves in pleasant feelings and retreat from those that are not. But by doing this we deny aspects of self and the reality we have created for ourselves.

We must awaken to see who and what we are identifying with. Whatever this may be is a role being played at this point in time and if this is not to our satisfaction it can be changed.

Many masks are worn to hide emotions deemed unpleasant. All this achieves is the inability to understand and process these emotions.

Sadness is one emotion that is a difficult one to express as it causes pain. However it causes more pain when suppressed as it gets stuck in the heart, causing blockages and/or the presentation of masking emotions such as anger, resentment, guilt, shame etc. The sadness will not be fully understood until these masking layers are peeled away.

This unveiling will reveal vulnerability and this can be confronting. The natural reaction is to put the defences back up and settle back into what feels like a safe place. This was a safe place at one time as it provided protection from being hurt in some way, but it does not serve the developing self.

The way through is to approach with compassion and care as under the masking emotions is a weeping aspect and when or if you allow yourself to feel the sadness associated with that aspect the tears will flow and flow they must until the well is empty.

Tears of sorrow uncovers the root cause of the emotion and sets in motion a healing response that cleanses the heart of pain and heals the emotional wound.

Short cuts, or trying to avoid feeling the emotion, undermines the healing power of being present, staying with the emotion, riding the wave of pain and allowing the tears to flow. Through the tears the sadness dissolves and from this emerges renewed strength and vitality. This is a truly blissful experience.

Choosing to be the follower or leader of thoughts has significant impact on the way life is perceived. The follower will go wherever thoughts takes them. Often this is misguided and aligned with unresolved issues or wistful thinking. The leader constructs thoughts consciously in the direction of their goals, wants and desires.

It is the responsibility of the thinker to choose whether to latch onto memories of the past, fast forward into the future or align thoughts with the present.

Living in the moment offers the opportunity to do something remarkable. That is to feel, hear, see and attend to our needs. The needs of the inner child, the inner adolescent and the adult self can be discovered by centering oneself in the moment.

How is this so? Whatever tries to steal the present moment has a voice and that voice echoes something from the past or projects thoughts of the future. That voice wants to be heard and attended to with the appropriate guidance.

Examples of aspects calling for attention are thoughts that focus on unknown outcomes. This causes worry, anxiety and unnecessary concern. Repeating or rehearsing conversations, can loop or jump from one to another and lead the thinker down a path leading nowhere.

Fortune telling what others think about you or how they will respond not only derives inaccurate conclusions but causes a gamete of needless angst and wastes valuable energy.

Thoughts of this nature can waste hours of precious moments. This is one reason why time seems scarce and disappears into nothingness.

Awareness and practice are needed to stop the thought cogs from grinding long enough to ask what is going on and what you need to do differently. It may feel like something comes on all of a sudden but with reflection it will be evident that there were many subtle clues that indicated the need to stop and take notice.

Being called to halt, taking a breath and re-evaluating where your thoughts are focused provides the perfect opportunity to recognize that time is to be cherished. Within time are the moments essential to do what needs to be done. If those moments are squandered it is like throwing away a priceless gift.

Want to get more time out of the day? Want to get more enjoyment from each day? Try being consciously aware of bringing thoughts back to the moment that you are in.

Try taking some deep breaths and clearing the mind of thought a few times a day. Imagine your eyes are the observers watching that thoughts don't interrupt your moments of peace. Employ an imaginary thought detective that rings the warning bell when harassing, detrimental or anxiety provoking thoughts enter your mind.

When interacting with others actively listen to what they say, while checking in with your own thoughts, feelings and reactions to what they say. This provides insight of significant value.

So much conversation is spent discussing trivial information or talking about the past or what is going to happen in the future that what is important right now gets overlooked. Having deep and meaningful conversations where intuition, knowledge and wisdom join and allows the emergence of something that enriches you.

Laughing is a healthy expression of enjoying the present moment. Going for a walk in nature and noticing the sights, the sounds and the smells is beneficial. Time spent in quiet surroundings connecting with self.

Spending quality, focused, time with a child or a pet is cherishing the moment. Sightseeing, animal watching, star gazing while thoughts are focused on what is being experienced in that moment is time well spent.

Any time you are consciously aware of your thoughts and how they affect the way you feel is embracing the moment. Stopping to check in with yourself and acknowledging how you are feeling enables the ability to make considered choices and to appreciate that every moment offers a chance to grow. For example, if faced with a frustrating situation the agitated mind will react to the frustration whereas a rational mind will be listening to intuition, analysing the situation and asking questions that facilitate awareness.

Questions such as:
How am I reacting to this situation?
How can I best work through this?
What is another way of looking at this?
Am I getting emotionally or energetically involved with something I don't need to?
Am I taking on a projection?
Is this triggering something that is unresolved from the past?
How can I best attend to this issue without blowing a fuse or suppressing what I feel?
These questions give clarity and enable good choice, helping to prevent post frustration. If

frustration and annoyance surface for no apparent reason or if the reason is being denied or if there is a general feeling of being ill-at-ease then something is hanging over from the past. Bringing this into the moment will reveal where a shadow is being cast. Using the above questions will provide the clarity needed to shift the shadow into the light.

Living blissfully comes from the realization that we can choose what flows from one moment to the next. Positive momentum is achieved by ensuring we are centered in the present and paying attention to what is occurring in that moment.

To Emphasis-Bringing yourself to the moment can take some practice and conscious awareness. Start by keeping an eye on your thoughts. Observing thoughts will give birth to an awareness that will gently remind you when you have faded into the past or disappeared into the future.

Suppressed emotion does not disappear. It remains and will want to surface at some stage. Emotion can become suppressed for many reasons, including when scorned, judged, abandoned, rejected and/or misunderstood.

Any form of abuse during childhood can cause emotional shut down, disassociation and any number of complications in the future. Reconnection and nurturing wounded aspects of self facilitates healing.

TECHNIQUE

Emotional development is a delicate process and a lifelong endeavour. One must be present to construct meaning to what emotions are trying to communicate.

Stop....Feel....Reflect.

As realization dawns new knowledge is derived and something that was simmering underneath surfaces. Carefully consider the appropriate tools you can use that will attend to what is being presented. An example may be to breathe while observing where the root of the emotion lies. While observing notice new understanding that arises and how perception can shift with this new awareness.

During the process it is important to stay present even if uncomfortable. Be on the lookout for thoughts that try to distract from the moment. This is an avoidance tactic. Stay centered. The emotion may bubble, scratch and claw its way to the surface, after which it can be healed. What comes from this is a clear mind that is void of thought and void of noise. From this space emerges a certain wonderment that after the storm one awakens to a blissful state of being where the only thing felt is a deep sense of inner peace and calm.

BE YOUR OWN THOUGHT DETECTIVE

To be a detective we observe, gather information and question. Being the observer is to notice what you are thinking by having thought check moments during the day and actively bringing thoughts back to the present.

This is like bringing them in for questioning so you may ask questions such as: were they regressing into the past or projecting into the future? What was I thinking about and what was I doing during the thought process? Are they emotionally charged? Are they self-enhancing or self-defeating? Are your thoughts getting in the way of what you want? Do flash-backs of past unsuccessful attempts interfere with what you want to achieve? Are there any repetitive thoughts? Are you being confronted by shadow aspects?

Begin to be aware of the hooks that pull you from the present moment helps gain insight into what is blocking the ability to be present. Past issues will continue to niggle unless they are processed effectively.

Why is thought detection important? Thought detection is important because without conscious awareness of what is going through the mind we are at the mercy of any of the aspects that exist within. Some of these aspects are misaligned with our higher self and what is in our best interest.

Thoughts are potent, they can lift up or pull down. Thoughts that pull down can come when least expected and cast a shadow on what would otherwise be a pleasant experience such as catching up with friends and/or family or participating in a favourite activity. If these thoughts go unchecked they can fast become a 'natural' way of thinking. Thoughts are attached to emotions that are attached to dissatisfied aspects of self.

These aspects will cast shadows if left unchecked and these shadows will build with intensity until acknowledged. It is these shadow aspects that lure us into chasing false satisfaction such as seeking materialistic gain, being overly concerned with appearance and trying to be someone we are not, which is seen in the creation of a false persona. Apart from possible short term gain, these things never lead to satisfying and fulfilling us in the way we think they will, in fact their attainment may accentuate feelings of discontentment and emptiness.

Satisfaction and fulfillment cannot be found outside of ourselves, they are found within. Going within requires presence. That is to recognize thoughts and acknowledge the thought, without getting caught up in it, and changing the thought. The more proficient we become at doing this the easier it becomes to be centered in the moment which is the place where the past, the present and aspects of self can be assimilated. This is putting the pieces together to create the whole. This is fulfillment which is the conduit to inner peace. Be present, be aware and find an inner state of bliss.

PLEDGE FOR BLISS

I create a blissful existence. I am centered in the present. My thoughts are aligned with what I want for now and the future. I am dedicated to creating the life I want to live. I let go of anything that opposes my wants, wishes and aspirations. I keep the company of those who are striving to be the best they can be and who aspire to achieve their dreams. I take responsibility for my own happiness. Discovering bliss in daily life comes from being present in the moment.

SUMMARY

- Moments are lost through thoughts that fade back to the past or dissolve into the future.
- Remain present in the moment of now.
- Experience everything in the present without the distraction of memories from what has been or preconception of what will be.
- True bliss is found in the clarity and calmness that evolves as positive momentum flows unhindered from one moment to the next.

Spiritual Quest

BLISS

I keep my thoughts centered in the present moment. I choose to think in ways that move me in a positive direction.

Blockage

Progress – for whatever purpose or pursuit – is likely to create barriers and obstacles. From these we can learn, grow & evolve.

Ever feel like you are standing in your own way? Do there seem to be barriers preventing you from achieving your goals and realising your dreams? Does doubt get in the way of your progress? Do you second guess your ability? This indicates that there is an aspect of self blocking your path and requires some attention to assist it forward. This is an inner defence mechanism that blocks in order to protect you in some way.

A blockages may be coming from past hurt that we do not want to revisit or would prefer to deny or suppress; the possibility of failure, or fear of not being equipped to handle what lies beyond the blockage can cause an intense reaction.

If you are feeling stuck, you are being confronted, either subtly or blatantly, by an aspect that requires attention. This aspect is a vulnerability and try as you might to avoid or deny it, unless addressed it will continue to stand in your way, until resolved. When you gain insight into this aspect of self and what underlies the vulnerability you become empowered to encourage and assist yourself forward. When a blockage steps aside, and it will when it has its needs met, then the feelings of liberation that will emerge from this will inspire a positive shift and momentum will flow again.

However the threat of uncovering what is blocking us can provoke a fight or flight response. We may try to avoid, run away or identify so closely with our limitations that we justify why we cannot do as we aspire. Or we might move from one thing to another without direction or focus to prevent having to confront what blocks us from doing what we want to do.

Feeling compelled to defend our viewpoint, belief or way of being prevents us from having to look too closely at the very thing that is holding us back. This can keep us attached to false beliefs, inaccurate view points and distorted perceptions. This is the definition of closed-mindedness.

Confronting as this may appear, the reality is that we would rather defend, run or harbour inner dissatisfaction than challenge a personal blockage. This avoidance is carefully disguised by excuses that justify why we are unable to manifest our dreams and desires.

Sometimes our reticence to uncover what is blocking us stems from childhood. The feelings linked to making a mistake or the judgment passed on a child's behaviour is often misinterpreted by the child.

The message the child receives is not limited to the behaviour or the mistake, but impresses itself on the person e.g. I did bad, I feel bad, therefore the only conclusion is I am bad. It is as simple as that.

Feeling 'bad' is a child-like description as they do not have the language to describe their feelings and are still developing their ability to express them.

If a child had the language they may exchange the emotion they deem as bad for words such as shame, guilt, inadequacy, uncertainty, unworthiness, vulnerability.

Children have even less capacity to rationalise what they are feeling and therefore often internalise or as is seen act out, melt down or express in other ways that are often deemed by adults as inappropriate. And while the consequent behaviour of an emotion may be inappropriate the emotions is always the driving force behind the behaviour, hence the importance of giving children the language to express what they are feeling and providing outlets for the emotion so that a steam pressure scenario is prevented or at least reduced in its capacity to explode.

The steam pressure scenario is a familiar one in adolescents, it seems hormones are the pressure releasing stimulants that see all that suppressed emotion surface and much to the parents and carers dismay erupts and spew outward.

When a child is experiencing an emotion ask how best to support the child to express it. When emotions become too big, when they are bottled up or reacted to in ways that create negative associations an "avoid at all costs" banner will hang heavily within the subconscious.

Later in life these emotions can be triggered and the banner will flap itself to remind the person of how to respond. Of course this can spawn into any number of behaviours and patterns of response. Including those displayed in childhood.

As we grow we become more resilient, however if the emotions associated with the "avoid at all costs' banner are triggered there will be a reaction. The reaction is the meeting of an aspect of self that has an issue that needs to be resolved. No matter how hard we push against this aspect it will not allow us thoroughfare until we acknowledge and attend to the emotion associated with this aspect.

Accompanying this aspect there may be feelings of frustration, doubt and feelings of defeat. A battle of wills is often encountered as the want to move forward encounters the aspect that wants to block the way. Acknowledging this blockage is part of the quest of self-discovery.

Example of encountering a blockage and moving forward

You have decided to do some study to seek a career aligned with your calling. You have chosen your course and are ready to sign up, but you read that part of the assessment criteria is to sit exams. Flash backs of sitting exams trigger a nauseous feeling associated with the past.

You feel intimidated before you even start and decide that study is not really for you and do not commence the study. This blockage is associated with an aspect that has had a negative experience with the prospect of studying and exams.

This was a personal scenario that I met within myself. I was not going to attend an examination due to a myriad of excuses. None of which held much merit.

Once I acknowledged that the excuses were coming from an aspect that had a negative association to sitting examinations I was able to use appropriate techniques and sat the exam. The experience of doing this exam was exhilarating, I had the knowledge and because I had eased any associated nerves I was delighted at how much I could recall.

After completing the exam I felt liberated, not only had I completed something I wanted to avoid but I knew that I had overcome a fear and worked through a blockage.

I expressed to the exam supervisor that I had thoroughly enjoyed doing the exam, a statement that was met with a look of surprise. This is an example of acknowledging and moving beyond a blockage.

My fear of exams evaporated and I cleared the way forward. Calling upon the strength of empowered aspects of self to assist fearful ones produces profound results. So much so that we surprise ourselves at what we are capable of.

There is nothing more liberating than breaking through the threshold of a boundary and achieving what was deemed unachievable. When the "avoid at all costs" flag is waving the associated emotions will cause us to want to escape, deny, defend or flare up.

When we arrive at this crossroad within self we have the choice of succumbing to our limitations and remain blocked, thus our goals remain distant dreams, or we can use our strengths to support our vulnerabilities and work through resistance. Acquiring new awareness helps us to break through personal limitations and in doing so we are infused with feelings of inner satisfaction.

Should you choose to continue and challenge a blockage do so with the understanding that there will be ups and downs. This is part of the process as we confront certain aspects of self.

Proceeding may trigger escape methods such as justification for action or non-action and excuses. Recognise these as an aspect attempting to block your path.

Keep moving or you may become stuck in non-serving mind-sets. Non-serving mind-sets cause us to stagnate and retreat into old patterns of behaviour.

Awareness that we are holding ourselves back enables the seeking of options, thus we empower ourselves to persist, resolve the blockage and break through limitations.

The amount of determination and courage shown will be greatly rewarded. A half-hearted approach does not provide the leadership needed to build confidence in less empowered aspects of self. Half heartedness dilutes energy and carries a wishy-washy vibe. On the contrast when we are committed our vibration is more dynamic and encourages us to be more tenacious.

From this perspective we activate personal strengths needed to face and overcome challenges. Find the rhythm of your own drum and walk to the beat, allowing yourself to take that occasional leap of faith.

This is to fully immerse self in this adventure called life. With this comes acceptance that, as with every adventure, there will be times when things go as planned, times when things will be chaotic and times when we find ourselves veering onto an unexpected path.

If our adventure takes an unexpected turn, the best approach is to redirect with faith that the new path is better aligned with hopes, dreams and aspirations.

Unexpected opportunities are meant to be and have the potential of becoming what you have hoped for. Summon the determination needed to move past what blocks you and see that you are capable of more than you thought possible. Overcoming blockages builds confidence and further enhances your ability to confront fears and limitations. Weeding out what we don't want for ourselves gives us the opportunity to realise what we do want.

The amazing journey of discovery plunges us into deeper exploration of who we are, with this comes the unveiling of what we are here to do. Thus comes the alignment of self with purpose.

When we can firmly declare who we are and what we are here to do we are accepting ourselves and our role on earth. Thus we become more attuned to our whole being and are able to access inner depth that was previously inaccessible.

As new awareness awakens we acquire heightened levels of compassion, acceptance, courage, commitment and self-confidence. All of which are wonderful companions to be traveling with.

When in the midst of challenge and conflict go within and allow yourself to be guided by your inherent insight and wisdom.

Experiencing an inner struggle, surrendering to inner defeat or defining ourselves by a limitation is testament that we have not properly dealt with an aspect that is holding us back. We will continue to come face to face with this aspect until we acknowledge it, attend to it and move beyond it.

How do we know when we are the victims of our limitations and are being blocked? When we find that instead of celebrating the achievement of our dreams, desires and aspirations we have excuses and justifications.

This can relate to any area of our life including relationships, business ventures, financial status, careers options and other significant life choices. Another indicator that we are being blocked is when there is a repetitive cycle of self-defeat and self-sabotage.

Aspects that may be blocking you and that you may be familiar with include:

The inner-critic :
"I haven't got what it takes"
The inner child :
"it never worked before"
The inner-judge:
"what will they think?"
The inner-victim:
"every time I try, I fail"

Other blockages are those emotionally tied to someone or something from the past. When you begin to listen you will become aware of what is blocking you and what it is linked to.

Whatever holds us back is linked to emotions that have not been processed effectively. This keeps us locked into mindsets that recycle thoughts of what was; what should have been or what could have been.

It is almost like we are grieving for the past and in doing so we forfeit a positive future. This is particularly noticeable in the recreation of similar circumstances.

Alarm bells should ring, if one finds themselves in the same situation over and over. Inevitably the same results will be produced unless one awakens and sees the attachment to the past, process it effectively and move on.

TECHNIQUE

Imagine yourself walking along a hallway. As you journey, you see different aspects of yourself requiring your attention at this point in time. You come to the end of the hallway - there is a door - it completely blocks your passage.

You sense an emotion arising within you. You know that you will find understanding of this emotion lying just beyond the door.

You feel something in your hand, you look down and there is a code that will unlock the door.

When you begin to use the code, you feel the emotion shift.

You reassure yourself that it is safe to open the door, that you will be protected.

The code is accepted and the door swings open. Standing on the other side of the door is an aspect of you that has been standing in your way.

You ask this aspect some questions about what it is afraid of, why it prevents you from doing as you desire, what it needs to help it move forward.

You accept the answers this aspects gives you with understanding.

Your understanding dissolves any apprehension and dissolves barriers.

You notice this aspect of yourself soften, you embrace this aspect and as you do you free yourself of the burdens of the past or fears associated with the future.

 Settle into a comfortable position. Take a deep breath in through the nose and out through the mouth

As you exhale you feel all tension leave your body.
Take another deep breath in through your nose.
This time you breathe in beautiful white light. The white light flows through your body cleansing and clearing as it flows into every cell.

You find yourself standing at the bottom of a mountain.

You want to climb the mountain as you know doing so will be liberating and enable you to uncover your personal strengths.

You take your first step onto the mountain path.
You are feeling determined to climb the mountain.
As you continue along the path you notice it getting steeper.

Your determination begins to waver and as it does you notice that there is something or someone standing in the way of your path.

It is blocking you from moving forward.

You look closely at this blockage or barrier and see what it is that is preventing you from moving forward.

You know you must move through the blockage or

you will stay where you are.

You acknowledge that while you may have put the blockage there to keep you safe.

If it no longer serves you need to move it out of your way.

Look at what your blockage is.

What do you see? It may be a sign, a word, an image, a person.

You speak to your blockage and tell it that you have outgrown the need for it to block your path.

The blockage accepts your words and moves to the side to allow you to continue your journey.

You continue your journey up the mountain releasing any other blockages that get in your way.

One by one you see and feel the blockages dissolve.

As they do you feel more and more empowered.

As you continue you feel your load lighten no longer are you struggling up the mountain.

You are moving more freely.

Your path has leveled out.

You are feeling free to travel your path.

PLEDGE

I release that which stands in the way of my progress. I will not retreat from what blocks me but will face it with renewed determination. I know that what lies beyond the blockage is freedom beyond what I have experienced before. I will approach with interest to ascertain what lies beneath. Once uncovered the blockage will dissolve and clear the path for me to move forward with ease. I recognise that blockages are aspects trying to keep me safe from perceived mishap. I assure these aspects that I am safe, that I am capable and that I am on the winner's path.

SUMMARY

- When one journeys to the realms of the inner self there may be times when feelings of restlessness, frustration and bewilderment accompany the traveler.
- There may be times when you just can't seem to move forward or when you plateau.
- A time when you are not progressing as you were.
- There may even be times when you feel like you want to retreat when you question all you have been doing and become disillusioned.
- What all this means is that you are experiencing an encounter with an aspect that, for whatever reason, is blocked.
- There are many reasons why this may happen. It may be an aspect of self has been protecting you from perceived harm so it blocks your progress.
- This is a vulnerability and if exposed there is fear that you may get hurt.
- Within this vulnerability is strength as you are able to gain insight into an aspect that is holding you back.
- When you gain insight into this part of yourself

you can coach and empower this aspect so it can move forward.

BLOCKAGE

I offer compassion and empathy every aspect of myself. I light the path for aspects that block my way so I may see my way clear.

Each of us possess a body that is capable of functioning without conscious effort, a mind that is capable of phenomenal feats and a spirit ripe with potential.

Spiritual Quest

Change

I am willing to make the changes necessary for my growth and development

When the winds of change blow in our direction, we can be certain that life as we know it will never be the same

Change clears the way for new beginnings.

Although change can be daunting it is always the conduit to personal growth. Change facilitates adaptation which builds resilience and resourcefulness. Change is the pathway to discovery. Through change we transform and evolve. Embrace change and allow it to lift you from your comfort zone and onto the horizon of new adventure.

Change is an inevitable part of life. The seeds of your destiny are planted in the opportunities change will bring. While the idea of change may cause inner discomfort it is the way to release the old and step into the new.

Whether we are willingly moving from or being forced out of our comfort zone, change can be challenging. There are aspects of our psyche that find change threatening.

These aspects do not like to be challenged and are inclined to remind us of our downfalls and vulnerabilities. This response may be unpleasant as the threat of the unknown makes these aspects feel unsafe and insecure.

On the flip side of this is that there are aspects of

self that have higher awareness and they know that change is imperative for our growth and development.

Although comforting to know we must also be aware of the inner conflict that may arise as parts of us aim to strive forward while others try to keep us where we are.

Be this as it may intuitively we know when we are being called to make changes, one telltale sign is a feeling of dissatisfaction that just won't go away no matter how hard we try to fool ourselves into believing that we are happy.

To facilitate change we must employ the higher aspects of ourselves to support those that are less able to accept the direction in which we are moving in.

Tuning into our inner resistance enables us to hear the internal dialogue the clouds us with doubt as it protests, discourages and deflates with words such as shouldn't, couldn't, can't, won't, don't and so on.

This inner monologue is attached to aspects that have an 'it is better not to try than to try and fail' perspective. However with awakening awareness we begin to acknowledge inner doubt and can apply techniques that will hush the voice of negativity and increase the voice of inspiration.

While change can fuel fear, it is always accompanied by opportunity. Life changes can be big on many levels. Whether it is a physical, emotional or circumstantial change we must find the thread that pulls us forth. Change indicates that you are on the path to discovering what you need to fulfil the ultimate purpose of your life.

TECHNIQUE

Focusing on the positive aspects of our being more closely aligns us with what we want to achieve. This will also assist us in accepting and adapting to change which enables us to focus on what we hope change will bring. We can project our hopes and dreams forward and be the positive creators of things to come.

By reflecting on the changes that have occurred in the past it becomes clear that, even if not evident at the time, change always facilitates personal growth. Resilience, strength, courage and determination are some of the many blessings change brings.

Change has the ability to revamp parts of, or all of, our life, bringing with it new inspiration and excitement. When change comes lift yourself upon its wings and enjoy the ride. Change precedes transformation. When change presents itself without warning make a conscious shift to embrace the promise of new opportunity. Open your arms to receive all that change will provide.

When confronted by change ask:

What opportunities will the change bring?

What has to be released to assist the change?

How can this change help me grow?

What am I resisting?

What do I fear?

What tools do I need to help me adapt to this change?

How can I best adjust to this change?

What can I do for myself so I can embrace change?

What is my inner monologue saying about this change?

How am I responding to my own inner thoughts and feelings?

Am I holding onto anything that is unhelpful?

Am I fully accepting of the change and allowing a natural progression?

PLEDGE FOR CHANGE

Change is essential to my growth.
On the wings of changes comes new opportunities, new possibilities, new aspiration, new ideas.
I embrace change and know that doing so enables me to transcend limitations.
Changes brings fresh hope.
Hope has the capacity to revitalise depleted energy and spark enthusiasm.
Enthusiasm dares me to dream.
I accept and construct a visual reality of what change offers.
Through my virtual reality I clearly demonstrate the direction I want change to take me.
As I attend to my perceived reality I notice shifts within myself.
These shifts are those necessary to embrace the new reality change brings.

SUMMARY

- Growth is found in change.
- One cannot find something different if they continue to do the same.
- Embrace change and allow yourself to make new discoveries.
- Change may be delivered in a variety of ways, be it to do with matters of the mind, the body or the spirit.
- Sometimes it is a wakeup call that instigates change.
- A shift is often what is needed to realign focus and make new discoveries.
- Change carries a seed ripe with potential and opportunity.
- Nurture and nourish this seed and be amazed at what blooms.

Spiritual Quest

CHANGE

I open my arms to embrace the opportunities change will bring.

Often the catalyst to change is proceeded by feelings of restlessness, irritation and uncertainty. This is the bridge of emotion we must cross if we are to be united with the pot of gold that awaits us.

Spiritual Quest

Clarity

Clarity is derived through reflection of the meaning and purpose of experiences

Clarity is found when the mists of the mind separate and give rise to clear thought.

Clarity emerges by engaging the skills of reflection and contemplation.

Connection to deeper levels of consciousness is obtained through a clear mind. Ideas are best explored and decisions best made when the mind is clear. Solutions to the most difficult problems surface when the mind is calm. A calm mind facilitates emotional serenity. Paint the images of your desires upon a clear mind and those images will manifest as imagined.

Reflecting on past and present experiences and the events and circumstances of our personal lives provides the insight needed to derive meaning of what is being presented. If there are issues that have not been processed they can have emotional, physical and/or psychological impact. Processing issues related to the past helps close that chapter and prevents it from being the prelude to the next chapter.

Indications that there is some processing required are when the same story about a past hurt is told over, thinking about a past event on a regular basis and recreating similar experiences. Unless this pattern is recognized and changed the story of the past will become the life story.

This requires that the story so far is bookmarked and the chapters of the life lived so far are reflected upon. Flicking through the chapters of life will make clear what remains unfinished and where emotional connections lie. Gaining this insight requires a certain distance be placed between the observer (you) and the experience/s.

Clarity cannot be found by being caught up in the emotions of the experience, it emerges by viewing the memory with the intention of deriving understanding. For example, there may be significant sadness associated with the loss of someone in the past. This sadness can become consuming if it is not processed and peace found in accepting the passing of the soul. Although the presence of the deceased may continue to be missed, the associated grief needs to be healed.

This is also true of the grief associated with lost aspects of self. It is actually this feeling of grief that can help uncover what this aspect is and reassimilate it back into our awareness.

Such aspects are usually those that have been buried due to any number of internal and/or external influences. For example if affection is meet with impatience or feelings of inappropriateness at being outwardly affectionate then it is likely that this aspect will go into mourning as it shuts down and hides itself away. This can be attributed to any aspect that shuts down; there is a deep feeling of hurt and sadness.

It may even feel that it is untouchable as it has been buried, denied, suppressed, but it is touchable and it will produce a physical symptom or symptoms that, if we take notice, will light the way through to this aspect.

An example of the emergence of a symptom associated with deep hurt and sadness is depression. In today's society treatment for this is directed towards the mind, of course this is a good place to start when the depression is consuming and action is required.

However, there is a twist, as although it may appear that the mind is depressed as it brings forth the thoughts, it is purely a messenger. In the case of depression it is the heart that bares the wound and feels the pain. And although we can shift our thoughts to reflect positivity and this does have good effect it is only part of the equation. Just as wiping our tears away doesn't dissolve the associated grief. We must trace the messages received from the mind to their roots and expose the underlying need. We then attend to the needs of a wounded heart first by recognising the hurt and sadness and then nourishing it with the love and compassion it needs. As the wound heals the sadness dissolves. But if the wound remains it will continue to tear at the heart, even in times of happiness the wound will ache.

Eventually the time will come when band-aid methods can no longer conceal matters belonging to the heart and one will feel compelled to look within. This is not reopening a wound; it is attending to one that is in desperate need of healing. Thus begins a journey that will, if one persists, provide the clarity needed to heal.

Going within starts by connecting with the heart centre to identify wounds that are yet to be healed. This is pulling back the band-aid to take a peek at what lies beneath. It may be murky, raw and sore, but it will also be grateful that you have the courage to acknowledge the pain. The pain will lessen in intensity and at the same time reveal its cause if approached with compassion and empathy.

This is the beginning of piecing together the

purpose of an experience and polar opposites will become apparent. For example where strength, courage, justice, equality, determination, tenacity and compassion are birthed from their opposites.

The potent forms of these qualities do not come easily but more often through a tedious, challenging process that had to be conquered. The roots of victory often wind back to a time when things were bleak.

It is clarity that shines the light on the roots that need a little tug so they can blossom into the insight needed to give meaning and understanding. This knowledge is particularly useful to assist stuck aspects forward in positive ways.

Reflection helps to make clear the associated learning from our experiences. Personal growth and spiritual awakenings are often the result of something that caused considerable discomfort that forces us to take notice.

Sometimes we arrive at ground level zero before we are confronted by an internal ultimatum that challenges us to move out of our comfort zone, forces us to take action and to find another way or continue as we are and face pending self-destruction.

Self preservation most often wins out and we begin to climb our way out of the hole we have dug ourselves into. Our inner light brightens each time we challenge and conquer negative thought patterns, each time we consciously take charge of spiralling emotions and each time we choose to break free of conditioned reactions.

Acknowledging what is being achieved and the difference it makes to our life is gratifying and paves the way for further progress. When the mind is clear of debilitating debris choices and decisions become easier and are better aligned with what is in our best interest.

Peace of mind is the conduit to emotional serenity. Can you see how important it is to stop the whirlpool and take the time to gain clarity? What emerges from clarity will fascinate and inspire new awareness and understanding and possibly new direction.

Design the images of your desires and bring them to life with colour and positive feelings. Be mindful of any negativity that surfaces. This may be the niggling voice of doubt that says "you can't do that!" "How ridiculous making an image and believing it can come true." "What sort of silliness is this?" "Surely you can't expect this to happen?"

The inner-critic loves to come to play when planning things that oppose its beliefs. Tell the inner-critic that you know there is some fear associated with putting yourself out there, however you are going to make your desires manifest and the first step to do this is to see clearly what it is you want. If the inner-critic continues, give it a good dose of confidence-building affirmations.

There may also be other aspects that come into play. Use the same technique and soon you will have silenced the naysayers and created some space for you to get entrenched in some super-stimulating creative visualization.

Remember that the naysayers in your mind are aspects that hold negative perceptions. They will not just fade into the background. They will continue to chime in with their worriers and doubts.

All you need to give in return is reassurance that you can do as you plan and will succeed. Each time you celebrate a success, no matter how small or grand, the naysayers will be a little less vocal and feel a little more confident in your ability.

Sometimes it can be difficult to navigate through

the mind chatter to find the clarity needed to define what it is you want. Unscrambling thoughts is not necessary. They are usually meaningless and have no means to an end.

What is required is an authoritative voice to guide you in the direction you want to go. Note: there is a difference between authoritative and authoritarian.

Authoritative provides self-assured guidance whereas authoritarian dictates and has the potential to cause inner rebellion. Being authoritative is to become your own Life Coach that lovingly motivates and guides you towards personal achievement. When you employ yourself as your own personal Life Coach you will see clarity starts to emerge.

Life Coaches have tool kits that contain tools, techniques and resources to assist clients on their journey. You also have an ever-growing tool kit equipped with all the tools and techniques you need.

When new techniques are introduced into your tool kit they may require some practice and perseverance before being mastered. The tools worthy of adding will be worthy of the time it takes to learn how to use them. There will be some that will be used often, others that will be used occasionally and some that come to the rescue when really needed.

> *Nourish your heart with compassion and empathy and you have discovered the recipe for miracles*

TECHNIQUE

Building Your Life Coach Tool Kit

Begin by breathing in through your nose and then exhaling through your mouth. Do this until you feel in-tune with your breathing. Gently let go of thoughts that enter your mind and continue to remain in sync with your breath. On the in-breath feel yourself relax and on the out-breath see your thoughts untangle and evaporate. There is no benefit in allowing meaningless thought take up space in your mind. Use your breath to calm your mind and body.

When you feel a void open within this is the gateway to your higher-self. Keep breathing into this space while letting go of all else. It is just you and this space opening up to the wisdom of your higher awareness.

Answers and insight are derived from this space. This is the emergence of clarity. Use this whenever you are feeling clouded or in a tangled web of thoughts that are going nowhere.

Gaining clarity requires focus. Make your heart centre the point of focus. Breathe into this area, feeling for any blocked energy, felt as discomfort. Keep breathing into this discomfort and on the out breathe imagine the blockage clearing.

This may be seen as a shadow, dark cloud or any colour moving from the heart area out through the breath and into a healing cloth that absorbs the blockage. As this is happening there may be an awareness of what this blockage is linked to. It is not important to go into the details, being aware of what it is enough.

Once this blockage has cleared, refocus fully on your heart centre. Imagine a beautiful white flower opening up in your heart area. The opening of this flower fills your heart with feelings of compassion, gratitude and joy. Connecting with these feelings regularly is transformational. If there is resistance to feeling these wonder-filled emotions then the heart can show you where the blockages lie.

If a blockage is detected look for a link. This may be preconceived ideas or ideals e.g. it should or shouldn't be like this or I should or shouldn't be feeling like this or behaving like that. Conditioning, which is emotional and/or behavioural response or reaction to external stimulus, e.g. something done or said, triggers the same response time and time again with the compulsion to react in the same way even after you proclaim that you will not.

Clarity provides the vision needed to evaluate where you are now and how to move forward. When we can clearly see how our thoughts affect our choices we have the power to create choices with new awareness. Conscious awareness is needed to guide our choices in the direction of desired outcomes. This is nurturing the seed of potential so it can blossom.

What preconceived ideas are standing in the way? Are there any perceptions that obscure the ability to be grateful for what one has, be compassionate to others and/or be content within oneself. If there are thoughts and ideas opposing those wanted then it is time to find where the misalignment lies.

Through conscious awareness we can follow our thoughts and uncover where opposing perceptions arise from. For example if one is opening their arms to receive abundance and continues to live in scarcity then thoughts and feelings surrounding what it means to live abundantly requires contemplation.

Unless this perception is changed, as it can be, then it will continue to be reality. Perceptions are formed through interpretation of experiences for example if there is negativity associated with manifesting dreams then the idea of doing such is doused with negativity before it has the chance to develop.

Such an association can form in any number of ways. If a child grows up in a home where the adults or significant others are consumed by worry over finances then believing the universe is one of abundance may be difficult.

It is likely that it will take considerable conscious effort on this person's behalf to dissolve the imposed belief of scarcity to one that supports abundance. There are many imposed mind-sets that can stifle the flow of abundance including lack of gratitude for what one has.

Gratitude has the power to ignite our inner light and uplift the soul; creating a feeling of warmth and a flood of feel good emotion. But if there is a perception that generates feelings of lack then we can feel miserable and unsatisfied with what we have.

Initially any personal reflection on a perception can cause confusion, although this may be a state we would prefer to avoid it is necessary if clarity is to be found. Confusion often signals that one is on the brink of breakthrough.

Remain the observer of the confusion, rather than being a participant and you will succeed in uncovering the root of a preconceived idea or a perception that keeps you captive in old formats.

Persevere through the discomfort and watch clarity emerge from the mists. The outcome is a shift in perception, which is to step from the shadows of worn out, unconsciously created, beliefs and into the light where new, more positive, perceptions are formulated. These perceptions will be those that are aligned with what you want for yourself now.

Conscious choices pave the way for achieving desired outcomes. The alternative is to leave it to the haphazard hand of fate to decide.

 Take a deep breath in through the nose and out through your mouth. Take another deep breath in through the nose and out through your mouth.
Bring your attention to the top of your head.
See the thoughts flowing through your head.
You are just observing at the moment.
You start to move your attention to those thoughts that provoke a feeling or emotion.
When you can identify one that you would like to explore bring it in closer and reflect upon it.
Remember that this is an exercise. It is a memory or an idea. It has no power over you.
You are an observer and the thought is communicating with you so you can gain clarity.
Breathe and know that you are safe.
Your thoughts are not happening now.
They are merely reflections of the past or a projection of the future, neither of which can affect you unless you allow them.
The purpose is to uncover the root of the thought.
What underlies that thought?.
Is there fear attached to the thought?.
Does that thought serve you or does it hinder you?.
You are lifting the lid on that thought so you can

see it clearly.

Through clarity you can choose to hold onto the thought and the associated perception and emotion or you can release it and choose thoughts that will steer you forward in a positive direction.

Now that you are consciously aware of the existence of this thought, if it enters your mind you have a choice of what to do with it.

That choice is to recognize it and why it exists and to calmly say "I choose to release what is attached to the past and select those thoughts that will support a future that is aligned with my highest good and purpose".

Stand back from your thoughts for a moment and just quietly observe them to see how they move and change.

That they really only have the power you give them. Now see your mind as calm and clear. Feel the serenity of being absent of thought.

This tranquil place of bliss is the space to use your mind positively and place an affirmation that will support you in a positive way.

PLEDGE FOR CLARITY

My mind is calm and from a calm mind I have the clarity needed to select only those thoughts that will serve me. I am consciously aware of the thoughts flowing through my mind and will choose those which instil feelings of peace.

Through peace I reach a part within me that is all-knowing and all-loving. This part of myself has my best interest at heart and will guide me in helpful ways. Each time I feel my thoughts are carrying me away I will be reminded of the aspect that holds my highest good and potential at heart.

SUMMARY

- Ideas and decisions composed with a clear mind connect with deeper levels of consciousness.
- Emotional serenity ascends from clarity of mind.
- Internal impressions create visual rendering, the attraction of like vision.
- The vibration of visual images formed through clarity project clear intention aligned with the path you seek.
- Send these images forth with faith that your creations will appear as you have imagined.

CLARITY

*I receive wise guidance
which allows me to reach my potential
with the love and support of my higher self.*

Spiritual Quest

Connection

As a multi-dimensional being the yearning to feel whole inspires the journey of self-exploration.

If there is disharmony in one there is disharmony in all.

Self exploration reveals the many dimensions that contribute to the whole of the being. When aligned with soul qualities there is an inner sense of fulfillment.

The core essence of all living things is energetic vibration. The higher self inspires meaning, purpose and the soul qualities of kindness, compassion, gratitude and joy. Mind, body, spirit unison creates a healthier, happier, purposeful life.

Conscious awareness combined with intuitive insight facilitates divine expansion. Knowledge and wisdom is obtained through an expanding consciousness. Connecting with the essence within is to see the connection to all.

The mind, body and soul are intimately connected. Together they make us whole and at the same time enable us to experience life from different perspectives, which gives rise to our multi-dimensional nature.

Understanding the different dimensions of our being assists us to experience life from physical, emotional and spiritual perspective, however to view any one of these aspects as separate from the others limits our perspective.

Becoming aware of the interlinking of mind, body and spirit is to see that they are in constant communication. The soul communicates through the heart, the heart communicates through the emotions and the emotions communicate through the mind and body.

Although it may appear as a linear process it is more likened to a grid like structure that enables the constant and essential interaction between the two worlds to which we belong-that of the spirit and that of our physicality.

Understanding the interconnection of these aspects opens a channel that enables the soul to convey deeper meaning and purpose. This is the same channel that invites the positive energy of the universe and attunes us to higher aspects of self.

The higher aspect of self assists the ego to evolve, which is the emergence of conscious choice aligned with increased awareness. The use of the word higher is not in the hierarchical sense but in relevance to the level of awareness.

When acutely aware we awaken to the soul aspects of our nature and in doing so we begin to piece together the symbolic nature of life.

Although understanding of what is communicated symbolically comes naturally, verbal language is developed from a young age and becomes the chosen method of communicating.

However we learn far more from what is not said, through body language, intuitively we know this, but often ignore what we sense and feel in favor of our conditioned form of verbal communication.

The same is true of symbolic language, intuitively we feel what is being expressed, but are less able to consciously interpret the messages. Like we developed our ability to communicate verbally we need to develop our ability to intuitive and consciously interpret symbolic expression. This is likened to learning a new language. At first we only grasp a few words, often picking up more via non-verbal messages, then we find ourselves understanding more and more until we are able to communicate effectively. When learning to interpret symbolic communication we are not focused on what is being presented but on what is being presentation represents.

Life re-creates itself is the most awe inspiring

ways when we grasp what is being communicated symbolically. Dreams become less cryptic and better understood through their symbolic representations. When this occurs, it becomes evident that a different level of awareness is being achieved and a whole new world begins to take shape. The senses shift gear and interpret from a different perspective. People, places and things become symbolic messages of what needs to be known, intuitive hunches are confirmed, thoughts develop into insightful ideas. For example, if an idea manifests in your mind remain consciously aware of the signs that indicate if it is worth pursuing.

Over the next few days or weeks there will be reminders of the idea in unlikely places. You may suddenly decide to go somewhere and while there you hear something, see something or feel something that resonates with the idea. I use the power of three to determine if I am on the right track. Usually it occurs in this order. First I see something that relates to the idea, then I hear something and then something occurs like an email, blog or post, that aligns with the idea. These three things indicate that the idea is worthy of further exploration.

There is no set way of gaining the meaning of symbolic representations, but what is consistent is that what is being interpreted will resonate within oneself this will be accompanied by an inner knowing. 'I think' becomes 'I know". This takes practice, patience and conscious awareness to attune to the signs and messages relevant to you. Before too long interpreting symbolic meaning will come naturally.

To receive confirmation just ask for it and remain aware because the answer will arrive. This may be met with skepticism at first, but once symbolic representations are experienced they cannot be denied.

The inner-skeptic may muster a scoff but at the same time cannot deny the irony of the 'coincidence'. Not even the inner-skeptic can deny the power unknown forces have on the physical world, although it certainly will try to discredit anything that can't be rationalized.

Note: While the inner skeptic has an important role, as it protects from gullibility, if given too much leeway it can scrutinize us into closed mindedness, a malady that squashes the wonder out of life.

Individual thoughts, feelings, beliefs and perceptions form the basis of interpretation, hence why a similar event will be experienced differently depending on the individual.

The perceptions of some are constructed positively and others are constructed negatively. This is the total sum of all experiences and how they were interpreted. Some people have been nurtured in ways that facilitate a positive outlook and some have not been so fortunate.

The reverse is true when some who have been exposed to negativity have somehow constructed a positive outlook. The common thread is that the outlook will determine how one exchanges energy with the environment, with others and with their inner self.

Money is a form of energy exchange. Some view money as their god and will dishonour themselves and others in the service of this man-made commodity that has no real value except that which we have been brainwashed to believe. This god is ruthless and allows human, animal and plant life to be sacrificed in its honour.

Relationships, families, communities and countries have been divided by this almighty god. However, money is the universal language and at this stage of our evolution the only language that has universal understanding. Hence the purpose it currently serves.

Energy is another universal language that is being exchanged constantly. As the nature of non-physical energy exchange is better understood and utilized it can have profound positive impact on all aspects of life. Whether aware of it or not, the subtle field of energy that surrounds you surrounds everything.

Energy carries variable vibrations; every individual has a unique vibe, based upon the inner and outer workings of their being. This is one of the aspects that makes us unique and also why different people give off different vibes.

Some we are attracted to, some we are repelled by and some we are neutral to. Thoughts and feelings carry vibration.

Those emitting negative vibrations will deflate and those emitting positive vibrations will uplift. We are all sensitive to energy. Some are more so than others and will quickly pick up a vibe regardless of what is displayed on the outward facade. This is extra-sensory perception, received intuitively and communicated by a feeling that gives us a positive or negative vibe. We cannot see this, but we know that what we are sensing is accurate.

This is also true when it comes to the special energetic connections shared with the people chosen to be partners and friends.

They speak the same energetic language, they understand us and we them on a level not shared with everyone. They know how we feel without words, they say what we are about to say and they intuitively know what we need. This is connectedness.

A personal shift in energy may strengthen, weaken or neutralize a connection. A connection can be weakened when someone acts in ways that oppose the virtues of another.

Neutralization of a connection can occur due to stagnation, lack of nourishment and lack of growth. Deeper connection is made when life is explored and discovered with compatible zest. Connection is made with people, animals, places and things. A deeper connection is made with nature by being in her presence and tuning into her harmonious vibe. This is uniting of soul energies.

SOUL ENERGY

Soul energy has no physical form but it affects the physical body. The soul communicates through our energy field and resonates at a high frequency.

The energy field that surrounds the body can be seen through the mind's eye and the physical eyes by those who are acutely attuned to energy. While vision of this may come naturally to some, it is available to anyone who applies themselves to developing the ability.

The energy field communicates inner thoughts and feelings with other energy fields. A good or a bad vibe is delivered through the energy field. Someone may be smiling and at the same time emitting a bad vibe based upon what they are thinking or feeling. The energy field has multi-consciousness and is perceptive of the thoughts and feelings of others. Every living thing has its own unique energy field.

When energy is looked at from this perspective it enables us to see that the same source of energy birthed every form of life. This interconnection weaves an energetic bond between all. However the strength of this bond is weakened by judgmental mindsets, perceptions that support disconnectedness and beliefs that divide and separate. If these things did not exist the world would be harmonious.

However it has come about that experiencing life in physical form contains the lessons the soul seeks, which includes everything that attracts our attention. Be it positive or negative if it's got your attention then exploration is required.

At the root of it lays valuable insight pertaining to soul growth. For example if disharmony in the world is attracting your attention then see how it relates to your own life.

The stronger the focus on the disharmony the louder your soul is calling you to take notice of what it is trying to communicate.

The journey of the soul is eternal with each of us having different paths to travel. We come; we learn what has been predetermined by our soul and return home where the soul processes the experience and derives the wisdom needed to evolve. There is a period of restoration followed by the continuation of the journey to different dimensions for the attainment of additional insight.

What this journey involves is a mystery and while much has been learned about life, death and reincarnation, this is only part of the complete picture pertaining to the soul. At the same time new knowledge is gained new mystery emerges.

The evolution of our race depends on being consciously aware of the connection shared with all living things which naturally include animals, plants and the subtle energies of the earth and beyond.

This begins by acknowledging that we are more than physical bodies. That contained within each of us is energy and that, by centering that energy in the heart center, one is heart-felt.

When centered in this energy the need to separate, judge and disconnect no longer exists and one feels compelled to strengthen the bonds that connects one to all.

Rising awareness sees behavioural shifts resulting in strengthened bonds within families, groups and communities. Supporting causes that advocate for animal, human and environmental rights coincide with rising awareness. Heart centered decisions and choices are those aligned with the soul virtues of love, compassion, humanity and honesty.

The yearning to feel whole is inspired by aspects of the mind, the body and the soul.

TECHNIQUE

Gently guide yourself to your centre
Breathe and focus on the mid-line of your body. Ask to see and connect with your higher-self.
See a white or golden light within you.
Allow this to manifest into an image of your higher-self.
You will know it is your higher-self by the love and compassion it has for you.
The more you tune into your higher-self the more you will hear its guidance.
Aligning with your soul's guidance gives you access to higher awareness and extra-sensory perception. This enhances the ability to understand the language of your mind, body and soul.

The intimate connection between mind, body and soul needs nurturing as they form the core of what manifests into your life. Harmony of one creates harmony for all.

A harmonious vibration attracts like vibration and enables a calmer solution-focused approach to the inevitable challenges life throws. While these challenges may see us faced with unforeseen circumstances that knock or bump us around, awareness of the mind, body, soul connection enables us to see that things happen to awaken us to disharmony and imbalance.

Making this connection is to listen to what is being communicated and approach in ways that facilitate positive outcomes. It becomes an intriguing adventure of looking for the clues that reveal the answers needed to strengthen the mind, body, soul connection.

PLEDGE FOR CONTEMPLATION

As a multi-dimensional being I am that of the body, that of the mind and that of the spirit. I nourish my spirit, I nourish my mind and I nourish my body which is to nourish my whole being.

There is no separation; what affects one will affect the whole. As an energetic being with a physical body, I give equal attention to my energetic and physical needs.

I choose healthy thoughts, healthy foods and healthy emotion.

Finding like-minded people is a blessing that will continue to encourage you and enrich your life.

SUMMARY

- Feelings of fulfilment exists in the alignment of mind, body and soul.
- Interconnection of these elements attunes you to the harmonious vibration from which your core essence resonates.
- Soul insight is channelled through mind, body, spirit unison.
- Centre yourself and step safely upon your path to divine expansion.
- Embrace multi-consciousness and unearth the secrets of your extraordinary gifts.
- Anchoring the perceptions of your higher-self frees you from singular consciousness.
- Expanded awareness allows you to see the connectedness of all.

CONTEMPLATION

*Contemplation gives access to the quiet space within
It is in this space that mind, body and Soul meet and
derive guidance, meaning and truth.*

*If preconceptions, judgements and beliefs were
suspended, the illusion of separation would dissolve
and in its place would be the connection shared
between humans, who as individuals are part of the
collective experiencing life with the knowledge and tools
available to them at that time.*

Contemplation

Contemplation through focused attention gives voice to your intuitive guidance

Contemplation provides the insight needed to make informed decisions.

Listen in silent contemplation to wise inner counsel. Contemplation digs beneath the surface of superficial thought to reveal higher-self perspective. Answers that resonate during contemplation are those that can be heeded with confidence. Have faith in the messages received during contemplation. Contemplation births realization and provides those "aha" moments. Trust that the information derived from contemplation will provide the guidance needed.

GUIDANCE

Contemplation is called for when faced with a decision, there is a need to find a solutions or when feeling clouded or disillusioned. Connecting with the higher-self is achieved through contemplation. This is felt by inner-knowing that resonates strongly without wavering.

The answers and solutions derived from contemplation can be trusted to be aligned with best possible options and outcomes. What is received may not be expected, but it will be accurate. Denying the feeling of inner knowing will not change the truth. Hush the chatter of the mind so wise inner counsel can be received.

Inner guidance cannot be pushed in the direction we want it to go. It moves in the direction of the truth. The truth is felt when thoughts and feelings align. If they are not aligned then further contemplation is required. This may uncover an aspect with a distorted perception of the truth, which means it will reject anything opposing its belief. This creates a blockage and may be the root cause of repeat patterns of behaviour and thoughts that sabotage progress. If this resonates, which is a deep feeling of inner-knowing that cannot be denied or dismissed, refer to the blockage reflection.

Find some space where you can sit in silence. Become the casual observer of your environment – just watch without thought or attachment. Everything just flows. If thoughts try to interfere, imagine that you have a feather duster and gently brush them away. Give your mind the task of taking note of what emerges from your contemplation.

Take a deep breath in and on the out breath feel yourself relax. Do this a few times and when feeling calm and relaxed bring your focus onto what you want to contemplate.

Explore the scenario from different perspectives; allow your mind to roam. Sometimes during contemplation the pendulum of the mind will swing fully one way and then swing fully in the opposite direction. Then it will swing to and fro until a balanced perspective is achieved. During this process the for and against information will be presented and this will evoke feelings. Feelings will guide one way or another until a clear picture emerges.

Notice what is thought and what is felt during this process.

Thoughts will try to take charge, following or tracing such thoughts to where they stem from will lead to an aspect that wants things a particular way. Awareness of what this is enables change. Change is necessary if thought processes are not aligned with your highest-good. Aligning with highest-good is to trust what resonates with inner-knowing. No amount of trickery can fool the truth which is revealed by being honest with yourself, opening your mind and rather than seeing what you want to see you see what is actually there. Be patient as it might take some time for information to filter through. Guidance comes from deep within, holds wisdom and resonates strongly. Mind-chatter is superficial and can be challenged. Hearing and feeling inner guidance gives composed understanding. With practice you will become familiar with true guidance and instinctively know the difference between being lead by the mind and guided by wisdom.

Contemplation gives access to the quiet space within. It is in this space that mind, body and soul meet and derive meaning aligned with the highest-good.

PLEDGE OF CONTEMPLATION

I receive guidance, personalized feedback, and deeper understanding through contemplation.
My mind is flexible, can think laterally and construct concepts that supports me in making wise decisions that are aligned with my highest good and potential. Being considered, reasonable and balanced in my approach enables me to see clearly and take the direction I need at any stage during my journey.

When mind chatter is hushed inner knowing can emerge.

SUMMARY

- As answers materialize trust what resonates within.
- Feelings of not being in sync with what you propose may be a sign that you are misaligned with your highest good.
- Take time to hush the chatter of the mind.
- Listen in silent contemplation to your wise inner counsel.
- Place faith in your ability to decipher messages.
- Realization is born through contemplation.
- Discover "ah ha" moments in which things fall into place and you intuitively know what to do.

CONTEMPLATION

I hear the wise counsellor within, it is that which speaks the truth and aligns me with my higher self and purpose.

The act of contemplation gives voice to intuition.

Spiritual Quest

Creativity

Creation is vision in motion

 *Construct life using the positive images of the mind.*

The conscious mind imprints the images the subconscious uses to produce the canvas of life. Every experience is sculptured by thoughts, feelings and perception. Their colour and vibrancy will be reflected in what is created.

If inner sight is clouded the vision of self will be dulled as will be the outlook on life. This reduces the ability to be the self-creators we are capable of being.

Focus determines outcome. Focusing in on one's imperfections will reduce the capacity to see what one is capable of. Honing in on qualities provides a constructive view that bolsters confidence.

An evaluation of personal attributes brings the focus onto qualities. At the same time we acknowledge our attributes we may also bring to light certain vulnerabilities. This is the development of self-awareness.

Every person has a mixture of strengths and vulnerabilities. This is part of what makes us unique and at the same time contributes to what we share with others.

What we focus on is emphasized. If we focus on our vulnerabilities then perception edges towards negatively, thus we will be receiving negative feedback.

If the awareness is directed towards strengths then the creative channels are infused with positivity. Becoming self-aware provides the opportunity to focus on strengths and to shift direction if vulnerabilities become the point of our focus.

As self creators being aware of how thoughts, feelings, beliefs and perceptions affect every aspect of self and how aspects of self affects thoughts, feelings, beliefs and perceptions.

Getting to know how different aspects of self influence us takes time. But the time dedicated will be well rewarded. There are some aspects that hide in the psyche and there are some that make themselves well known.

They are heard through the inner-dialogue and they impose their thoughts, feelings, and beliefs upon the mind. This is not a split in personality these aspects are part of the whole, they contribute to our character forming the self we identify with. If the perception of any of the aspects that make us who we think we are is askew with our wants, wishes and desires then we need to identify the aspects causing the misalignment and make necessary readjustments.

Misaligned aspects can catch us up in mind chatter that is unhealthy and non-beneficial. The negative voice within belongs to such aspects.

None of which has anything to do with who we really are but the self that has been constructed through interpretation of experiences.
Mind chatter creates a barrier that keeps us separated from higher-aspects of self. When trapped in the thought churning factory very little happens as the focus is on menial, meaningless and uninspiring topics or on personal insufficiencies. This is disempowering, self-destructive and prevents access to the inner-realms of creativity.

Disengaging from the thought churning factory requires conscious awareness and active engagement with the creative-self. This can be done in many ways song, dance, writing, painting, meditation, yoga, cooking, crafting, knitting, drawing and the list goes on. Discovering what you enjoy is a matter of try until you find or acting on an inkling.

Everyone has a way of connecting with their creativity it may just require trying a few different things to discover what that is.

Moving to the rhythm of the creative mind hushes the conscious chatter, enabling the mind to open and expand. An open mind attracts inspirational ideas. Feelings of inspiration, enthusiasm and optimism arise when engaged with the creative-self.

Becoming the quiet observer of self is to see the differentiation between the whispers of the inner-being and the drone of meaningless thought. Hushing thoughts so the inner whispers can be heard is to be thought aware which is to be the directors and conscious creators of self.

Becoming aware of thoughts is the first step toward conscious creation. If noxious thoughts are detected they need to be transformed into healthy ones.

Using affirmations forms good thought habits, the proof can be found in the benefits of using an affirmation for just a day. They will also make you aware of unhelpful thoughts that are having a negative effect.

Recognizing negative thoughts, negative thought patterns or insistent thoughts that prevent affirmations from taking hold leads you to discover the aspect behind those thoughts.

The aspects will almost always hold a view that opposes the affirmation. This requires some work so that the perception of certain aspects can be acknowledged and shifted.

Reflecting on what is being presented by an aspect provides insight into the inner most thoughts and feelings. This is using strengths to assist vulnerabilities.

Uncovering where vulnerabilities lie can be done by tracing the thought back to its roots. This may lead to something that was said in the past or an impression received.

Breaking down the role you take within the family, relationships, friendships, career and any other area of relevance will provide insight of the messages received and how they were derived.

To gain truthful answers about the impression you hold about yourself ask questions such as what judgments do I place on myself? How do you perceive myself? How do I feel about myself?

Use a journal to write down the answers to these questions, be honest and you will be amazed at the insight gained and the aspects you will uncover.

It is these aspects that are not moving in the same direction as you or are not moving forward as they could. One such aspect is the inner-critic, which is an aspect that finds it difficult to move past perceived barriers.

Often recognizing an aspect is enough to help it shift, or some inner-coaching may be required. This is to activate the inner-mentor.

ACTIVATE THE INNER MENTOR

If the inner-mentor needs assistance it will guide you to find the information or knowledge needed to enhance your awareness. It will then motivate you to implement the techniques that will assist a change in perspective such as focusing on strengths rather than on areas of weakness.

Finding strengths is to screen self through positive eyes. Write down your strengths. Ask yourself what someone else might say is a strength of yours. Think of what you might say about yourself if you were writing your autobiography.

Note your qualities. This may be that you have a compassionate nature who genuinely cares about the welfare of fellow human and animal beings.

When you have done an honest appraisal of your strengths/qualities pick one and state it to yourself. Listen for anything that opposes what you say. The inner-critic may interject with criticism or there may be another aspect that disagrees with what you say.

These aspects distort the overall perception of self, hence the need for them to be aligned with a positive view.

Realigning an aspect that holds a negative view point begins by acknowledging what is being said and then counteracting with a positive statement.

Acknowledging an aspect's view point is important so that it feels heard, whereas continuous overruling may alienate and cause it to become repressed the ramifications of such will become evident sometime later.

Dealing with aspects as they arise develops a foundation of trust, respect and honesty within oneself.

This facilitates a transparent relationship with

the inner self and lights the channel that enables higher aspects of self to flow through, thus seeing the emergence of the true self.

This is an example of acknowledging and counteracting an internal statement based on a belief "I can't do this" acknowledge this inner statement by saying "this does present as a challenge, but I have encountered challenges before".

Then counteract with "every day I am coping better and I am capable in many areas such as (insert something from strengths list)". Use this counter statement as an affirmation to reinforce the positive statement.

Being aware when an aspect is trying to distort or cloud a positive view of self enables you to attend to that aspect by acknowledging and countering the statement.

If strengths/qualities are reinforced and kept at the forefront of the mind vulnerable aspects have less impact.

Creating word cards to reinforce qualities helps to shift the focus onto positive attributes. This is the true definition of creativity as you are consciously creating the person you want to be, reflected through the qualities you now acknowledge, nurture and actively demonstrate. This is to be the most amazingly creative being.

Take some nice deep breaths in through the nose and then exhale out through the mouth.

When you are feeling comfortable and relaxed allow your mind to create the following vision.
You find yourself floating above the clouds. In the distance you see a figure coming towards you.
You feel a sense of familiarity and as the figure moves closer you see it is a wise guide.
When the guide reaches your side he/she smiles, you feel at ease and trust this guide.
Together you sit upon a cloud.
You speak first and ask why he/she has come.
The guide answers in a wise gentle voice telling you that they have been with you all along and have been waiting for you to acknowledge them.
You nod with understanding.
You talk for some time and then he/she hands you a note.
On the note is a message that says: You are the

conscious creator of self and you have the capacity to shape yourself any way you desire.

You look at the guide who nods and smiles.

You continue to read the rest of the message.

It says: *Express yourself to the fullest, you will prosper in all your endeavours, remember your qualities and utilize them each and every day.*

You sit quietly for a moment and digest the meaning of the note.

You feel empowered, inspired and courageous.

You and your guide exchange knowing glances that the note speaks the truth.

Together you rise; you thank your guide for being with you.

They have awakened something that you have always known deep within, and are now consciously bringing into your awareness.

You also know that following your heart will guide you to exactly where you need to be.

You bid your guide farewell and watch as he/she walks away and fades into the clouds way beyond.

You now return to your body awakened and invigorated with creative energy.

You are a magnificent creator.

PLEDGE FOR CREATIVITY

Everything I have in my life today is testament to the creative being that I am.

I choose to colour my creations with positivity.

I am aware of what I say and what I do as this is what I will create.

I see myself, my life and others in a positive light.

This is how I choose to see my world and this is how the world will be reflected back to me.

Focusing on my qualities enables me to see the talents and skills available to me.

SUMMARY

- What you imagine you can create.
- Reality is a product of the sketches held in the conscious and unconscious mind.
- Life's lessons place a brush stroke on the canvas of life.
- Imperfections are not separate but part of the divine self.
- Sculpt life until it blossoms into a masterpiece.
- Acknowledge that experiences are the pearls from which wisdom is derived.
- Be courageous and step out of the comfort zone.
- Unlock the creative centre, unveil the truth and project positive images until they mould into reality.
- There is a new world waiting to be created, embrace the journey.

CREATIVITY

I consciously create the person I want to be, by acknowledging, nurturing & actively demonstrating my unique qualities.

Spiritual Quest

Dream

Tap into your dream account and access the power of your creative visualization.

 The conscious creation of dreams requires continual reinforcement of the visual images aligned with desires, wants and wishes. This is using the language understood by the subconscious, which is the power that motivates the formation of all goals, aspirations, ambitions and endeavours. Continual reinforcement of the visual images and the associated positive feelings that emerge forms the basis of dream manifestation. Be bold, be brave and inspire the imagination in the direction of your dreams.

To dream is to fly beyond limitations and return bearing the blueprints of something others deemed impossible. Unlock the potential that awaits.

Night-time dream interpretation: The symbolic meaning of dreams can be found through interpretation.

A dream journal and a dream meaning book are great tools to assist with dream interpretation. Before falling asleep ask that the events of the day be processed swiftly to clear the mind, so it is more receptive to the signs, symbols and messages presented in dreams.

Dream content draws attention to aspects of the past that are yet to be processed, provides insight into current issues and allows one to gain glimpses of possible future occurrences.

Recording the contents of a dream in a journal helps uncover the relationship to what is presented to the past, present or future. The symbolic meaning of people, places, animals and concepts can be understood by taking a closer look at what they represent in the dream.

Often they relate to some aspect of the dreamer for instance if a lion enters a dream it can represent different things, depending on what is relevant to the dreamer.

The image of a lion could mean that there is fear that is interfering with the ability to empower oneself or that courage is needed pertaining to a project, an idea or the pursuing of something the dreamer feels is out of their grasp. Intuitive guidance is a wonderful resource to use for interpreting the meaning of dreams.

Repetitive dreams indicate that attention is needed in relation to some area of life. Unravel the meaning and something of significance will be revealed. If dreams are dark then this could indicate that there are shadow aspects begging to be explored.

Dream interpretation provides the clues needed to unlock the secrets hidden in the subconscious. Being aware of what stands in the way enables the release of old patterns.

Releasing the old creates space for the new. This liberates the spirit with more freedom to function as it is destined to. Thus arises new perspectives, new ways of thinking and a newly empowered state of being.

As these shifts occur it becomes apparent that dreams can be created consciously. The manipulation of the subconscious mind for the benefit of aligning higher-good with reality begins the creation of a different kind. From superficial wants emerges something with significant depth. Materialistic acquisitions become less attractive and heart-based purpose is sought.

Fill your dream account with self-belief, make heart-based choices and nurture your unique qualities and you will be pleasantly surprised at how easily your dreams can become a reality.

TECHNIQUE

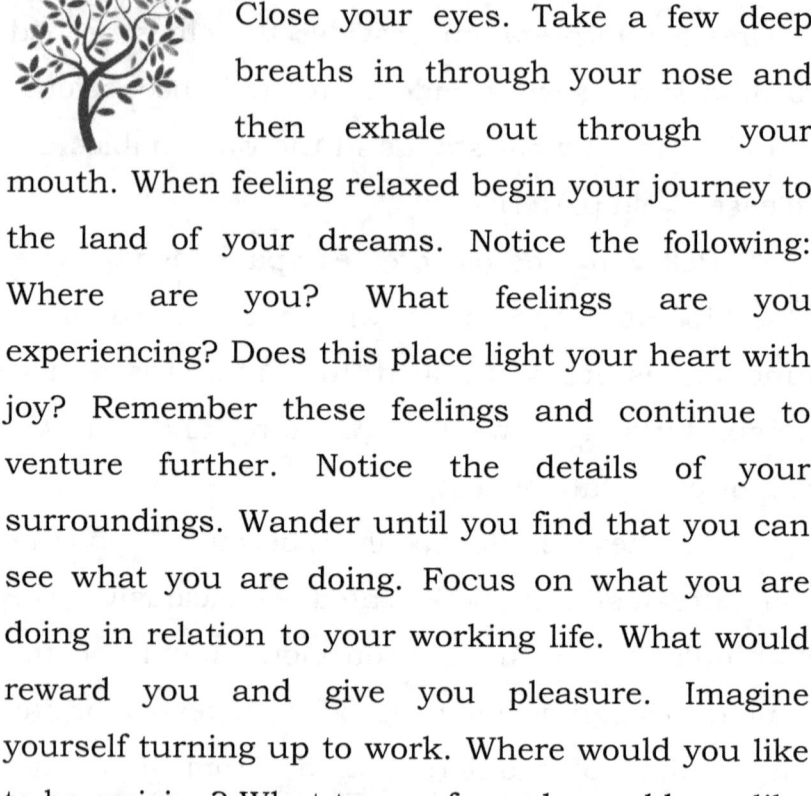

Close your eyes. Take a few deep breaths in through your nose and then exhale out through your mouth. When feeling relaxed begin your journey to the land of your dreams. Notice the following: Where are you? What feelings are you experiencing? Does this place light your heart with joy? Remember these feelings and continue to venture further. Notice the details of your surroundings. Wander until you find that you can see what you are doing. Focus on what you are doing in relation to your working life. What would reward you and give you pleasure. Imagine yourself turning up to work. Where would you like to be arriving? What types of people would you like to be working with or would you prefer to work alone?

Once you have a good overview of where you would like to be and what you would like to be doing wander further to who you would like to have in your life. The types of people you would like to be surrounded by. When you have a good idea of who they are wander further to focusing on what you would enjoy doing for yourself and what you would like to be doing with others. When you have done this wander further and as you do see all the things that you believe would enrich your life.

Visiting the Solutions Tree: You see a tree up ahead, on it are notes containing possible solutions to any issues you may be having. Think about the issue and state it either out loud or to yourself. You reach up and pluck a note from the tree and open it. This is a reasonable and doable solution.

You know that you can implement this solution and it will have good effect. You can visit the solutions tree whenever you have a dilemma, issue or seek insight.

When you are ready to return feel yourself safely grounded in your body. You are present and ready to consciously create the visions of your dreams.

You are a master creator of your dreams and will find ways of achieving whatever it is you desire. See it, feel it, affirm it and you shall have it.

PLEDGE FOR DREAM ENHANCEMENT

My dreams, desires and aspirations are intuitive insights providing me with a blueprint of a possible future.

I will use the inner and outer resources available and dreamscape this possibility into reality.

I am the director of my destiny; today I take charge and guide my life forward with positive momentum.

I inspire! I plan! I act! I receive! My life is as I dream.

Believe in your ability to be a powerful, conscious creator of your dreams.

SUMMARY

- During dream time the subconscious mind presents many visions.
- Whether the messages of your dreams are cryptic or understood, all are symbolic.
- Consciously imprint your desires into your subconscious mind and it will create your external environment to align with your inner vision.
- Acknowledge the strength of your creative talent as evidenced through your dreams.
- Anchor your belief in visual effectiveness.
- Transform your reality to appear as you dream it to be.

DREAM

*I awaken to the destiny of my dreams.
All I wish for and desire can be achieved.*

Spiritual Quest

Embrace

*Embrace all aspects of self with the kindness
and care they require as they are part of what
makes you whole.*

 Understanding the inner aspects of self is to tune into thoughts, feelings and emotions and uncover what they are communicating. Feelings act as radars that guide the direction of choice.

Although we can suppress our emotions we cannot deny what we feel. Emotions are expressions of the many aspects that are identified as self. Surfacing of emotion that is linked to a wounded aspect needs to be embraced with the compassion it deserves.

Every time we embrace an aspect that needs embracing we are granted the gift of understanding where limitations and vulnerabilities lie. This facilitates and inspires an empowered self.

There are many aspects that contribute to the whole of our being. These aspects are heard through thoughts and felt through emotions.

The surfacing of denied or suppressed emotions can be unpleasant, but they give us insight into unconscious aspects of the psyche. Unconscious does not mean invisible as they transmit energy and have contributed in some way to the formation of who we are.

This is who we identify with, which is the

compilation of our thoughts, emotions, beliefs and perceptions. This is the manufactured self, not the real self which ultimately is the soul.

However our thoughts and feelings are very real to us and therefore require our attention. Because if ignored these aspects will continue to present themselves in unsatisfactory ways, such as interfering with relationships, friendships, finances, career and the way we think and feel about ourselves.

Another repercussion of suppressed emotion is the manifestation of acute or chronic disease. All emotion is energy; suppressed emotion is often associated with a negative experience and as such will carry a negative vibration.

Negativity opposes flow and causes blockages, which present as health complaints. This does not mean that we are to blame for the manifestation of illness.

The issue is arising from an aspect that requires attention and until it is attended to it remains caged in the same mind-set, feeling the same negative emotion. The way to best serve such an emotion is to acknowledge it, feel the emotion attached and process it.

Vulnerable aspects block and limit us in some way. Rather than being shunned or rejected these aspects need to be embraced, nurtured and comforted. When embraced in this way the tendency to define what can't be done is exchanged to what can be done.

Often it is through our vulnerabilities that we discover just how strong and courageous we are. This is the beginning of self-acceptance which creates a solid basis on which self-love is built. Part of self-acceptance is to give ourselves permission to feel our emotions.

Embracing emotions transforms them so they cease to have negative influence. An example of an aspect that has a negative influence is the inner-victim which believes that no matter what it does it is destined to fail, it will attract the wrong relationship, that everything bad happens to it and that success, should it happen, would be jeopardized.

The inner-victim sees itself as the pawn rather than the conductor of life, believing that we are the victims of our circumstances, that the world is against us and that there is nothing that we can do about it. Evidence that supports inner-victim perspective will be sought and confirmed from various sources including the media and through association with like-minded people.

The inner-victim can go completely unnoticed, as any aspect can, as the way it thinks and feels is accepted as normal. This has been proven and reinforced through experiences that align with its perception.

Recognizing the inner-victim requires attention. Thoughts such as 'oh this always happens to me', 'it is just the way it goes', 'I can't do anything about it', 'no use even trying', are some of the many inner-conversations held with the inner-victim. Feeling defeated, deflated and blamed are felt by the inner-victim.

There are times when most of us hear these negative internal comments, dismissing them soon after. This becomes different when the inner-victim dominates and the negative thoughts are constant companions.

The inner-victim is one of the many aspects that needs to be embraced and shown an alternative perspective. This is done through a healthy dose of positive internal dialogue, patience and persistence

The inner-victim will become active and reminded of the dire consequences should its beliefs be threatened. The challenge is shifting a mind-set that has been active for years. This is where diplomacy, kindness and compassion is needed, for one cannot dissolve an aspect, one can only reshape its perspective.

Ultimately, shifting the inner-dialogue to encourage the inner-victim to think differently is the most effective way of transforming a negative outlook to one of positivity.

While the inner-victim will still exist it will have less impact on how things are perceived. Getting to know the different aspects is imperative to transcend limitations.

As with all self-limiting aspects the inner-victim needs to be convinced that there is another way and this can only be done by consciously and constantly reinforcing a new perspective.

Half-hearted attempts will not be successful, only the strong-willed will instill the trust needed for the inner-victim to re-evaluate its position. Luckily, whether acknowledged or not, each one of us has this strength. It is a matter of cultivating it.

Once cultivated it will be a significant asset of

great value. Ask yourself which aspect is guiding your current perception? Listen, feel and all will be revealed.

As certain aspects loosen their grip and no longer have the hold on our thoughts and feelings we move closer to discovering the essence of who we are. Hence uncovering the magnificence qualities of our soul. This is something worth striving for.

While certain aspects can cause emotional discomfort they provide opportunity to grow. Denied aspects become the shadow that dulls our light. They become vulnerabilities that disempower.

Have courage, look within and illuminate shadow aspects through acknowledgement and awareness of their existence. Recognize limitations without being tripped over by them.

At the core of vulnerability is the ability to discover more about the different aspects of self and how those aspects may be influencing the overall perspective.

What has been accepted as a truth may not be true at all and is merely an aspect that needs to be embraced and shown another way of seeing things.

Fearful aspects desperately need to be embraced as they construct significant barriers that block the way.

Embracing fear dissolves barriers. The result is the freedom to become empowered human beings. As empowered human beings we have the ability to change our life any way we choose and in doing so we make our contribution towards shifting into higher consciousness.

Approach life optimistically. Unfurl your defenses, trust your heart and infuse your life with love. Be authentic and attract like authenticity. Imagine your heart dispersing light energy that fills up your entire body.

See this light energy wrap itself around you in its embrace. Breathe into the heart centre and feel the love radiate into every cell of your mind...body...and soul... continue to do this until you really feel this love flowing through you. Being embraced by love dissolves fear, and nourishes the whole of your being.

TECHNIQUE

Feel love and warmth fill your heart centre. The love grows in intensity as it swirls. The energy of love may be represented as pink or green light.

You feel it flow down your arms. You can feel your arms laden with beautiful loving energy.

As you stand in an abundance of love. You see someone walking towards you looking.

This person looks bewildered and unsure as they approaches and does not know how you will receive them if they show themselves.

As you take a closer look you recognize this as a vulnerable aspect of yourself.

You invite this aspect to come to you, but it shies away in fear that you may reject it.

You walk to your vulnerable self and smile warmly, it softens and begins to feel less apprehensive.

You then take your loving arms and embrace your vulnerability.

It melts into you, absorbing the compassion and understanding you infuse into it.

As the aspect moulds into your embrace, you feel the vulnerability is dissolving and in its place is strength and confidence.

PLEDGE TO EMBRACE SELF

I embrace every aspect of of me, as that is what makes me complete.

I know my qualities and strengths and use these to support my vulnerabilities.

I accept myself as I am and embrace this self to become all I can be.

I acknowledge my potential and utilise my inner resources to coach this to fruition.

SUMMARY

- Embracing limitations and vulnerabilities initiates the uprising of hidden strengths.
- Surfacing emotions seek your understanding, embrace them with compassion.
- Accepting all of oneself is the foundation of unconditional love. This is to exchange viewing self through the eyes of ego for viewing self through the eyes of the soul.
- From this evolves the confidence to expand

through imagined boundaries and discover all that you are capable of.

EMBRACE

*I lovingly embrace every aspect of myself.
I choose to focus on my strengths and support my
vulnerabilities and by doing so
I am being authentic to myself*

Spiritual Quest

Empowerment

Self Empowerment gives me courage needed to do as I am destined

You are an Empowered being capable of extraordinary things

Self- empowerment is to know the intimate details of our inner self. Our inner selves are composed of various aspects and although they are part of the whole of our being, they are unique in their interpretations, thoughts, feelings and beliefs. Our beliefs are formed in various ways based upon our interpretation of our experiences and also from what has been imposed upon us during the early years of our development.

Beliefs are reinforced through internal dialogue and perceptions that are aligned with our beliefs. Anything can appear to be true, even what it bogus can be real to us if we believe it to be.

The monster under the bed, even though bogus, is real for a child. Although rational thought eventually dispels the monster the predisposition to make our beliefs real continues. Beliefs in scarcity, in separation, in failure, in hierarchy are all examples of false belief.

Religion is an example of beliefs built on the unknown. These beliefs dictate how we 'should' think, feel and act, even if it means judging, shunning and harming our own brothers and sisters on earth that share the realness of being human. This places free will, which is the ability to think, feel, explore and discover for ourselves in the confines of domination. That is the impact our beliefs have on us. Are they real? Not really.

Beliefs are powerful and if geared negatively towards self are extremely detrimental. Negative belief about self is disempowering.

Disempowered aspects impact the whole. This happens through thoughts, emotions and beliefs, which are intricately interconnected. Thoughts stimulate emotions which are linked to beliefs about self and others.

Thoughts are communicated through the inner-dialogue. The inner-dialogue is connected to inner aspects of self. Some aspects of self are disempowered and hold a negative view.

These aspects generate negative thoughts. If unchecked these thoughts become the predominated way of thinking. If they go into overdrive they take over the emotions.

Negative behaviour is the expression of thoughts and emotions that are spiraling in an unfavourable direction. When thoughts and feelings cast a shadow they adversely affect well-being and sabotage happiness.

The effect is further disempowerment presented in numerous ways such as thoughts, feelings and behaviour that is self-defeating, self sacrificing, uninspired, guilt ridden, angry, despondent, dissociative just to name a few.

Catching ourselves before we are pulled into a downwards spiral is empowering and unties the intertwined thoughts/emotions/reactions cascade from occurring. This is to be emotionally aware.

Emotional awareness develops through increased awareness of what is happening when it is happening and applying tools and techniques that facilitate communication where emotions are expressed in a way that acknowledges what is being felt and enables positive outlet.

Being emotional aware is to develop the capacity to be objective about what is being experienced subjectively. And it happens that life provides many opportunities in which we can practice and develop emotional awareness skills.

Life exposes us to a variety of situations that enable exploration of our external and internal worlds. Some experiences will evoke pleasant emotions and some will evoke unpleasant emotions. Pleasant emotions are desired, they are dynamic motivators.

The desire to satisfy the need to feel pleasant emotions lies at the core of most of our endeavours. In opposition to this is the desire to avoid unpleasant emotions.

Uncovering the emotions that have caused pain goes against instinct. However, at the core of unpleasant emotions are aspects of self that yearn for attention. They make themselves known through thoughts.

When thoughts are negative it is probable they are linked to an aspect that is reflecting something from the past.

These aspects are stored in the subconscious, which not only communicates with every cell of the body, but exists in every cell of the body. Which means that every cell has memory and is emotionally intelligent.

The mind is in constant communication with every cell of the body, if the mind is disturbed then every cell in the body will be effected. The predisposition of a person will determine the outcome, which is often expressed as a health concern of some form.

The body houses the soul and the soul will flag disharmony by sending messages through the body. If the attention needed is not received then our well-being is in jeopardy.

When attending to the needs of the body it is important to remember to attend to the underlying needs. To ignore what lurks beneath disempowers and denies the opportunity to discover, learn and grow.

Uncovering what underlies a symptom requires objectivity. This is done by observing what comes forth with empathy. This approach is to become the witness of the emotions. The witness can gain objective insight without becoming attached to the experience or the associated emotion.

This process may trigger emotions and stimulate emotional release. This is where empathy is required to assist the emotional aspect through the shadow so it can emerge into the light. This does not mean that experiences have to be relived; it does mean that the emotion attached to the experience is acknowledged.

Acknowledging emotion is to become consciously aware, this is an empowered state.

Being empowered is to have choice and in that lays the ability to find and utilize tools and techniques that aid the process of becoming emotionally aware. Emotional awareness is the key to self-empowerment.

TECHNIQUE

Start by breathing into the solar plexus, the area near your navel.

Take a deep breath in through your nose and then exhale out through your mouth. Imagine your breath is flowing into your solar plexus area. Repeat a couple of times or until your breath is flowing smoothly and your thoughts are at rest.

When you are focused and comfortable notice any stirrings or discomfort in this area. Ask for guidance. This can be done silently or out loud. Then just observe. Notice any emotions that may arise. It may be easy to try and escape the emotion by dismissing it or allowing thoughts to intrude, but try to remain present and stay with the emotion.

An emotion may be represented as a feeling,

a vision, a word, a message or a memory. Watch as you would a movie. As you watch ask yourself what is being communicated? What does it mean to you? Is this serving or non-serving? Accept what comes up, without interjection. You are creating a safe space where you are allowing your emotions to express themselves. You are getting to know vulnerable aspects of self.

This awareness enables vulnerabilities to be supported. This can be done by using the mind's eye, which constructs the visual images of the mind and give phenomenal insight. Look and appraise honestly and without judgment. Be kind, be compassionate and allow your true self to emerge. The most magnificent being resides within. Seek and discover. Infinite possibilities await you.

When an emotion surfaces it will bring with it a realization of something that it is associated with. If it is associated with an unpleasant experience and is not attended to then it will, at some stage or another, cause disruption in some area of life. This is where the phenomenal power of the mind can be utilised to reconstruct the unpleasant experience to one that reflects positively.

By reconstructing the image the associated

memory changes and the associated emotion transforms. For example, fear in any form is an emotion that is mentally and physically disempowering.

Uncovering the reason for the fear, which may be associated with a childhood memory, will shift the perspective.

This shift is empowering as the aspect that was previously cowering in fear can see that while it may have been a scary experience as a child there is no need to carry that fear.

Fear that is associated with an experience will react the same way it did when first triggered, regardless of the amount of time that lapses. An effective way of addressing fear is to ACKNOWLEDGE it and TRANSFORM it.

Empowerment is found when we have the courage to recognize aspects of self that are disempowering. Acknowledgment and assimilation of these aspects transforms choices into those that will achieve desired outcomes.

SELF-EMPOWERMENT

Following is a personal experience I will share about the powerful effect of transforming a negative experience using creative visualization.

Healing Asthma

I once visited a hypnotherapist. As I was leaving we were talking about how crippling fear can be. She put her hands on my shoulders and looked me in the eye and said "No Fear". Those words triggered something in me and for the rest of the day they replayed over and over in my mind.

In bed that night I just allowed myself to listen to the words to see where they took me. After a minute or so my breath got caught in my throat and I could feel an asthma attack coming on. It was like my mind was trying to block me by diverting my attention to the asthma.

I just kept focusing on my breathing while silently repeating the words "No Fear" I knew that if I could move past the symptoms of the asthma I would uncover something. Suddenly my focus switched from the breathing and I went back in my mind to a memory from long ago. I saw an image of myself at about two years of age I was in hospital standing in a cot crying out to my mother who was walking out a door. I felt frightened and bewildered that my mother was leaving me, perhaps I did not know if she would ever come back.

Penetrating through the noise of my crying come a harsh voice growling at me and telling me to lie down.

The combination of being separated from my mother and being growled at was extremely distressing and I began to cry louder. I then felt a sharp sting across my leg which made me fall onto the mattress and start sobbing.

The person who had growled at me and whose face in the vision I could not see, walked off, leaving me there sobbing. I didn't get much more that night, but knew that I would try again the next night.

The next evening I took myself to the same place and again it triggered the asthma. However it dawned on me that I was no longer the little girl crying in the cot, I was an adult observing what had happened. I then began to feel like I was like watching a scene in a movie.

There I was as a frightened child in hospital the

night before I had an eye operation.

The realisation was profound and provided the insight needed to pin point what had triggered 'my' asthma. So intense was the fear combined with the grief of losing my mother, as a two year old her disappearance was a loss, that the physical response was the symptoms of asthma. Note: The lungs are associated with grief and sadness.

The day after piecing this together I called my mother and she confirmed the vision saying that she wanted to ease me to sleep before she left, but the matron had told her it was best she left straight away as to linger would make it worse.

Hearing my cries made my mum turn around and re-enter the door, to which the matron ordered her out saying "go away, mother" my mother did as ordered against her will.

My mother says she will never forget how upset she was having to leave me in such as state. She also confirmed that from that day on I started having trouble breathing and shortly afterwards was diagnosed with asthma and put on puffers, which I continued to use until I changed the memory of that day so long ago.

CHANGING THE MEMORY

The following evening I repeated the same process of breathing while saying "No Fear" With less resistance my mind showed me the memory. I began to sob as if I was my two year old self again and was being left by my mother in that strange place.

I felt as though I was releasing what had been suppressed all those years ago. After allowing myself to express the emotion I took conscious control. Through my mind's eye I changed the scene.

I replaced the unkind matron for a kind, caring nurse who bundled me up in her arms, sat in a rocking chair next to the cot and sang to me while gently rocking. When I fell into a peaceful sleep the nurse put me in the cot and I slept soundly, awaking to my mother's smile. I did this every night for a month.

Over the course of the month I noticed that I was using the puffers less and by the time the month was up I no longer needed to use puffers.

From that time until now I am only confronted with asthma occasionally. If I believe stress is a trigger then I go back to the scene of me in hospital and recreated the pleasant experience and the asthma subsides. It has become apparent that whenever stability is threatened, as was the case in the hospital all those years ago, it triggers the same emotional response which results in asthma.

The asthma calls me to attend to my emotional needs. Using my mind's eyes I creatively visualized a new scenario. I supported the vulnerable inner-child through my visualization, by uncovering the reason for the fear and exchanging the negative experience for a positive scenario the fear dissolved and to my relief this healed the aspect that was an asthmatic.

The mind's eye can be utilized in profound ways to assist emotional healing. This can be done by recreating a scenario, by infusing the emotion with light, and embracing the fearful aspect with love.

For example, feeling unlovable can be traced back to an aspect that at some stage received the message that it was not lovable. This perspective can be changed by infusing this aspect with love.

Feelings of worthlessness can be exchanged for feelings of worthiness. This can be done for any aspect that holds a thought, feeling or belief that causes it to react in ways that is detrimental to your well-being. Practice, patience and perseverance are the essential ingredients needed for the task.

RELEASING NEGATIVITY

If an aspect is carrying negativity allow your mind's eye to form a picture of what negative energy might look like or imprint an image of a dark cloud, grey dust or black smoke. Whatever image is created see it fall to the ground and be swallowed up by the Earth. When it goes into the Earth it is neutralized and can no longer exert a negative effect. This clears the aspect of its negative perspective, it can then be open to exchanging the negativity for positive.

Creating Positive Vision: Create a vision in your mind of what you desire. Place your picture in a seed and visualize yourself planting the seed in your solar plexus. Nurture this seed with positive intention.

See and feel your seed grow and blossom and know that it will become what you intend. Check in on a regular basis to feed your desire positive energy. Enjoy the rewards of this exercise, it is testament of the power of the mind. Once aware of emotional triggers we are no longer at the mercy of things we have no control over, instead we are able observe and attend in positive ways. This is what it means to be self-empowered.

Please note: It is highly recommended that the support of a trained therapist be sought if there has been emotional disturbance, emotional imbalance or abuse of any kind. Although our minds will not allow us access to places we are not ready to go, even touching on certain aspects can cause intense emotional discomfort. If this happens while attempting a creative visualisation STOP and seek a trained therapist to support you through this stage of your journey.

TECHNIQUE

To untie the tangled emotion breathe deeply into your Solar Plexus. Count slowly to 5 or 10 and feel the knots untie and release.

Repeat twice or until feeling calmer and able to respond rationally. Responding rationally is the way to attend to the underlying need without suppressing emotion. The emotion and the need is attached to an aspect that encountered an experience that it did not have the maturity or insight to understand. To uncover the underlying need is to ask the inner-self "what is causing this reaction?" Tune into the answer. Once the reason is revealed it can be understood and provide an alternative perspective. This process helps diffuse intense emotion and intercepts reaction, providing the space to respond in ways that attend to needs through rational, heart-felt communication. This is positive communication and captures the spirit of our empowered self. The empowered self offers choice, enabling qualities to be revealed and vulnerabilities to be nurtured. Practice is the key to success. Apply patient determination.

Persevering when faced with inner-resistance

offers great personal reward. Every aspect has something of significance to share. Once understood, an aspect which was previously disruptive will assimilate into the whole and become one with self. This is the path of developing an empowered self.

PLEDGE FOR EMPOWERMENT

I am empowered to do what is right for me. I possess the tools and techniques to manage myself in ways that create positive outcomes. I assimilate all aspects of self to create a confident, self-assured, emotionally aware me. I design and drive my destiny in the direction of my dreams.

SUMMARY

- Connect to your own unique thoughts, feelings and beliefs.
- Release that which has been imposed upon you.
- Leave the past behind.
- Open the door into the future.
- Become centred in your own divine power.

- Discover your true identity by anchoring into your sense of self.
- Move the wheel of fortune in the direction of your dreams so you may see the opportunities and infinite possibilities awaiting you.
- Step from the shadows and become the driver of your destiny.
- Create positive intentions.
- Treat yourself and others kindly.
- Uncover your divine self and embrace your inner light.

EMPOWERMENT

*I claim the throne to my empowered self.
I honour myself with the life I wish to live.*

While we cannot push ourselves past the threshold of our conscious awareness we can choose to be open to seeing beyond what we currently know. This is to welcome conscious expansion, which is hugely empowering.

Spiritual Quest

Energy

You are surrounded by your very own subtle field of energy

Every aspect of mind, body and soul is energy.

Every thought and feeling is constructed by energy transmission. Surrounding the body is an energy field. While this field can be seen, it is essentially perceived on a subliminal level. Energy is transmitted in two ways, either positively or negatively. Energy vibrates at different frequencies. The lighter the energy the higher the vibration.

The higher self is the soul aspect of self, is an example of something that vibrates at a high frequency. Love, happiness and gratitude vibrate at a high frequency and will resonate with like vibration, hence they will attract love, happiness and gratitude.

Energy will accept or reject the vibration being transmitted from another. If there are aspects transmitting a low vibration they will attract low vibration energy. Aligning with positive vibration is to think positively, feel positive and respond positively. Energy cannot be deceived. It senses all. It projects the inner vibration of a person and will attract like vibration. Attraction and aversion are dynamic characteristics of energy. Aligning intentions positively is imperative to receiving positively. Positive energy makes us feel inspired and motivated. When energy is doused in negativity it becomes drained and depleted.

Energetic scanning helps detect thoughts and feelings that may be inadvertently projecting negative energy. If things are not aligning as hoped a scan is recommended.

If negative thoughts are moving through the mind, sometimes they loop or go on replay. This affects the vibration of the entire being. Some of us are more sensitive to this than others.

Those who are sensitive need to exercise caution when exchanging energy. Feelings of heaviness or of not feeling ourselves may signal that the energy of another has rubbed off. If allowed to hang around it may penetrate the energy field and weave its way into thought patterns, feelings and behaviour. Not thinking, feeling or acting like oneself calls for immediate energetic cleanse. See Techniques.

Attuning thoughts, feelings and emotions positivity is to travel in the light. If thoughts, feelings and emotions are clouded one travels in the shadows. Being aware of the energy projected by thoughts enables the implementation of tools and techniques that facilitate a positive shift.

Shed the mask that prevents you from displaying your true self. Notice when inner thoughts and feelings are not aligning with what you desire. Realign with positive affirmation. Avoid hiding behind yourself, be open, be honest and see the real you.

Sometimes we fear what may be presented, however when we uncover the underlying vibration we are emitting we can see how and why we are attracting certain things into our life. Address inner objections to your desires, for they unconsciously defy your wishes. Attraction of positive energy requires the generation of positive thought. This requires us to be mindful of what we are thinking from one moment to the next.

Everything is energy

TECHNIQUES

Energetic Cleanse

Smudging is a way of clearing the debris that sits in the energy field. Stand on a piece of Earth. Light a Sage smudge stick or Sage incense stick. Waft the smoke up the front of your body, over your head, down your arms, under your arms, down your back and down your legs. Using a feather disperse the smoke. See it going into the earth taking with it all energetic debris. This is an effective way to self smudge or you could have someone do it for you.

Visualisation

Picture yourself surrounded by your own field of energy. Place a silver cloth around yourself. The cloth will absorb any negative energy in your energy field. After a moment take the cloth off. When the cloth is removed it takes any negative energy that has been casting a shadow over you. Lift the silver cloth into the sun. The sun shines upon the cloth transforming the negative energy into light.

Self-Hug

Give yourself a hug. Fold your arms over your heart pull your arms in towards your body and embrace yourself. **Affirm:** *"I see all negative energy leave my energy field. I now see my energy field as radiant and full of positive ions that attract wonderful things to me. I am loved."*

OBSERVATION

Ever notice how the people in our lives change as we do and if they are resistant to change they fade out of our lives? This is due to the shift we make within ourselves which shifts our perception of how we view ourselves and how we view others.

If we are focused on our faults to the detriment of our qualities then no doubt those around us will be viewed in the same light. I love seeing the different people that flow into my life. I am also awed to see how the outer world reflects back what is going on within.

If I am feeling restless I will be greeted by agitation from those I come in contact with. If I am calm I am greeted with patience and consideration.

This is based purely on the energy I am transmitting. This is very useful as I can check in with myself and ask what is going on in me.

The same is true in relation to those who have a permanent position in our lives; these are the main characters of our life story and have been carefully selected based on what we need to learn at that stage.

However, there are some people we hold onto for longer that required and if the relationship if less than satisfactory it can become toxic. We always know when we have reached this point, but it is our choice to continue to hold on or let go.

When we let go one of two things will happen they will go and stay gone or there will be a transformation and there will be a reunion and the circumstance will be renewed.

Letting go is not always easy due to invisible agreements. These agreements are put into place to protect each other from experiencing things we fear such as rejection, worthlessness, guilt, shame etc.

The deal is that so long as we don't change we can continue the façade that keeps us safe. What this does is limit our ability to confront our fear, to face up to our shadow and to grow. All of which can feel threatening and so we choose to stay where we are in an unpleasant place of dissatisfaction, in the company of those content to share the experience and therefore also protected from having to face what they would prefer to ignore. It is a crafty arrangement that serves all in a non-serving way.

Should one of the parties awaken the change detected will threaten those sharing the silent contract. When the contract is broken it forces choices that will cause significant changes in a relationship.

If the choice by one party is to stay where they are the relationship will most likely dissolve and eventually the parties involved will go their separate ways. If the choice is to make the necessary changes that facilitate growth, then the relationship will strengthen. In these cases visions of miracles are shared and individual destinies are entwined.

PLEDGE FOR ENHANCING ENERGY

I allow my soul to infuse my mind and body with an abundance of positive energy. I see myself and others from soul perspective. I understand that the source of universal energy that flows within me is the same that flows within every living thing. I accept that each of us have different levels of conscious awareness and are at different stages of our evolution. I live and let live. Everyday I evolve emotionally, cognitively and spiritually. I am at one with the universe and I know that what I give is what I will receive.

SUMMARY

- While this field can be seen, it is essentially perceived on a subliminal level.
- You cannot deceive this sphere of intelligence as it is all seeing and all knowing.
- Attraction and aversion are dynamic characteristics of this energy.
- It projects your inner vibration and will attract like vibration.

- Aligning your intentions positively is imperative to receiving positively.
- Douse negativity so you may see the manifestation of your desires.

ENERGY

*My energy field is radiant
and full of positive ions.
I attract wonderful things into my life.*

Spiritual Quest

Enlightenment

Enlightenment is to incorporate
spiritual evolution
into human existence

The enlightened path is walked by those who choose to see the miracles in everyday life.

Surrender to the eternal journey of self-exploration and discovery.

Enlightenment is the evolution of the soul through human experience. It is accepting that trials and tribulations are part of life and knowing that their presentation serves a purpose.

All that life presents has choice attached. Living through higher purpose is to decide whether we get bogged down by the details of a problem or situation or surrender worries to higher aspects of self.

Surrendering cares to the higher self gives access to broader perspectives and understanding of life's events and experiences. This helps us to harness greater awareness of what happens and why. Energy expands as awareness grows, which is in contrast to the energy that is drained by the trivial details.

When perception widens bigger picture perspectives are gained. This brings focus into areas of significance, which includes life goals, aspirations and life purpose.

Maintaining a clear view of aspirations and goals is to listen to the voice of wisdom and clear away clouds of doubt. The evolution of our spiritual selves is to approach each day with a warm heart, an open mind and positive attitude.

Enlightenment is a gradual process of achieving heightened awareness, inner stillness and life balance. Achieving such is the amalgamation of the mind, the body and the soul.

This may seem like a challenging feat, especially when just to keep pace with the daily influx of internal and external stimuli can be challenging.

There seems to be more that pulls us away from the enlightened path than encourages sure steps upon it. The construction of high rise offices and shopping complexes are favoured over the building of ashrams where people can take time for meditation and quiet reflection.

Many businesses are more focused on the bottom line than on employee well-being. The home is full of devices that make noise that distract with incoming data and information that bombards the senses. But all those things, while distracting, contribute to our growth.

Challenges push us towards the pinnacle point that leads to breakthrough. If we didn't reach this threshold we would remain in a comfort zone as unaware beings hiding under a rock of superficial existence.

When we experience discomfort we are being challenged to wake up and do something. That is enlightening. Although we may fall back to sleep, our slumber will be shorter and our awakened state more potent each time.

Another important aspect to reflect upon in the uncovering of the enlightened self is choice. Choice is single-handedly the most powerful thing we do each moment of every day.

Choice is aligned in one of two ways. One is to align with ego and the other to align with soul. Soul aligned choices have significance, meaning and purpose.

These choices move towards the enlightened state of being. For example we can choose to be problem or solution focused. By choosing to be problem focused we emphasize and retain the problem.

In contrast to this, if we choose to be solution focused we evoke higher thought and guidance which helps to navigate the problem or dissolve it altogether. Other examples of choice exchange include choosing to construct new behaviours that produce desired outcomes in favour of retaining old habits that reinforce undesirable behaviour.

Choosing to construct positive thought that encourages and motivates in exchange of tuning into self defeating inner monologue promotes positive self belief in favour of retaining outdated, non-serving beliefs.

Choosing to be open to discovery and being prepared to make life enhancing changes is to walk the enlightened path where we find ourselves awestruck by what was previously taken for granted, accepted as part of life, or as not being anything of significance.

This is to be aware of the intent behind the choice, why the choice is being made and to explore possible outcomes.

Being mindful will highlight factors influencing choices and facilitate awareness of associated thoughts and feelings. Taking this into consideration and then projecting the possible outcomes of the choice helps to broaden the view.

By projecting the outcome of a choice into the future and asking if that is how you want your future to look is an effective way of gaining insight before making a choice. Of course, as with anything in life, there may be a few unexpected occurrences attached to a choice and readjustment may be required.

When alterations and adjustments are needed flexibility is an essential asset to employ. This directs us towards growth and development which is essential for soul growth. Knowing that the core of every experience contains the lessons needed to evolve is to be enlightened by the profound insights that comes from this knowledge.

Enlightenment is a gradual process of awakening

One must be brave and courageous to venture into the realms of the inner-self for it is here that the truth of who we are is discovered. Within this resides true enlightenment.

Making Enlightened Choices

Breathe deeply into your belly. Repeat a couple of times until feeling focused and relaxed. Bring your focus into your heart centre, feel the warmth and love. Gently breathe into this area. Relax your neck and shoulders, feel them drop down and as they do you feel the rest of your body relax.

Scan your body for areas that are still holding tension. Relax them one area at a time using the breath. Inhale into the tension and when you exhale release the tension. Feel it loosen and fade leaving you feeling calm and relaxed.

Tune in and actively listen to what the body, the mind and the soul is communicating. Stopping for a moment to attune to your body and asking what do you feel? Attuning to thoughts. What do they say? Attuning to the soul. What do you want? Not the superficial wants and desires, but the heart connected desires, the ones that come from higher aspects of self. Take a moment right now to ask these questions and reflect upon the answers.

This is the beginning of something transformational.

Call your Higher-Self for guidance

Imagine your higher-self as you think it may look like or allow an image to manifest in your mind. When you sense the connection with your higher-self bring a vision of a past choice in mind. What aspect of yourself did you use to make this choice. Did it feel the same as when connected to your higher-self? Notice the different perspective when making a past choice compared to the perspective taken when aligned with your higher-self. The higher-self provides insight and clarity and therefore choices are aligned with your best interest.

Setting intentions through higher-self perspective gives access to deeper understanding which enables choices that align with what it is you are meant to do. The decision making process is based on gathering evidence that supports self-development and soul-growth.

Insight into what this looks like is obtained by being present and attuning to the messages received from your heart and intuition. The guidance delivered through these channels is enlightening.

Affirmations are an effective practice that

activate and open these channels more fully. Choose an affirmation that resonates with your heart and repeat every day for one month.

After that month the ability to be heart centered and to tune into your intuition will be enhanced. This will contribute to a significant shift in perception that aligns more purposefully with higher aspects of self. Over the period of the month notice changes that occur.

You may meet aspects of yourself that are resistant to shifting their perspective. The ego, who prefers to be heard first, may object.

The ego-self needs retraining so it can accept that there is no hierarchy when taking a holistic approach to life. All is one and one is all.

This is a difficult concept for the ego aspect, as it sees itself as a separate entity and determines worth in ways different from soul perspective.

The spiritual self inspires the ego, which latches onto the idea and provides the motivation needed to get the project started. However it is the spiritual self that maintains the longevity of a project by maintaining the much needed passion and drive that retains the momentum. Whereas the ego will become distracted and dwindle.

It is evident that both aspects of our nature are necessary as is the need to maintain balance. Should one dominate we find ourselves ungrounded and challenged with living in the physical realm or we become absorbed with our physicality and become egocentric.

When balanced we approach our physical lives with spiritual perspective, which is to exchange selfish egocentric choices for ones that are selfless and have higher purpose.

Making Choices

Write down some significant choices you have made. What process did you use? What was the primary focus of these choices? Who was the primary focus of these choices? What did your feelings tell you about the choice you were making? How did you feel after making the choice? e.g. happy and content or doubtful and unsettled. How did you make your choice? Through rational thought? Intuitively? Or a combination of both? When you made your choice were your thoughts reflecting positivity or negativity? What were the influencing factors that helped confirm your choice? Was there a desire that was driving your choice? Evaluating the choice making process identifies what needs to be addressed to enhance future choices.

Making choices aligned with your highest good and taking right action requires awareness.

An Enlightened View of Self

Write down something positive about yourself. This may be a quality that you recognize in yourself or a quality you would like to possess. Having positive thoughts about yourself is encouraging and promotes self-esteem. State clearly what it is you see or want to see. Notice any thoughts that object when you state this quality about yourself. Upon detection of an opposing thought clearly state the following "while this may have been a past view of myself, I now choose to accept the new belief." Follow up by re-writing the positive reflection. Restate your positive reflection several times a day until it becomes a mantra. Within a short period the positive belief will be anchored in the mind and with continued positive reinforcement it will be received at cell level. When this happens the old negative belief has been fully exchanged and the positive belief is now fully accepted.

Take the time to visit the place within where mind, body and soul merge. From it comes inner-peace and serenity that will expand into every day.

PLEDGE FOR ENLIGHTENMENT

As an enlightened person I am aware of how my thoughts and feelings effect my actions and reactions. All experiences have meaning and purpose from which I learn. This is the quest of the spirit. The essence that gave me the energy to sustain life. Through expanded conscious awareness I evolve into all I can be. I am present, aware, insightful and ready to grasp opportunities that come my way. I can arrange the present in ways that facilitate the manifestation of my hopes, dreams and desires for the future.

SUMMARY

- Enlightenment it is to achieve inner calm while working through the trials and tribulations of life.
- Harnessing understanding and maintaining awareness throughout the twists and turns of your journey is the secret to living as an enlightened being.
- Surrendering cares to your higher self will assist in the processing and management of life's events and experiences.
- The awareness shared through your higher self places you firmly upon the enlightened path.
- Perceptions are transformed to align you with your destiny.
- Each day is sparked by the light of inner awareness.

Spiritual Quest

ENLIGHTENMENT

I am an enlightened being walking my destined path with love in my heart and light in my life.

There is no one thing that grants us an enlightened state of being. Enlightenment is a compilation of experiences from which we discover and learn. The more we uncover and understand the more enlightened we become. The ultimate discovery is the unveiling of who we truly are. This is to experience a state of pure enlightenment.

Spiritual Quest

Expression

I express myself by channeling my thoughts, feelings and emotions positively

Open, honest expression deepens the relationship with self and transforms communication with others.

 Thinking one thing and expressing another is unhealthy and harmful to the relationship shared with self and with others. Expressing thoughts and feelings honestly facilitates good communication.

Honest expression requires emotional responsibility. This is taking responsibility for your feelings and exploring why they have surfaced.

Openly discussing what is being felt and why facilitates understanding. Being emotionally responsible counteracts blame. This opens communication channels because there is no need for anyone to become defensive or be offended.

This does not mean that feelings can't be hurt by others, they can be. What it does mean is that blaming is dis-empowering as it takes away the opportunity to reflect on personal perceptions and interpretations.

Reflecting on these things creates awareness of how we can be affected by others and why. Sometimes there will be repeat incidents and if so this needs to be considered and rectified.

Repeat emotional reactions signal that there is an aspect that has an unmet need that requires attention. The people we invite into our lives are there to assist, even if it does not appear so at the time, as they are the ones who will trigger emotions, challenge beliefs and provoke the aspects needing attention. Often this is an aspect that blocks progress, limits potential and holds outdated beliefs.

When emotion surfaces conscious awareness is gained and the need to deny, ignore or suppress an aspect no longer exists it can be expressed and in doing so it is being attended to. This is being brave enough to air vulnerability.

Barriers come tumbling down and enable authentic expression, which is to express and communicate inner feelings honestly. This is to own one's feelings and communicate them without shame or blame.

The way another responds to what is being communicated will be based upon their own inner perceptions and interpretations. Being open and honest enables authentic communication which encourages others to drop their defenses and express in a similar way. This form of expression deepens the connection with self and transforms relationships with others.

Signs that what is being expressed is not aligned

with thoughts and feelings. Covering up emotions or radical expression are signs that there is misalignment.

Honest expression is to align what you say and do with the way you think and act. If you feel that it is necessary to speak and act differently to how you think and feel, you are not being true to yourself and there will be a nagging feeling of not fitting in with yourself or others.

Second guessing what you do or say, feeling wishy-washy and unsure are signs that you are not expressing your truth. Expressing how you really feel may arouse fear.

When fear rises its head we tend to retreat back to our comfort zone. This keeps us operating within the confines of our boundaries and reinforces our limitations.

Speak out and be yourself, this will attract the people who need to be in your life. The people who like you for who you are naturally are the ones you want in your life. Those who prefer the person you pretend to be are not needed. Deciphering who is who takes an honest approach and an abundance of courage.

How do we express openly and honestly when there

is confusion about how we are feeling and why? If inner evaluation of feelings has not been done then it is likely that there is a misalignment of what is being felt and what is being communicated.

It might be that we are communicating in ways that is not effective or that we are not attending to our needs and we are getting a figurative 'shake up' in the hope we will start paying attention. This can be confronting, especially if we don't like what we see or if we would prefer not to know. Don't despair.

Expressing thoughts, feelings and emotions honestly is healthy expression.

What we see may be magnified so we take notice. What we do with this is personal choice. We can ignore or look at it and see what pearls of wisdom are being offered. This concept is easier to reject than accept because what we see in ourselves is justified through our reasoning, hidden because it has been suppressed or rejected because we cannot accept that aspect of ourselves.

To effectively express ourselves we first need to understand what we are feeling. How we are feeling our emotions? Why these feelings are being triggered? When we feel these feelings? Who we are holding responsible for our feelings? Asking ourselves these questions gives us room to explore our feelings and emotions. This leads to clarity. This gives us the space to seek positive solutions and attend to our needs in a positive way.

Have courage enough to express your vulnerabilities. It is the strong who speak their truth without fear. Expressing from the heart is like being witness to the petals of a flower as it awakens to greet the first day of spring.

When the behaviour of others draws our attention it can be that they are reflecting something that needs attention within ourselves.

Thoughts trigger emotions and emotions trigger behaviour. Underlying the thoughts are beliefs based on perceptions and interpretations of experiences. Profound awareness is found by tracking how this process occurs within yourself.

Take a deep breath in through your nose and exhale gently through your mouth. Repeat this a couple of times. Clear your mind of thought and focus on your breathing.

When comfortable and relaxed think about a recent situation that caused an emotional reaction. Notice what happens in your body just by thinking about this. Reflect on the situation.

What happened that caused the emotional reaction?

Did the emotion come up by itself or was it a prior thought?

Was it something said or done?

How did you respond? Was there any associated behaviour?

Did you express how you were feeling or did you keep your feeling to yourself?

If you expressed yourself how did you do this? If

you didn't why not?

What happened afterwards? Were you able to let it go or did you continue to think about it? When you have finished with your reflection, breathe into your heart centre and connect with your heart energy.

Bring all your awareness into this area and feel yourself filling with love.

Send this energy to your throat area and feel it fill with love. Then send this energy to your solar plexus, the area near your navel. See this area filling with love.

When emotion is evoked honour yourself by acknowledging the emotion and expressing it as it feels for you.

Stop...Breathe...Consider and Respond.

Breathe into the heart centre. Take your focus into this area and imagine it filling with pink light. Visualize bringing this pink energy into the throat area. Set the intention of communicating through the heart with love and being authentic about how you feel. Be honest with yourself about how you feel and express with sincerity.

PLEDGE TO ENHANCE SELF-EXPRESSION

 I express my thoughts and feelings honestly. I live my life according to what is right for me, free from the opinions of others. My mind is strong and capable of making sound decisions. My thoughts are constructed with positivity that carries through to all my endeavours. I communicate in ways that ensure my message is received as intended.

SUMMARY

- Thoughts and feelings are generated by perceptions based upon inner beliefs and as such cannot be controlled by others.
- Taking responsibility for your emotions is empowering and allows you to better understand what you feel and why.
- Allow others to see your vulnerabilities, for they are part of what makes you whole.
- Authentic self-expression is to express openly and honestly from your heart.
- Peaceful and positive solutions are found by attending to your emotions with considered response rather than instantaneous reaction.
- Creative expression adds dimension and substance to who you are.

The only person you can change is yourself. When we change we find things around us change. There will be those in your lives that are not accepting of your change and they will drift away. Let them go for they are not meant to accompany you for this part of your journey. They may rejoin you in the future, but if not then your paths are not aligned. You will find those whose paths do align will join you. Whether they travel with you for a short or long period is irrelevant. It is what they bring with them that matters. If they bring the things that encourage you to expand and evolve then they are good companions indeed.

EXPRESSION

I listen and communicate through my heart. I am safe to honestly and openly express my thoughts and feelings.

Thoughts tainted with negativity do not go unnoticed. They will reveal themselves one way or another.

Spiritual Quest

Flow

I release myself into the flow of life
to be carried upon
the wings of Angels

*Open your arms in readiness to go with the flow
moving you in the direction of your dreams*

 *Universal energy that flows within all of us.*

This energy can be cultivated positively or negatively. When positive, our thoughts lift our vibration and aligns us with the positive universal energy and sets the inner vibe accordingly. When thoughts are negative they lower our vibration and aligns us with less evolved aspects of self.

These aspects need help so they grow and evolve. They have formed their perception on the way experiences have been interpreted. To enable growth the lens which the limited aspects of self sees through needs to widen its angle and broaden its view or it will remain restricted.

This is opposite to being in flow. When in flow we are focused and at the same able to see bigger picture perspectives. Being able to transcend limited views and become open minded is one of the purposes of life and part of human evolution.

If life is viewed through a lens that is attuned to the shadow aspects of human nature such as greed, jealousy, doubt and distrust, then one is not living life to its fullest capacity and is hindering expression of soul qualities.

Soul qualities are expressed through heartfelt feelings of compassion, kindness, acceptance, forgiveness, joy and peace. Experiencing flow is to be totally absorbed in what you are doing. It is drinking in the pleasure of seeing, hearing, feeling, and smelling what belongs to the moment being experienced.

A heavenly space is one spent immersed in the moment while experiencing all of what that moment presents.

Meaningless thought, or any that trigger less evolved aspects of self, stifle flow. Less evolved aspects are attached to emotions such as greed, jealousy, envy, resentment and other dense emotion that dull and diminishes. Whereas being in flow is associated with feelings that are light and uplifting.

TECHNIQUE

Exercise for insight into how thoughts can elevate or reduce mood.

Think of something that makes you feel happy. It might be a person, a place or an experience. Absorb yourself in it for a moment. Notice how you feel while having this thought. Now think of something that is unpleasant. Notice how your feelings change accordingly. Also notice the density of the emotions as you feel them.

Those that have unpleasant association are dense and restrictive compared to those that uplift. This gives instant insight into how thoughts and feelings affect our vibration – high and light – or low and dense.

Thoughts and feelings are composed of energy. This exercise shows that energy is not some mystical force, but something that exerts an effect every moment and with every thought.

We exchange energy in many ways. One way is through our experiences. Life is a series of experiences that contain various lessons from which we learn. How the experience is interpreted will determine the exchange, be it negative or positive. Positive interpretation is to identify what has been learned from an experience.

Recognizing the symbolic nature of an experience is to see how it is directly associated with growth and development. For example, financial hardship when viewed from a materialistic point of view could be considered a negative experience due to the significant impact it can have on our lives.

However, this point of view is focused on loss which limits the ability to see what can be learned from the experience.

Merely shifting perspective from loss to what can be gained sees a surge of positivity into the equation. A journey within for some internal reflection will determine the real reason for the financial burden and provide insight into possible ways forward.

What flows from this will be something of significant greater value than the perceived loss. Awakening to this enables the ability to take purposeful action to break free of constraints. Great minds of the past and present know this and persevere until they successfully penetrate self-constructed limitations and fulfil their potential. This attunes the inner self with a positive vibration. What flows within flows without and shapes success into a masterpiece of your own creation.

Holding on causes narrow vision that keeps us locked into past ideals. This is restrictive and causes stagnation. The longer we abide by outdated rules the more staid we become. Becoming set in our own ways reduces flow to a trickle.

Loosening the grip on preconceived ideals provides the room needed to discover new meaning. As meaning expands a spark of fresh ideas emerge and freedom to explore arises.

Give yourself permission to enjoy doing something totally of your choice at least once a week. Doing something enjoyable enables you to tune out all distractions and focus on being happy. Tuning out from the buzz of the external world gives access to your inner sanctuary, which is where you connect with the universal energy that flows within. This is the foundation of inner peace.

When attuned to this positive vibration it flows outwards and attracts "like" energy. This is energy synchronization and will bring to you the energy with the potential needed to manifest your desires.

When you step into flow it is as if things have been magically orchestrated, such as being in the right place at the right time, seeing opportunities when they come your way and seeing potential in things that were previously overlooked.

When in-sync everything else fades into the background leaving you immersed in your own state of bliss. Being in the flow of life is like playing a game of chess where, even when challenged, you intuitively know what move will put you in a winning position.

TECHNIQUE

The Thought Carnival

Find a space that you can get totally absorbed in something you enjoy. When in the space, tune out all distractions and remain focused on what you are doing. Totally lose yourself in your enjoyment. Be captivated by the pleasant feelings this brings to you. When thoughts enter your mind watch them float through without hooking onto them. This is your precious time. Use it wisely. If you find yourself hooking onto thoughts and unable to let them go try visualizing yourself at a carnival. You are watching the rides trying to decide which you will go on. Each ride represents your thoughts.

THE GHOST TRAIN

There is the ghost train that goes back into the past. As you watch where the thoughts are going ask: "Is that where I want to go?" If yes, ask why? Is there something unresolved? If so, then commit to attending to this at another time.

THE ROLLER COASTER

The next ride you see is the roller coaster. These are the thoughts that run from one into another and another. You end up thinking about something without knowing how you ended up there and why.

The *Thought Roller Coaster* shows you how some thoughts take you to great heights while others make you plummet. The thoughts on this ride are mostly random and scattered.

THE MERRY-GO-ROUND

The next ride is the merry-go-round. The thoughts on this ride go round and round in a circle. This represents the replays, the rehearsals and the repetitive stories that continue to play. This ride must be stopped before you get stuck on the continuous cycle that have a tendency of forming into a spiral causing confusion and doubt.

DRIVING THE BOAT

The next ride is one worthy of your attention. This requires you to get into a boat and be the driver. You drive the boat along a canal. There are thought alert signs posted on the sides of the canal.

Some are necessary such as reflection required and some are warnings such as whirlpool alert, rapids approaching or distractions ahead.
The boat ride is slow and deliberate. It requires you to be consciously aware of thoughts that threaten to take over and detract you.

When you leave the carnival you will have a good idea of where your thoughts take you, how to identify what ride you are on and what to do when you are stuck on a ride and how to get off.

Practice being thought conscious and utilise techniques that assist moving from non-serving to beneficial thought patterns.

PRACTICAL AWARENESS TECHNIQUE

On a piece of paper draw a circle in the middle and write your name in the middle of the circle. Draw a line out from this line and write an experience, an event or a situation that persists. Then draw another line from here with what that experience entailed. e.g. was there another a person involved? What you were doing? How did you feel? Write your answers down. Then draw a line out from the questions and write in that circle the outcome of the experience.

Ask yourself: What was learned from the experience? Would you like this experience to be different? If so in what way? If you were to have this experience again how could it be different?

By looking at experiences in this way we gain insight into how things are aligning or misaligning. This offers something tangible to look at and reflect on. From this we can see our way through things that we might be stuck on. We can find the gem of the experience eg. what was learned.

When we are out of sync with what we experience we can get caught up, miss opportunities and overlook things that are worthy of seeing. Hence why being in the flow of life is important as it allows the opportunity to identify things that we may not have been awareness and by expanding our awareness we expand our relationship with life.

Life is an amazing journey forming part of what is your Ultimate Destiny.

PLEDGE FOR FLOW

I am one with the Universe. The same energy that flows within me flows within all. I let go of beliefs that contribute to feelings of separation. What I give I shall receive. When I embrace I am embraced. I am in flow with the same energy I project. I choose to harness the energy aligned with my hopes and desires. I see opportunities when they arise and am fully aware of the synchronicity occurring in my everyday life. I go with the flow that gives rise to the wave of my destiny.

SUMMARY

- Life is an amazing journey forming part of what is your ultimate destiny. Your destiny is an evolutionary process, expanding through your experiences.
- Resistance opposes the flow and stifles growth.
- Stepping through the barrier of resistance is to discover that you can challenge and succeed.
- Declare your desires and believe them real.
- Revitalized zest for life exudes outwardly.
- Energy is magnified to its capacity and will positively affect the law of attraction.

- Accept change as a blessing for it is the conduit to revitalized energy and renewed inspiration.
- Getting into the flow ignites one with joy and enthusiasm.

FLOW

I flow effortlessly with the universal energy contained within me.

Spiritual Quest

Forgiveness

Freedom is found through Forgiveness

Forgiveness prevents the future from suffering the same fate as the past.

Whatever has been done has been done, it cannot be reversed, but it does not have to continue to cause emotional havoc. Forgiveness is an almighty healer and prevents past suffering from leaking into the future. One does not have to forget to forgive. Forgiveness is for the forgiver, so they may heal past wounds.

Forgive yourself. Release blame, shame and guilt and forgive yourself of all perceived errors and mistakes. We are all students of life and as such mistakes are inevitable. Perfection is subjective and therefore does not exist.

Accept that whatever you have done in the past was done with the knowledge you had at the time. Forgive yourself for not knowing that which you now know. Set your intentions to do good and serve your higher purpose.

Forgiveness frees us from being energetically tied to the past. If we still hold a grudge or hostility towards something or someone from the past it overshadows what we do now and in the future. While we may have moved away from the experience itself, if we have held onto any associated emotion this will embed itself in our life somehow. Thorns of the past must be removed or we risk them being the burdens of the future. Emotions associated with the past do not go away they emit a vibration. This vibration has the capacity to attract like vibration. Hence the possibility of recreating a similar experience, but mostly there is a nagging feeling that stifles our ability to find happiness.

Unresolved emotion festers and consumes part of our identity. Past hurt can be so subtle it goes undetected and we accept it as being part of who we are. But ask yourself if what you feel now was there before? Were are not born bitter, resentful or hostile? We are not born with these emotions, they are created by our experiences. We are born pure and innocent. That is the truth of who we are.

We construct our personality based on the thoughts and emotions arising from our experiences. Our thoughts and emotions are not the complete picture of who we are, but rather aspects of us. We must wade through and identify the layers of these aspects to uncover the truth of who we are.

This is the return to innocence which shows us that ultimately our core essence is love. Love in its essence is gratifying, empowering and balanced.

Unfortunately, there is little known about true love. For so long it has been associated with romance. Romance is a type of love, it makes us feel good as it nurtures the need to feel accepted and loved. This may fulfill that need for a short period, but cannot replace the connectedness we yearn to feel. This is found when we connect with our own inner source of love, the life force, our essence.

This love can forgive, as it perceives higher purpose to all life's experiences. When we are unable to forgive we block love and dam up our life force.

When love ceases to flow as it should we are left with a gaping hole that seems impossible to fill. Any attempt to do so only emphasis the void.

While most of us are aware when there is absence of this vital life source, we accept it as the way it is and continue to seek it from other sources, which are usually those that are external to ourselves.

Love that comes from a need has conditions and

will never completely fulfil us. Because as soon as the love is not servicing the need it sours and dissolves. Compare this to love that is that is found within oneself. This lights us up and floods the void dissolving all associated need to obtain love externally. From this we attract what is not based on need, but genuine connectedness.

How do we move beyond emotions that block our access to what lies beneath? Through forgiveness. Calling upon the inner resources that have got you this far. Assemble your strength and declare that you forgive yourself.

Calling upon the essence of forgiveness will help dissolve the pain, heal the hurt and allow love to flow again. There will be different reactions to what is being said here depending on individual interpretations and individual experiences.

Some may feel repulsed, revolted and maybe enraged at the thought of forgiving some of the atrocities that have occurred and to entertain the thought of forgiveness is beyond comprehension.

Some may want to stop reading in utter disgust at what is proposed. Some may disbelieve that it is possible to forgive someone or something that is unworthy of forgiveness? How can we forgive someone or something that should be punished or who has done the unforgivable?

Reading on will explain the power of forgiveness and why it is important. But first understand that forgiveness is for the benefit of the FORGIVER and not the forgiven. This is a powerful statement. Read it over to fully embrace what it means.

FORGIVING IS FOR THE FORGIVER.

Forgiveness is the path to peace. Holding negative emotion towards someone does not punish them. We may think that not forgiving someone gives them the punishment they deserve, but in reality the one being punished is the holder of the emotion. This is self-punishment.

Lack of forgiveness intensifies toxic emotion that pollutes the mind, body and soul. Slowly this drains our energy. This is a double tragedy, as not only was there suffering associated with the experience but it is perpetuated by what we do to ourselves. We literally self-destruct. What sense does this make? We are punishing ourselves, no one else. Taking this perspective goes a long way towards healing.

If forgiveness still seems like an impossible task ask yourself "how does holding on help me? "what will I lose if I let go?" Do you feel they will win and you will lose if you forgive? Their journey is not your concern. The law of cause and effect, the karmic law, will make all things equal at some point in time. We need only be concerned with how we travel. While there is an emotional link to the past we continue to drag past things into the present and the future. Ask "do you want to maintain a link with this past experience?" If not, do what is necessary to cut loose the threads of the past and take control of your journey.

Every one of us has had experiences that have caused anguish and emotional turmoil. Forgiving is not excusing or forgetting. It is cutting ourselves free from the emotional attachment, which gives us freedom and the opportunity to create the life we wish for ourselves. Who wins? The forgiver, as they will be moving into a brighter way of being.

Note: The forgiven are not freed by forgiveness it is the forgiver that is freed. There are those who seek the path to peace and those that continue to travel attached to the past. The path chosen is one of choice.

TECHNIQUE

You see yourself sitting upon the healing throne. Attached to you are threads. These threads are hanging out of you and may be attached to a person, a place, an event, or circumstance. Theses threads are heavy. Imagine now that you are releasing these threads one at a time. See each thread loosen its grip.

As each thread detaches take it in your hand and infuse it with love. As you let the thread go free you feel yourself freed from its burden.

The love you infused into the thread sees the associated emotions healed. This process may take some time and practice.

There may be some threads that are challenging and some that may resist being extracted. Keep persisting.

Physically burning some thread or string as a visual representation of the imagined thread will help to consolidate this practice. The string as a symbolic representation of the thread being released is powerful reinforcement. As you let go of the threads affirm: *I forgive all past hurt. I release the negative threads of the past and create the life I wish to live.*

Note: Forgiveness comes from within. There is NO need for physical, emotional or energetic contact or connection to another. To forgive is to extend kindness towards oneself. It is recognising the emotions attached to past hurt and extending a hand that connects with the wounded aspect of self. This is the extension of empathy, not sympathy. Sympathy can turn into pity whereas empathy holds the space needed to find the light in which to heal.

PLEDGE OF FORGIVENESS

I give myself the gift of forgiveness.
When I forgive I release myself from pent up emotion that serves only to keep me attached to old hurt.
Through my loss I have gained, through my hurt I have healed, through my sadness I am touched by compassion.
Through compassion I forgive.
Through forgiveness I am released from the past.
I am now free to embrace new approaches and be liberated by the abundance that now flows into my life.
Life flows, love flows, I flow.

SUMMARY

- It releases you from being energetically tied to the past.
- Forgiveness dissolves emotional turmoil.
- Whatever has been done has been done, take from it what you want and leave the rest.
- While the past may have been determined by what was occurring at that time, the future does not have to suffer the same fate.
- By forgiving you step into the next moment free of the burden you once carried.
- Forgiving and forgetting are different, while one need not forget in order to heal, forgiveness is imperative.
- Forgive yourself for everything.
- Release blame, regret and guilt.
- Set your intentions to do good and serve your higher purpose.
- Accept that whatever you have done in the past you did with the knowledge you had at the time and that is all anyone can do.

FORGIVENESS

I forgive myself and others. I now see that our actions are triggered by our inner perceptions & the condition of our inner being. I choose to derive meaning from my experiences & move on in a positive direction.

Holding onto past hurt is detrimental as it infiltrates other aspects of our lives. For example, hoarding bitter emotions will cause bitterness; harbouring resentment will make one resentful; harvesting hostility will make one hateful. If emotions are not healed they fester which causes them to intensify. This can be such a subtle infiltration that is goes undetected. We accept this as being who we are, while at the same time there is an inner knowing that there has been a morphing into something opposed to who we are. This inner conflict creates turmoil and if not attended to it can become a black hole of despair. Forgiveness is the light that infiltrates this inner conflict so we can reawaken to a new way of being.

Spiritual Quest

Happiness

Happiness is an inner feeling of elation

In the pursuit of happiness there is a tendency to look externally. But the real source of happiness lies within.

The quest for happiness begins by looking at how thoughts are structured. If thoughts are positive feelings will reflect this.

If thoughts are clouded by negativity feelings will reflect this. If feelings are low they create a lowly vibe which attracts other lowly vibes. Challenges feel like unmovable obstacles, daily tasks feel like huge chores, navigating life seems like a difficult, perhaps impossible, task.

If thoughts and feelings go unchecked it can feel like the pleasure is being squeezed out of life. A dismal picture that can be changed through thought awareness and shifting perception from a negative frame to one that reflects positivity.

Becoming aware of the effect thoughts have on feelings and the effect feelings have on emotional well-being provides a sound platform on which to build an inner state of happiness.

Note: The use of the word negative is for identification purposes and associated with the effect it has on our well-being. It does not make such thoughts or feelings wrong or unimportant.

All thought and feeling is important as they provide vital clues to the workings of the inner self and the various perceptions aspects of self have.

Shifting thoughts into happy mode shifts feelings to reflect the same. Think of something happy and notice what happens to your feelings. Feelings follow thought. Things flow more smoothly when in a positive frame of mind.

While being happy all of the time is an unrealistic expectation and would go against the up and down nature of life, we can weave a strong vibration of happiness into our energy fields. Doing this helps build the resilience needed to deal with the ups and downs when they are encountered.

Resilience is a safety barrier that protects us from being pulled into a spiral of despair when things don't go our way and helps us deal more effectively when faced with challenges. Resilience provides the flexibility needed to bounce back.

Bouncing back is to navigate thoughts into positive context. Thoughts that provide the narration to an experience affects the impact the experience has. For example in the case of a lost sporting tournament or not gaining a well earned award, feelings of disappointment may well be natural, however it is the thoughts that accompanying the feeling of disappointment that will harness the greatest impact.

If thoughts acknowledge the loss and then embrace the overall experience as positive e.g. what was gained, what was learned, how the experience contributed to growth then overall the tournament will serve in positive ways.

However if things don't turn out as hoped and is accompanied by thoughts of hopelessness, personal insult and character defamation then that may well be the undoing of someone.

If the disappointment of losing or not gaining what was expected is feed with negativity the ability to bounce back will be reduced. However if the disappointment of things not turning out as hoped is utilized to fuel a positive approach then bounce back mechanisms are engaged and will serve to propel one forward.

Thoughts can be problem focused or solution based, the choice lays with the thinker. Negative thoughts oppose, whereas positive thoughts facilitate an inner state of happiness.

Thought awareness begins by recognizing inner monologue. This is the internal voice that we identify with as being who we are. This internal voice chats away all the time. It tells us what it thinks of us, it tells us what it thinks of others, it tells us what to do and how to do it. It maintains a continuous stream of conversation.

The inner-voice speaks in the same tone, in other words it is always identified as being our own voice, however it does represent many aspects of ourselves. One such aspect is the inner-critic.

The inner-critic is an aspect that brings to mind memories of perceived failure and reminds us of personal inadequacies. The words of the inner-critic resonate with the images embedded in the psyche, many of which were formed during childhood when there was lack of understanding and the inability to rationalize what was happening at the time.

Many of the impressions held of self are false. Unfortunately these false impressions appear very real and stand in the way of happiness. There are a multitude of reasons for this, including not feeling worthy of happiness, disillusionment of what happiness is and pushing happiness away due to fear of the consequences that may follow should one allow themselves to be happy eg.

disappointment or sorrow. All these things affect the way we feel about ourselves and impact on actions and behaviour.

Added to this, the inner-critic thinks it knows what others are thinking which reaffirms the negative opinions of the inner-critic and other dis-empowered aspects of self.

These aspects are at the core of our worries as they are focused on whatever burdens them, be it fear of rejection, humiliation, failure, loss etc. Worry of these things, on a subconscious level, sends thoughts into turmoil.

Such worry filled thought are an antagonist to happiness. When worry comes to douse happiness it will appear with merit, a reason worthy of the worry. The outcome of which may see such things as the happiness found in a relationship fall under scrutiny.

The proposal of something good occurring such as a job opportunity, a friendship, a journey or the presentation of a new path to follow will be fraught with concern. This douses the positive vibe happiness brings before it even gets a chance to shine.

This is a form of sabotage driven by the

subconscious, from this comes the emergence of repetitive negative thoughts and uncharacteristic behaviour. It is during this time that one needs to be aware of the small voice calling from the distance. This is the voice of awareness, calling you to recognize what is going on so that you can take conscious control of what is happening before the possibility of happiness erodes.

Taking conscious control is to use affirmations, reframe negative banter into positive self-talk and create positive visual images. Using techniques that enhance positive thoughts and images of self attunes to the vibration of happiness. This is the definition of authentic happiness as it is not dependent on external sources, but is derived from within.

There are things that we can do that help elevate mood, which in itself may not change a situation, but it does make us feel better, which dramatically improves coping skills.

*Listen to uplifting music

*Wear bright colours

*Buy flowers to bring into the home

*Eat fresh food to revitalize the body

*Breathe deeply and inhale the essence of life

*Practise thought awareness and use positive affirmations

*Reframe negative self-talk into positive self encouragement

*Post positive quotes where they will be seen on a regular basis

*Create a vision board of happy images

*Tune out negative conversation

*Replace self-criticism with constructive self-feedback

*Choose the company of positive people

*Turn off the news

*Laugh!!

PLEDGE FOR HAPPINESS

Every day I notice moments of happiness. I stop and absorb these moments. I am fully present and take time to appreciate what is in my immediate environment. My happy thoughts create happy feelings. I smile often, laugh loudly and think and speak kindly of myself and others.

Note: Happiness is not a steady state of being achieved by reaching a certain level on the happiness scale that guarantees everlasting happy feelings. Happiness ebbs and flows just like we do. Accepting this improves overall happiness as it dissolves unrealistic image of what happiness looks like and allows us to see that we are not missing the happiness boat, do not have to climb to certain heights to find happiness or have a predisposition to low happiness levels.

A formula for happy feelings is to exchange negative thought for positive engagement.

SUMMARY

- Happiness is an inner feeling of elation, vibrating so strongly it infusing every cell of the body with light.
- Feelings of happiness radiate outwards and touches everything it comes in contact with.
- Light-hearted, jovial, gracious feelings flow freely.
- Embracing the glow of inner serenity, is the key to lasting contentment.
- Contentment forms the foundation of emotional well-being.
- Happiness sparks the light that infuses life with joy.
- True happiness is found by being heart centered.
- Heartfelt thoughts are filled with compassion and kindness towards self and others.

Negativity is renowned for knocking the sparkle out of happiness. Look negativity in the eye and laugh out loud.

Spiritual Quest

HAPPINESS

I am radiant with inner happiness and joy.
Happiness flows into all aspects of my life.
I am centered in my happy place.

Happiness is an inner feeling of elation, vibrating so strongly it ignites our core, spreads through our entire body and radiates outward touching everything we come in contact with.

Spiritual Quest

Harmony

A harmonious state is achieved through regular visits to your inner sanctuary

 *Inner-harmony is created through inner-balance achieved by connecting with the core of the inner being.*

This is the soul. The soul activates heart awareness. From heart awareness arises compassion. Awakening heart consciousness is to fulfil the aim of the soul and the purpose of having a human experience.

Knowing this is to construct an alternative view of life and broadens the perspective of why we are here and what life is about. At the same time the view broadens it shifts and becomes internally focused. This is the point of reference from which everything revolves.

If there are aspects that are unbalanced in their perspective and approach then attention is required. Balancing inner aspects of self will see a ripple effect that begins the realignment process. First step is to become soul conscious.

This can be done through the breath which calms and relaxes and connects you with your essence. Inhale through the nose and hold 1...2...3...and exhale through the mouth. Continue until there is a natural rhythm and flow to your breathing. Bring your focus onto the breath, rein in all thought. Be still, stillness of body.....stillness of mind.....all is calm and relaxed.

The merging of mind, body and soul occurs through the breath. All is one. Your inner world is all that exists. This is a moment shared with your wholeness. Once touched this space of inner serenity will be remembered and can be recreated by focusing on the breath. What emerges from the nothingness is your soul.

It is void yet present, it is empty and full, it is nothing and everything, it is light and has significant depth. When it communicates it will reflect compassion, it will be non-judgmental and harness vast insight.

Capturing the essence of the soul can only be done through personal experience.

Breathe and focus...Breathe and focus...be still...be aware...

This is the creation of inner-harmony. One minute a day of this practice can transform your life as it will become an instant place of retreat when overwhelmed, overburdened or overextended. Taking this minute of reprieve enables you to regroup, refocus and establish balance. This creates a more functional platform to work from.

When centered within self you become more attuned to heart energy. This works to broaden perspective, soften judgment and enhance empathy towards ourselves and others. This filters into the mind and assists with being focused in positive ways. The harmonious vibration this creates will flow into every aspect of life.

TECHNIQUE
Centering

Picture a line going down the middle of your body, bring your thoughts to this line, focus on the line. Breathe in through your nose. Exhale through your mouth. Continue to do this until you are completely focused on this imaginary central line.

If you feel pulled from this centre bring your focus back through the breath. Imagine a field of energy around you. This may be seen as a white or coloured haze, a white or coloured line or a white or coloured cloud.

Imagine bringing this field of energy towards your body and smoothing the edges so it looks like you are standing in an oval balloon. This enables you to be centered in your own energy and prevents energy leaking or being drained. You may already see the energy field around yourself and/or others with your physical eyes. With practice this sight can be developed further. Whether seen or not it can be sensed through the mind's eye.

Create inner harmony

Centre and focus on your breathing. Disconnect from external disruptions. If something or someone is drawing you away from your centre or disturbing your inner harmony take a deep breath and focus. Repeat the word "Calm" in your mind. Resist being pulled outward from your place of inner centeredness.

Retract your energy inward by imagining the field of light surrounding you and comforting you with its embrace. You are safe and protected. Breathe and listen to your kind inner voice welcoming you.

You are entering inner stillness. Feel the energy of your heart centre. Make peace with yourself through this centre. See and feel loving reflections. Breathe...Focus...Relax. This is your temple, a place of solitude. This is inner-harmony.

Spiritual Quest

PLEDGE FOR INNER-HARMONY

Harmonization of my mind, body and spirit creates inner peace and harmony.

By creating a state of inner harmony I feel relaxed and calm. These feelings flow into all areas of my life.

I am focused, clear and attuned to a harmonious vibration that fills me with a satisfying sense of well-being.

SUMMARY

- Channelling logic through the heart centre forms non-judgmental perceptions towards self and others.
- Use your heart when generating your view of the world.
- Love dissolves antagonism, allowing the assimilation of all aspects of self.
- Inner harmony evolves through this merging of all into one.
- Immense pleasure emerges from this alignment, giving rise to true lightness of being.

HARMONY

*I harmonize all areas of my life.
I choose to live in harmony with myself, with others and with the beauty of nature.
I connect with my inner stillness and create a harmonious existence.*

Inner-Harmony and emotional well-being is born from self-talk that encourages, supports and inspires.

Spiritual Quest

Healing

We all have the ability to heal ourselves and others

 *Each one of us has been blessed with a beautiful gift of healing.*

Developing this aspect of ourselves is to make an intimate connection with our higher selves and with the universal energy.

The universal energy is our essence; it is pure source energy. It can be perceived through colours, feelings or sensations. This energy has profound healing ability that once experienced cannot be denied.

Accessing healing energy is done by calming the mind and freeing it from thought. When we create a quiet space within we bypass mind chatter and connect with higher aspects of self. The more often we connect with our higher selves the more attuned we become to how it communicates.

Higher self communication is perceived visually, aurally and kinaesthetically, with one of these modalities being the primary source of perception. Although one sense may be stronger than the others, increased awareness and connection with the higher self will see all senses work together in unison.

Visual perception is received as images in the mind's eye. This is like viewing a movie screen.

Communication through auditory channels is like perceiving a written message, hearing a word (same as own inner voice, but different to thoughts) or messages that inspire you to act, such as to call someone or to say something that happens to be the right thing at the right time.

Kinaesthetic perception is to feel, to get a hunch, sense something, pick up a vibe, there may be a tingle or a prickle.

Although there are many similarities to how we perceive our higher-self and other subtle energies we all have unique ways of interpretation. Some people may feel or hear a subtle stirring before receiving insight. Some people get an image or a 'newsflash' which provides insight. Sometimes it is like a download of information that forms a concept. These are just a few examples. Whatever and however the higher-self is perceived it will reflect something of significance.

Our higher-self will provide guidance and higher perspective. It is a choice to acknowledge and take heed, but should your choice oppose higher guidance another path will lay before you in the hope you will choose that which is aligned with your highest good and purpose. This will continue throughout the lifetime. Your higher self will not abandon you, even if you ignore it or deny its existence.

Our spiritual selves are not weighed down with the layers our physical selves are burdened with. These layers form the personalities and beliefs we identify as being who we are. But in fact they are fabricated constructions there to aid the learning we are here for. But as we are in constant contact with our physical bodies and physical environment we become attuned to our physicality and less attuned the more subtle spiritual selves.

Re-attuning to our higher-selves requires delving into the layers that block access to our spiritual awareness. When we do this there is a dawning of something magical, an enlightening moment like the magnificence of a baby being birthed upon this earth and at the same time being connected to its source energy.

There is a certain awe and innocence to being in touch with our spiritual selves. It is like meeting the ultimate life partner that loves unconditionally, is forgiving of mistakes and prepared to do what is necessary to see you reach your potential.

When we entered the world we had no

preconceived ideas. The soul births with the mission of clearing past karma and to learn through experience what is required to evolve. This requires alignment with the higher self to ensure that intention and conduct is of the highest integrity. This automatically lifts our vibrations and creates a closer connection to higher self principles.

Frequency of connection is important as the more often we connect with our higher selves the more aware we become and the better able to attend to our spiritual needs. Spiritual awareness and alignment is something our world has a significant lack of and is the root cause of a majority of the woes of humanity.

If each of us took personal responsibility to realign with our spirituality the world would make an instant transformation. Spirituality is not based on a set of beliefs, and is not derived from dictatorship or preaching, but rather from guidance that empowers us to discover our inner light. Everything that emerges from this will reflect the essence of true spirituality which is based on love, honesty, integrity and joy.

If individual decisions were based on these

principles collective decisions would reflect this. This would eliminate destruction and choices that hurt, maim or kill other living beings on this planet. If every individual aligned with their spiritual selves and lived in accordance with the principles of love, kindness and compassion then the idea of world peace would not be a whimsical concept but an achievable reality.

World peace starts inside the heart of an individual. Heal thyself first, thus begins the healing of aspects of self that opposes heart-based kindness, caring and compassion.

To ascertain which aspects require healing requires an energy assessment. This begins by taking notice of what you think and what you say for the next twenty-four hours.

Notice any tension or imbalance in your body, such as clenched fists, grinding teeth, sighing, shoulder position, neck position, any discomfort in any area of the belly, back discomfort and its location, hip or knee stiffness.

Underlying the seemingly innocent tightness in the neck or clenching of the teeth is a message. If more subtle messages such as getting some rest or having a massage are ignored then how else is your inner self going to communicate if not through your body? Once the messages of the body are received some significant self-healing can be done. Inevitably things that can no longer be buried will surface.

Nestled at the root of this disharmony is the code that will unlock the courage, strength and stamina needed to heal the aspects of self that require healing. Thus begins the development of a beautiful and unique relationship with the inner-self.

Nurturing a relationship with self will uncover false aspects which are based on false perception and uncover the true essence of who you are. False perception develops from misinterpretation of an experience.

Re-evaluating the experience will shift the perception. For example: when your parent's got angry at you for voicing your opinion did that mean that your opinion was worthless or did it mean that your parent's behaved according to what they were experiencing at that time. Does feeling good have to have a cloud hanging over it due to the possible impending doom? Did the message "enjoy it while it lasts" get a strong hold in your mind and continues to be associated with feeling good and often dampens those feelings?

All too often we have conformed our real selves to meet the approval of others, notably the adults in our lives. Even the most outwardly successful person, however that is measured, will have something that shadows them.

Everybody has a story to tell and every one of those stories will have a certain impact on the way a person conducts themselves and how they perceive themselves.

False perceptions of self can easily become who we identify ourselves with. Transforming these perceptions can be assisted by tapping into the true essence of who we are.

With this comes the ultimate realisation that what we have perceived as being our true nature is only representative of traits and characteristics that have been constructed.

Dropping these constructed aspects of who we are enables the real self to develop. This starts by differentiating between what has been constructed are part of the personality and what exist naturally as higher-self qualities.

Reconfiguring the personality to reflect higher-self qualities is dynamic. What emerges from this union are the qualities of love, hope, compassion and joy. These higher-self attributes carry a higher vibration which naturally lift spirits, gives hope and inspires personal growth and healing.

We all know what it is like to be in the presence of people who uplift and inspire our spirit and we all have the ability to uplift and inspire others. We only need move out of our own way and allow the qualities of our higher-self flow through us.

Beyond the veil of physical existence is the energetic realm. There is nothing mystical about this realm. The mysticism comes from perception based on physical attachment and the belief that if it can't be seen it doesn't exist.

Science debunks this myth. Everything that is perceived as solid is not; it is made up of energetic particles. Look at a wall, it looks solid? But the fact is it is vibrating with tiny particles called atoms, which emit energy, a wall is energetically dense, like most matter, but it composed of energy just the same.

All energy has a vibration and the higher our vibration the better able we are to connect with other higher vibrations. Simply put, if the vibration rate is low it resonates with lower vibrations. If vibration has a higher frequency then it resonates with energy that has a similar frequency. Non-physical beings exist beyond the veil of physicality. They have a higher rate of vibration as they are not bound to the density of a physical body and the density of this plane of existence.

Physicality naturally has a lower vibration rate, however we can increase the vibration by aligning ourselves with the vibration of positivity. This can be achieved through meditation, visualisation, affirmation, positive thought and exercise such as Yoga and Tai Chi. Increased vibration energises and enhances our overall well-being.

It is not unusual for people who meditate, pray, chant and use positive affirmation to have a higher vibration, which aids their connection with higher vibrating beings such as spirit guides and angels.

Most of us have encountered spirit guides and angels and although we may not have been consciously aware of the encounter, intuitively we know that we encountered such.

Most of us have stories, whether we choose to divulge them or not, about times when we felt a presence, felt helped or guided in some unexplainable way; or when we have witnessed or perceived something out of the ordinary.

Our minds create barriers that undermine our faith in what we perceive intuitively. It takes time to re-establish faith, but upon achieving this there is no doubting the existence of realms beyond this one. It is through this shift that we become more attuned with the subtle fields of energy that exist everywhere.

Our brain carries messages through electrical charges, from one nerve cell to another our brain orchestrates the workings of our bodily functions. This in itself confirms the affect energy has on us.

Energy facilitates everything we do. If this energy it interrupted or negatively charged it can cause all sorts of disturbance in the mind and body.

However, by setting our energy into positive mode, which is assisted through the power of intention we can reprogram ourselves in ways that facilitate healing. This process does take dedication, persistence, patience and time, but it can be done.

When it is our intention to heal we gain

conscious access to our higher-intelligence. This inherent intelligence is what produces new cells, keeps our heart pumping, keeps us breathing and digests our food, it maintains all our bodily functions without us having to think about it.

The anatomy and physiology of these functions can be explained, as can the working of the master powerhouse, the brain.

However the brain is a physical entity. What is far less understood is workings of the mind. The mind expands beyond physicality, to where remains undetermined. Within this lies an innate source of power and when we tap into this we awaken the inner-healer.

Through this aspect flows universal healing energy. This amazing resource of energy that flows within us can be used to heal ourselves and others.

If energy is stagnant healing will get it flowing. If it is scattered, healing will calm. If energy is blocked, healing will help release it. Getting into the groove of healing will awaken you to a whole new world.

Healing flows into and out of our aura. The aura is a field of energy that surrounds us. The colours seen in the aura and the vibration carried by the aura reflect our inner vibration. This vibration is produced by the energy centres. For detail see Energy Centres at the back of this book.

The energy centres are wheels of energy that govern specific areas of the body. For example, the heart centre is connected to the heart, if love flows freely through the heart centre the heart is healthy as is the giving and receiving of love. If there is a blockage or disturbance in heart energy it can manifest as physical illness. The manifestation of a physical ailment can be a blessing in disguise as it alerts us to energetic imbalance.

We are here to work upon our spiritual growth, not our physicality and although we have to attend to the physical needs of our body that is not the purpose of our existence.

Our physical body houses our soul and as the temple in which our soul resides we must ensure we do what is essential for its health and at the same time ensuring we nourish our soul.

The aura is another channel for soul communication. It exchanges energy with other energy fields, it communicates our thoughts and feelings and provides clues that help us ascertain where there is imbalances, blockages and leakage.

Our aura expands and contracts according to what is going on in our life. It will display physical illness, emotional state and broadcasts the state of the energy centre. Each centre relates to different areas of our being, although they are often viewed as separate they function as a whole, if there is imbalance in one energy centre this will affect the others.

The aura can be seen by the physical or the mind's eye. Detecting the colour of the aura comes naturally to some, a good start to seeing the aura is to put your index and middle finger together in front of a light coloured wall. Slowly move your fingers apart and you will see a slight haze surrounding the fingers. This is a field of energy. Next try standing someone in front of a white or cream coloured blank wall and see the same haze around their body, it may appear slightly white. With time and practice colour vision will begin to develop, if not through physical sight, then through the mind's eye, which is an intuitive perception of the aura. The same is true of the energy centre, they can be intuitively perceived through the mind's eye. Interpreting the state of the energy centre provides much information about where healing is needed and whether there is an energetic imbalance, blockage, leakage, excess or deficiency.

TECHNIQUE
Tune into your inner healer

Focusing on your breath, breathe in through your nose, bring your breath down into your belly and then exhale. As you breathe in again, feel your breath ignite the spark of your inner healer. Imagine that a light or flame jumps to life within your abdomen, awakening your inner source of healing.

Whenever you are feeling ill, hurt, worried, burdened etc, whether it be emotionally or physically focus on the light in your belly; see the light expand through your entire body and going to where healing is needed. Fill the area up with the light, feel it mend, nurture and heal whatever is in need of healing. With practice this will begin to occur naturally and you will find yourself calming and soothing through your own inner healer.

Tuning into the Universal healing

Focus on your breath. Take a couple of deep breaths in through your nose, draw it down into your belly and then exhale out through your mouth. When you exhale imagine tension releasing from your body. When you are feeling relaxed, imagine yourself being surrounded by beautiful white light energy. When you are feeling safe and secure in your white-light cocoon imagine the top of your head opening and a golden light flowing down from above into your crown area.

This energy flows down and cascades through your entire body, filling you with love. Imagine it going to any area you feel tension; allow it to dissolve the tension. When you have finished imagine the golden light withdrawing from your body and as it leaves the top of your head your crown area closes. Take some deep breaths and continue to enjoy your day.

 Take a deep breath in through your nose. Feel the warm air flow into your belly and then exhale slowly through your mouth.

Take another deep breath in through your nose, draw the air down into your belly and then exhale slowly through your mouth.

Take another breath in through your nose, bring the air into your belly and allow it to continue to flow down into your legs and extend out through your feet. Extending like roots out into the ground.

Your breathing returns to normal as you bring your focus on the roots extending from your feet into the ground.

As you connect with the Earth you begin to feel all tension dissolve into the Earth.

You feel safe, protected and completely relaxed.

You find yourself sitting with your legs crossed in a large room filled with crystals.

The crystals sparkle brightly creating a matrix of colour throughout the room.

You are mesmerized by the breathtaking colours that surround you.

You begin to tune into the colours.

The crystal colours begin to separate and as they

do you tune into their individual colour.

The first is a rich ruby red. As it vibrates you feel the area in the base of your spine begin to tingle. The tingle gets stronger and stronger and transforms into feelings. Feelings of being safe and secure within yourself.

You know that you are safe and have a natural ability to survive in this world.

Your attention is now drawn to the vivid orange. It pulsates and connects with you instilling feelings of inspiration and creativity.

You know that you have unique creative talents. Your focus now turns to the vibrant yellow and as it does you notice your naval area begins to tingle. As the tingles gets stronger you become aware of feelings of balance, confidence and harmony.

You absorb these feelings. Own them as they belong to you.

Your awareness is now drawn to the magnificent emerald green that floats towards you.

You breathe in this emerald green. It flows into your heart-centre filling you with feelings of love and acceptance of yourself.

You now become aware of a tingle in your throat area.

You bring your attention to a blue coloured spiral moving slowly towards you.

You breathe the blue into your throat area. It gently embraces you. You gain a sense of clarity and know that you are able to express yourself more freely.

You are now drawn to a magnificent shade of purple. You are captivated by it.

You feel the area between your eyes tingle, this is your third eye awakening. As it opens you find the images of your imagination begin to sharpen.

You focus on the purple and feel enlightened by its presence.

White swirls of light begin to form through all the colours. You breathe it in. It is invigorating. As it swirls through you it cleanses and clears any residual negativity.

You are a beacon of pure white light energy.

As you experience this energy remember that you can call upon whenever you need healing. Connect to this brilliant white light energy for ailments of mind, body and spirit.

This is your inbuilt natural healer.

Please note: Seek professional medical attention if there are any concerns regarding your physical, mental or emotional health.

PLEDGE FOR HEALING

I am an energetic being living within a physical body. When the vitality of my energetic self is nourished I am well. Physical ailments signal that vitality dwindles. I can call forth my intuitive healer and attend to my energetic needs which will inert a positive effect on my physical body. By recognising that my inner sage and modern mind can be incorporated I have at my fingertips ancient ways and scientific advances. I can evoke wisdom and methods beyond current comprehension. Energy heals, I am energy, hence I have the power to heal and be healed.

SUMMARY

- The power to heal is an amazing gift.
- Surrounding each of us is an energetic field.
- This field emits subtle energies that communicate with the energy field of other living things.
- This is our connection to the source energy from which we came.

- One who peers beyond physical existence lifts the veil to reveal the magical realm of energy.
- Beyond the booming voice of the mind is a quiet space within.
- From this stillness comes a vibration that has the power to restore, revitalise and rejuvenate.
- Through the breath we connect mind, body and spirit from which emerges the essence of who we are.

> *Our higher-self is part of who we are. Every time we align with compassionate, kind and intuitive aspects of self we are channelling the qualities of our higher self.*

HEALING

*Within me lies divine healing ability.
As I expand into the essence of my existence I transcend all limitations and discover my inherent gifts.*

Connecting to our spiritual selves sees similar awe and innocence as a baby opening its eyes for the first time.

Spiritual Quest

Hope

Hope is that which flickers gently in the background of all of your endeavours and experiences

Hope keeps our dreams alive and gives us strength during times when faith dims.

Hope flickers gently in the background of all of our endeavours and experiences. Hope gives rise to the inspiration that transforms wishes into reality.

Hope always looks forward and is what sparks the power of possibility. When possibility is sparked we add dimension to our thinking. Lateral thinking enables us to branch out and seek alternative ways of doing things.

Hope is a powerful motivator and a great companion that assists us when faced with obstacles. Hope encourages, empowers and sparks enthusiasm. This opens the doors to opportunity. Opportunity somehow manages to maneuver fate in our favour.

Hope comes to the rescue when faced with challenge and crisis. It is the seed of strength when abandoned by all else. Hope will be there to comfort through the shadows of doubt. There is no such thing as false hope. However there is false attachment, where we hang hope on something or someone that is not part of our destiny.

The disappointment faced when hope flickers will spark new hope that will lead to something that is aligned with our destiny. As this moves into our radar and manifests we can rest assured knowing that all is as it is meant to be. Hope held with conviction is a conduit to the manifestation of miracles.

Hope provides the strength needed to navigate obstacles, combat challenges and encourage during crisis. The spark of hope is what keeps us going beyond what we thought we are capable of. Hope is our inner promise that no matter what happens we will endure and succeed.

Life is the journey on which we endeavour to find meaning and purpose, hope inspires the way. If life is void of hope, it is void of meaning. This can cause us to be lost in a shallow existence until hope is rediscovered. How does one rediscover hope? Look into your heart and be embraced by the warmth hope brings.

Reigniting hope may see a shift in direction, significant life changes, redirection of focus and re-energized feelings of inspiration and motivation. Hope is the gift we all must unwrap to appreciate the power contained in its essence.

TECHNIQUE

Hope embraces us and provides the light needed to kick-start our dreams. Light a single yellow candle. Look into the candle. Allow all thought to fade away as you bring your focus into the flame. Imagine the energy of the flame moving into your heart centre. Breathe it in, feel the power, feel the warmth it gives. Allow it to spark heartfelt hope. The combined energy of hope and passion is a phenomenal force. Utilize this to its fullest potential and be amazed at what comes your way. New hope sparks new opportunity.

PLEDGE OF HOPE

I hold my hopes to the light and ask for the energy needed to kick-start them into reality.
The sacredness of my hopes are worthy of sanctum.
They will not be tarnished by inner or outer doubt.
They are precious and are infused with the same source energy from which I was delivered onto this earth.
I build on the whimsical nature of hope and watch as it transforms into a dynamic pillar of strength and provides the power to fuel all my endeavours.

SUMMARY

- The force driving your dreams and desires is found in the hope that what you wish for will come true.
- Hope rises as inspiration gently calls you to awaken to the beauty contained within.
- Being held in Hope's embrace is to find comfort in knowing that everything is as it should be.
- Hope assists the forward direction of your journey in positive ways.
- A trickle of Hope can yield great power.
- Hope can be held when faced with challenge and crisis.
- It is the seed of strength when abandoned by all else.
- As a lifelong friend, hope makes a delightful companion.

HOPE

*Whatever I may face
I call upon the comfort of hope
to give me strength.*

Imagination

Your imagination creates the visual images of your mind.

Imagination is a divine gift capable of conjuring images into reality.

Stretching the imagination is to awaken to limitless possibilities. Imagination comes before creation. Using the imagination in constructive ways sees miraculous things emerge. Greatness can be achieved by first imagining such. If our imagination is set free it can go to unimagined places. This may be the conduit to an amazing new idea, an invention, an insightful plan or a vision of a path to follow. This can be reinforced through the use of the imagination in the form of creative visualisation.

Creative visualization has the power to stir excitement, instil confidence and actively engage the resources needed to manifest aspirations into reality.

Imagine lying on the beach listening to the waves lapping gently upon the shore while receiving a relaxing massage conjures a picture of peace and tranquility.

Imagine writing a novel and holding a framed certificate acknowledging it as a best seller conjures a different, but equally compelling image. Using the imagination to inspire and motivate towards goal achievement is utilizing a natural talent to achieve greatness.

If the excitement felt when visualizing something that is enjoyable is infused into a desire, a goal or a dream it provides the energy needed to jump start a vision. If this is done every day or as often as possible that vision will move from the mind and cast itself into reality.

Goal achievement is motivated by the visual images produced by the imagination. See, inspire and act upon the positive images seen in the mind's eye. 'Living the dream' is not just a saying. It is something each and every person is capable of doing.

Knowing how and actually doing it is where misalignment can be seen. There are many reasons for this including lack of belief in the power of creative visualization reinforced through the inner voice of doubt. This can undo the most powerful visual image.

As soon as the voice of doubt starts to object the image starts to decompose and fade. The mind turns its attention to the mundane and the impact needed to firmly embed the image into the subconscious is lost. Being aware of this empowers the action needed to hold the image and maintain the infusion of positivity. If this is done every day the results will be testament to the power of creative visualization. Try it and see.

To enhance the power of a visual image flood the image with positive feelings. Stand guard and protect the image from the destructive voice of doubt. If it is detected use a positive affirmation to shift negative to positive. Never give up on your vision.

There may be set-backs, there will be challenges from internal and external sources, there will be highs and lows. But those who are able to write the story of success are those who have honoured their vision and moved past obstacles and mastered the internal and external challenges.

Even if you stumble in the shadows the vision of your desire must remain pointed towards the light. Infuse your vision with positive energy, nurture your vision with the belief it is possible, attend to your vision daily and one day you will look around and realise that your vision is no longer a vision, but your life. Try it and see.

TECHNIQUE

Conscious Creation

Create an image of what you desire. Visualize without reservation. Give your picture colour and belief. Hold this image in your mind, feel it as if you already have it. Immerse yourself into your picture. See, feel and hear every detail until the image is firmly planted in your mind. Tune into the positive feelings that arise. They are great motivators and will emerge whenever the image is brought to mind. Use cut outs of what you desire and place them where you will see them every day. This will impress upon your mind what you desire and allow that energy to flow and attract like energy. This is how to combine the power of intention and the law of attraction to manifest the images of your mind into reality. This is the playground of your mind. Get your dose of creative fun daily.

TECHNIQUE

Imagine a giant golden bubble. This golden bubble is radiant and glowing. It is empty in readiness for you to fill it with a picture from your imagination. Begin to visualise what it is you wish to create.Focusing on creating the image of one desire at a time enhances the power of the image rather than distributing focus which scatters energy and diffuses power.

Find physical representations of your desire to reinforce the image and anchor it into the subconscious. Believe that you already have what you desire. Bring it into your waking world. See it, feel it, smell it, hear it, be it. It is yours. Start enjoying it now. This may seem like an unusual thing to do, but those who have used creative visualisation successfully know its power. You are one of those people.

You have real life examples of how you have utilized creative visualisation. Believe, because you can. Use your imagination...

PLEDGE OF IMAGINATION

My imagination creates the visual images of my reality. I utilize this to maximize my manifestation capacity.

I imagine.

I reinforce.

I create.

This is a divine gift of phenomenal power. Imagination, desire and action are a magnetic combination that will see the materialization of my dreams.

SUMMARY

- It is the base from which all your creations evolve.
- A divine gift capable of conjuring your impressions into reality.
- Combine imagination, desire and action to fulfil the hope held in your aspirations.
- Stretching your imagination beyond imposed boundaries is to awaken to limitless possibility.

- The greatness of your being can be recognized through the ability to imagine such.
- Purposeful activation and focus is the key to rekindling child-like wonder of wishing your dreams true.
- Create, play, enjoy and watch the manifestation of an enchanting existence.

Allow your imagination to be the artist that creates the images of your desires. Infuse these images with positive energy and watch as they are transformed into reality.

IMAGINATION

I infuse all thought with positive energy. I unlock the wonder contained in my imagination and choose to form my reality based on the images I create with positive intention.

Spiritual Quest

Inner Child

Your inner child is as much alive today as when you where a child.

 *The essence of the child lives within each and every one of us. This child is as real today as it was when you were a child.* It remains as an aspect of self, complete with its own thoughts, feelings, perceptions and beliefs.

We exist as layered aspects that combine together to create who we identify with as being who we are. These layers are the infant, child, adolescent, adult and elder.

The inner child is the child-like aspect that forms part of our psyche. It is the keeper of memories and of our inner-most secrets. The child self needs to feel safe and be nurtured.

The beliefs and perceptions held by the inner child affect who we are today. While certain beliefs from childhood are debunked as we mature, there are still underlying beliefs about self and the workings of the world that are held true.

These beliefs form perceptions that construct our outlook on life. If the inner child has opposing views, unfulfilled needs and unexpressed emotion, they can be triggered and cause a reaction.

What triggers our inner child is often unknown to us. Something bubbles up from somewhere deep inside and causes us to behave in ways that are beyond our conscious control. Child-like tantrums or child-like withdrawal are examples of inner child reactions. Our inner child may have never learned how to express themselves rationally and continues to react automatically to triggers. Automatic reactions will continue until we acknowledge our inner child.

Getting to know our inner child will provide amazing insight into our current beliefs, perceptions, motivations, talents, fears, annoyances and emotional triggers.

Our inner child holds emotional memories, self-limiting beliefs and fears; it also holds core values, natural enthusiasm, sheer determination and is naturally optimistic, although this may be concealed by any conflicting emotion the inner-child identifies with.

When we first approach our inner child it may present itself as an emotion. This emotion may be one we are familiar with as it would have been triggered numerous times. Sitting with the emotion is like taking our inner child by the hand and saying "I am listening." If we try to escape the emotion, that is like saying "go away, it's too hard,

I don't want this burden." Which is what we have been saying to our inner child for as long as it has been denied as an aspect of self. How would you react or respond to someone who has denied your very existence? With this in mind it may be that your inner child may greet you with anger or may dismiss you. Take heart your inner child may be upset at being ignored for so long.

Building a relationship with the inner child may take time as your child-self may feel vulnerable, be distrusting, angry, sad, repressed, withdrawn or any other possible scenario.

A wounded inner child may experience a period of grief as it comes to terms with whatever occurred. As unique individuals, an encounter with grief will be personal as will be the way any associated emotion is processed. Patience, empathy and perseverance are essential during this time. But perseverance will be well worth it.

As the consciously aware adults in our inner child's life we can love, nurture, accept and guide the little being inside.

Ponder what you enjoyed doing as a child as this will be a way to encourage inner child communication. We all have different learning styles and the best way to entice inner child communication is by using the style preferred. This may be visually through pictures and images, auditory through song and music or kinaesthetically through painting, drawing, building or crafts.

Once we have engaged our inner child it will be more receptive to receiving our love and healing. Love, understanding and compassion help to establish a positive relationship that enables us to cooperatively find solutions and fulfil the needs of our inner child.

Building a positive relationship with our inner child is the first step to forming a solid relationship with ourselves. Gaining trust and being accepted by our inner child makes us more trusting and accepting of ourselves.

The more loved our inner child feels the more we love ourselves. The more we attend to the needs of our inner child the more we meet our own needs. The more encouragement we give our inner child the more we will see our natural qualities and talents emerge. A happy inner child will see the emergence of a joyful adult.

Know thyself is to know the Inner Child

To know the depth of oneself is to acknowledge the inner child. Base beliefs, core values and perspectives are established as children. These are formed when there is a lack of emotional maturity and rationalisation ability. This demonstrates how this can cause conflict when the same perspectives are carried through into adulthood. Also carried through into adulthood are the memories, some of which contain unresolved emotions, unfulfilled needs, counter-productive beliefs and distorted perceptions.

Although this may sound like a lot to work through, especially if the inner child is resistant, connecting with the inner child is well worth any work that is required. Our adult selves can become a parent to the inner child. This begins by being consciously aware and attentive of the inner child.

Conscious awareness is paramount to our personal growth and development as we can more easily identify inner child perceptions and how they affect our adult point of view. Increasing our conscious awareness requires us to be open-minded, active seekers of knowledge and to be active participants in the development of soul qualities. Approaching life in this way, as consciously aware beings, we facilitate awakening on levels that will amaze.

If there has been ill-effect from others who have demonstrated a lack of conscious awareness, meaning they have acted in ways that have hurt, harmed or devalued the amazing being that you are, please refer to the chapter on forgiveness and commit to healing wounded aspects by gently guiding them with love and acceptance.

Being empowered in this way can reverse detrimental effects and establish new foundations on which to grow. If the fundamental building blocks of love, nurture and stability were absent in childhood, they can be established by the adult self. This is to parent oneself and provide the essential components needed for the inner child to receive the love, nurture and stability it deserves.

Acknowledging your inner child is to uncover some of the hidden aspects that may be interfering with your happiness. Reaching out and connecting with the child within is to discover the hidden aspects of your identity.

The journey of life is full of ups and downs. Sometimes life flows and sometimes it is stagnant.

Sometimes we are happy and our needs are fulfilled and sometimes we are not happy and our needs are requiring our attention. The key is to accept that there will be highs and lows. The idea is to find the highs in the lows. This is the blessing that comes in disguise.

An aspect that contributes significantly to the highs and lows of life is associated with our inner child. An inner child reaction may be felt as a shift and then, without warning, we see our emotions change. We might find we plummet from the heights of happiness into emotion that seems to come from a distant place within.

What triggers an emotional reaction from our inner child may be unbeknown to us but can have considerable effect on what we are doing at the time. Identifying triggers and the effect they have on us helps to determine areas of sensitivity, our raw points.

If feelings of worthlessness were triggered there are many different emotions that may emerge and from which there will most likely be a behavioural response. Outbursts and withdrawal are examples of behaviour with an underlying emotion.

As children we based our worth on the feedback we

received from the significant adults in our life. What is worthy of mentioning here is that the adults in our lives saw us from their perspective and projected this perspective onto us. We hear this perspective through our inner monologue.

Children do not have filters; words and actions are absorbed by the subconscious like a sponge. We become what the adults in our life reinforce. If a child is criticized for who they are and what they do their self-esteem will be greatly diminished.

As children we do not have the capacity to declare "I know they love me, they are doing the best they can with the tools they have". Criticizing a child sends the message that they are unlovable and so it is more likely that unhealthy criticism is absorbed and will be heard as the inner-critic for years to come. This critical voice batters the self-esteem. Even if we put on a false bravado, we cannot hide the truth from ourselves.

Acknowledging this goes a long way to being able to change the voice of the critical inner-critic to one that supports and nurtures a healthy self-esteem.

Recognising that whatever the voice of the inner-critic says is a projection of what was in the mind of the parent or significant older, thus not ours to hold, can help make a dynamic shift. Through this shift we can exchange the critical voice to one of praise and positive guidance.

By taking on the parental role we can champion our inner child and build our self-esteem so it flourishes. At the same time our inner child shifts its perception and understands that certain beliefs are merely a subjective projection from someone else, we will see our adult perception shift.

However if we try to shift our perception without considering our inner child's perspective, we may end up with a battle of wills and the core belief will remain fixed. That feeling of going forward but being held back is an example of the inner child rejecting what is being proposed.

We must start at the roots and build from there, otherwise we are at the mercy of the beliefs held by our child-self. Understanding what these beliefs are and shaping them to better reflect what we want will see shifts in perception that align with our adult selves.

By using affirmations and actively

encouraging our inner child we champion ourselves to success.

Imagination - Children use their imagination to transform everyday objects, places and things into things of wonder and intrigue. Whatever can be conjured by the imagination can come to life. Children do not query their capacity to turn a cubby house into a palace or a stick into a wand.

Adults can also use their imagination such as when conjuring up a holiday, a dream home, a dream car, a dream partner, a dream job. We also use our imagination when picturing what our current day looks like and what the next day will look like.

We imagine our to-do list, the bills that need to be paid, the credit card bulging, the mortgage and our current bank balance. As adults we use our imagination for the mundane. This is a huge under-use of a powerful resource.

Children are like magicians with their imaginations, but as we grow we revert to being less creative. Except for those who remain connected to their inner child. Effective use of our imagination will empower the vision of our dreams.

Infusing our vision with positive feelings reinforces what we want and we will find ourselves on our dream holiday, living in our dream home and holding hands with our dream partner. If we tarnish any part of our vision with doubt and negativity we are telling our subconscious to bring the negative version of our vision.

Framing thoughts and visual images to match the picture of our dreams reinstates our ability to transform the mundane into the magnificent. There is a child inside that would take great delight in recreating the magic.

Determination - Children are quietly determined. They do not give up easily. They will somehow find a way of doing what it is they want to do. Most don't entertain the idea of failure, they are too focused on what they want to achieve. Previous attempts provide them the feedback they need to make adjustments until they find the winning combination.

We need to apply this same determination as adults when striving to achieve our goals. Determination will see us through the toughest of times and direct us onto the path of success.

Success being the result of determination, faith and positive focus. This is the winning formula that we can give as a gift to our inner child.

Optimism - is a child-like quality. The world to a child is abundant and colourful. As we grow our wonder-filled view of the world gets hazy. We become more black and white in our view, possibly due to the years of brain training and rote learning that tends to actively develop our logic and at the same time passively squelches our creativity.

At a young and influential age the paint pellet is exchanged for a pen and the blank cavases that received our innovative creations are exchanged for formulated worksheets. And this is the way it stays throughout our formative years. Is it any wonder that our rose-coloured view of the world dims? Our mind requires both academic and creative stimulation to see the various dimensions and array of colour life presents.

Enthusiasm - Children exude enthusiasm. The ability to transform a word into a vision or a feeling can have a child jumping for joy. The words party, puppy or pony will have a child overflowing with enthusiasm. Adults tend to dull the exuberance of an excited child. There are many reasons for this, including avoiding over-excitement which can be challenging to deal with, the moulding of appropriate behaviour and the taming of emotional expression.

What is exciting for children can often mean work for adults. The responsibility that goes with adult life can squash feelings of excitement so that it makes it difficult to meet the child at the same level of enthusiasm. However if enthusiasm is culled to the extreme then in later years getting excited about anything will prove challenging. If enthusiasm is stripped due to thoughts of the work, effort, time, etc. take some time out to play and regain child-like vision. To do so will see one reinvigorated with enthusiasm.

Resilience - A child gets on with things. A child may feel an emotion, but does not dwell. An incident that occurs is dealt with then and there and they move onto other things. If a disagreement happens it is resolved and the same children will be playing happily moments later. However, resilience begins to fray if there is repeat exposure to negativity or if any stage of development is not mastered. Thus we see different characteristics emerge; the child will not seem themselves.

This is the time to act and seek to engage the child and provide the support needed to ensure the best possible transition through this period so the child does not become stuck or begin to hone in on negative thought patterns. If negative thought patterns become engrained they will become the way of thinking.

When we feel a certain way and don't really know why, it is possible that an emotional reaction has been triggered in the inner child. If a vulnerability is exposed or we feel affronted we might see the inner child jump into defence mode. That may be to yell, sulk, hit out, get huffy, withdraw, detach or disassociate. Recognising inner child behaviour is the awareness needed to give to the inner child what it didn't receive in childhood.

Please know that what our parents and carers did, they did with the awareness and knowledge they had at that time. This is not to excuse some of the things done, but it does help to understand that people cannot be expected to know more than they know. However, once there is awareness then it is important to be on par with the insight this brings.

On the journey of self-discovery there comes a time when we arrive at the realisation that in order to love fully we first must love ourselves. Self-love becomes the theme and, try as we will to achieve this, what we receive is the inner child defending its position of not being lovable.

Telling ourselves that we are lovable over and over has an effect on the subconscious. However if the opposite is believed by the inner child then the affirmation will be rejected by that aspect of our psyche. Thus begins the process of discovering the root cause that opposes our attempts of self love.

When we arrive on Earth we are connected to the source from whence we came, but over time this connection weakens. Arising from this are feelings of abandonment, rejection and loneliness.

When these feelings escalate there is further severing of the connection to the source resulting in behaviour that opposes the moral principles of human conduct. This is seen in the atrocities that occur, all of which is ego-based that influences the mind to such a degree that certain untoward actions can be justified by those who believe the illusion of their perceptions. Ego-based perspectives, which are those that oppose love, compassion and joy, denies access to the source of who we are. Underlying this illusion is a profound truth that has power to transform lives.

Reflecting on our childhood beliefs and perspectives begins the rekindling of the connection to the core of our being. With this comes the realisation that we are never alone, we are all connected through the same source that sparked our energy in the first place.

The love and joy felt through the reconnection to the essence of who we really are will see the inner child rejoice and as it does feelings of loneliness, abandonment and rejection will dissolve and the essence of the child is reborn.

Peep through the eyes of the inner child and be touched by the essence of magic.

TECHNIQUE

*Please Note:* The questions here may trigger certain emotional reactions. If there was childhood trauma or abuse it is recommended that before doing inner child work one seeks the support of a trusted professional.

Journaling is an effective way to scribe thoughts, feelings, beliefs and perceptions of the inner aspects of self. Begin by reflecting on a favourite childhood memory. What do you remember about it?

Now reflect on yourself as a child.

What did you enjoy playing?

What did you wish was true?

What did you pretend was true?

Who were the significant people in your life?

What messages did you receive from the people in your life?

Were your parents or carers emotionally responsive?

How did the people in your life respond to your needs?

What message did you get about expressing your emotions?

Did you enjoy social activities or prefer your own

company?

What key words would you use to describe yourself as a child?

What qualities did you have as a child?

Were these qualities recognised?

Were you praised more for who you are or what you did?

Reconnecting with our child-self is a return to innocence. Our true essence is held in the heart of the little being within, this is a true reflection of who we are before we begin to interpret the world based on our physical experience.

If we stripped away everything that influenced us and returned to our birth state we would see a picture of purity. A free spirit with immense potential.

What happens from the moment of birth is dependent on factors beyond our control. It is not until later years that we have the opportunity to become the masters of our mind, the managers of our life and the orchestrators of our destiny.

When we arrive at this stage of our journey we must be prepared to heal the emotional memories of the past, become aware of inner conflict presented by certain aspects and counteract ingrained inner-dialogue. This requires us to stand tall, be courageous and do what it takes to reveal our inner light. Contained within this light is the ability to become a beacon not only to ourselves but to others so that they too can find the courage to reveal their light and so on. Are you ready to awaken and shine your light?

Connecting With the Child Within

You are going on a journey to meet and gain insight into the feelings and beliefs held by your inner child. You are going to unlock hidden secrets such as the hopes, dreams, wants and wishes that the inner child has or had. What has disappointed, upset, bewildered or overwhelmed this child. You are going to be the parent of this child to make it feel safe, secure and know that it is loved unconditionally.

Imagine yourself going to meet your inner child in a place you feel comfortable or a place you would think a child would feel safe. If you close your eyes you might find that your imagination takes you to a place. If vision is not transpiring initially think of a place you like to be or a place you liked as a child. Set the intention of meeting your inner child. You may receive a vision, have a feeling or remember something that represents the child.

This is the inner child communicating with you. The more you visit your inner child the more it will trust you and be willing to express itself. Much insight is gained through the insights of your inner child.

 Take a deep breath in through your nose then exhale out through your mouth.

Take another deep breath in through your nose then exhale out through your mouth.

Take another deep breath, this time you breathe in beautiful white light. This white light fills every cell with its purity.

This white light flows through your entire body and you can feel yourself fill with its love.

It flows down your legs and down into your feet.

It flows out of your feet and into the Earth.

You can feel yourself connecting with the Earth essence.

Your white light roots go down, down, down, into

the Earth.

You are feeling grounded, safe and protected.

You and the Earth are one.

You feel a warm feeling in your white light roots.

It is Mother Earth's energy responding to you.

She sends her love through your white light roots.

The energy flows through your entire body filling you with warmth and love.

As you feel these feelings of warmth and love you tune into your heart beat. Your heart beats to the rhythm of your essence. You see a spark of light in this area. With each in breath you notice that this spark of light gets brighter.

As you watch this light grow you notice that there is someone standing beside you.

The bright light has aroused the curiosity of the child within.

You look at the child and smile.

The child looks at you with innocent eyes.

You kneel down to meet the child at its height.

You request permission to ask the child a few questions.

Respect the child's answer. It may take a few practises before the child is ready to communicate. Although you are meeting a child, this is a very wise being, it has much knowledge about the truth of who you are. You can learn from your inner child and in exchange you can provide the security and comfort a child needs to grow.

When you feel that you have spent adequate quality time with your inner child you say goodbye for now. Remind your child that you will try to be there for him or her and that you are becoming more aware of how it communicates. Ask if there is anything special that it would like you to know. When you are ready slowly come back to where you are and settle yourself firmly into your body. Wrap your arms around yourself in a warm embrace and as you do breathe in pink and green light to represent the love you have for your inner child.

If one wants to know themselves they must first get to know the child like being within.

PLEDGE FOR THE INNER-CHILD

My inner child is an aspect of me.

I take this child by the hand and offer my ear to hear what it has to say.

I shall listen. I empower this child with the love it deserves. Love is the essence it needs to grow.

As my inner child grows so do I. As he/she accepts who they are I also accept myself for who I am. Being me is everything I need.

I am worthy, I am lovable, I am able, I can and I will.

Unless we understand the workings of our inner child we are not completely in synch with ourselves.

SUMMARY

- The inner child does not dissolve and go away because our bodies grow and our minds mature.
- The inner child is the keeper of memories, has insight into our inner most secrets and is a co-creator of our life experiences.
- Much information about oneself and the reasons for thoughts, feelings and actions is contained within the memories of the inner child.
- Reach in, take the hand of your inner child and find out how it feels, what it thinks and what it wants.

We have the choice to resolve what is unresolved from childhood or to allow it to resolve us.

INNER CHILD

*My inner child is loved and nurtured
as every child should be.*

Denying that we have an inner child is like denying that we were children. Our bodies will grow and our minds will mature, but our child like self will remain.

Spiritual Quest

Inner Sanctuary

My inner sanctuary is a place
I can go to relax, gather my thoughts
and take some time for myself

The inner sanctuary is your inner retreat

 Your inner sanctuary is a place you can go when in need of some space to collect thoughts, centre yourself or take some time out. You can visit this place even when in the mists of turmoil. When feeling unsettled, restless, overwhelmed or anything that makes you feel ill-at-ease visit your inner sanctuary. It is a space where you can be at one with yourself.

Feelings of serenity and positivity established while visiting your inner sanctuary will transfer to daily life. This has the long term benefit of creating permanent feelings of inner calm. Calm mind, relaxed body, balanced emotions set a harmonious vibration to your day.

Connecting with your inner sanctuary requires the bypassing of the conscious mind, silencing mind chatter and being void of thought. Ways of doing this include meditation, guided visualization, using mantras and deep breathing. Having a space to escape the noise and busyness that accompanies living in today's society is the foundation of well-being, which is to be a well-being.

Creating your inner sanctuary begins by thinking of a place that makes you feel relaxed. It might be a place you love to visit, it may be the size of a temple or the size of a hut, it may be somewhere in nature or a cathedral. Whatever your sacred space looks like in your mind's eye, when there you feel secure and calm.

Designing your inner sanctuary will use visual, auditory and kinaesthetic modalities to create a picture of your beautiful space on your mind's eye screen. Visual is to impress the image of what you want your inner sanctuary to look like. Be it an island, a forest, a temple or a room this is your sacred space. Kinaesthetically you can connect to the feeling of your inner sanctuary.

Start by breathing in through the nose and then exhaling out through the mouth and as you do let go of tension. Continue to do this until you are feeling calm. Now take yourself into the image of your inner sanctuary whatever that may be. This connects the feeling of calm to the visual image of your sacred space. You can add some sounds.

If your inner sanctuary is a forest you may hear the birds singing, the sound of a waterfall flowing and the feel the mystical ambiance that surrounds you. What you see, hear and feel accentuate the feeling of being a real place of retreat. This may come naturally or may take some time to create. Once created spend some time in your inner sanctuary. Familiarize yourself with how it looks, sounds and feels. This will become the place you visit to gather your thoughts, ponder ideas, to reflect on issues or areas that need your attention.

If virtual creation of your inner sanctuary proves challenging, you may like to cut a photo from a brochure or find a digital image of something you like and print it out to have nearby until the image of your sacred space becomes visible in your mind's eye.

While experiencing this place take in everything you need to anchor it into your memory so it can be recalled at other times when there is no physical or digital representation. There are no limits to what you can create on the screen of your mind's eye. This is your personal virtual reality screen; the possibilities are boundless.

 Take a deep breath in through the nose and then exhale out through your mouth.

Take another deep breath in through the nose and then exhale out through your mouth.

Take another deep breath this time you inhale beautiful white light. The white light swirls through your body touching every cell with its essence. The white light revitalizes you and makes you feel relaxed and at ease.

You notice the white light form into a ball of brilliant light. This ball settles gently in your heart area. This is your connection to your higher-self. You look into this brilliant ball of light. It fills you with feelings of peace and tranquility.

As you continue to gaze into the light you see it transform into the most beautiful place you have ever seen. You feel so comfortable in this place. It is the most comfortable place you have ever been to.

You take in everything that is here.

This is your Inner Sanctuary where you can come to recharge, to reflect and to take some timeout for yourself.

Your Inner Sanctuary is your creation and will be

here whenever you need to retreat and find inner calm

You only need think of this place and you will automatically feel its presence. Feeling its presence will bring you instant calm, peace and tranquility.

You remain here for several moments, drinking in its beauty and the feelings of absolute bliss

You know that you can visit this place whenever you wish

You know this place by the aromas, the sounds and the sights

You know every detail of this place. It is yours.

You continue to spend time here until feelings of inner calm are bestowed

When you are ready, return to the space you are in. You are becoming more consciously aware and are bringing with you feelings of inner calm and serenity

Your awareness slowly returns to your legs, and now your hips and up into your stomach and chest. You are now aware of your arms. You are conscious and feeling relaxed, refreshed and have with you a visual image of your Inner Sanctuary.

PLEDGE TO CONNECT WITH YOUR INNER-SANCTUARY

My inner sanctuary is where my mind, body and spirit meet. This is where I retreat to find the quiet space within. In this space I feel safe and secure. Spending time here frees me from mind chatter and allows me to process and find clarity. This is the source of deeper knowing. Here is where I get to know the rawness of my natural state of being. I am accepting of the real me. There is no pretense, no agenda. I am a well-being.

Connect with your inner sanctuary by attuning to the harmonic vibration contained within.

SUMMARY

- You can visit your inner sanctuary when you need time alone.
- Your inner sanctuary can be created in any image that pleases you.
- It may be the image of a tropical island, a meadow, a forest, a cave, or a silent void.
- Your inner sanctuary is your sacred space, it is calm and harmonious.
- The inner sanctuary is a place for contemplation and helps to replenish energy.

INNER SANCTUARY

My Inner Sanctuary is a place I can go to relax, gather my thoughts and take some time for myself.

Spiritual Quest

Inspiration

I listen to the inner whispers of my inspiration

Allow the petals of your creative ideas to unfold and blossom into magnificence

Allow new ideas to emerge and manifest through your creative spirit.

Being inspired by your own inner guidance captures the energy that brings into focus your unique talents and gifts that when utilized align perfectly with your hopes and dreams.

Inspiration yields phenomenal power. It triggers the motivation needed to drive our dreams into reality. Although powerful, inspiration is also vulnerable and likely to dissolve if exposed to doubt. Hence the need to nurture inspiration.

This is done by being around inspiring people, going to places that provide inspiration and having a positive approach, especially when attending to thoughts and feelings that cast dark shadows over attempts to be optimistic.

When the seed of inspiration is nurtured natural creative talent emerges. Tapping into your creative centre gives access to greater opportunities and possibilities.

Every aspect of your life reflects your creativity. If what you see does not appeal then it is time to get creative.

Recognizing that you are the creator of your

reality and taking a constructive look at what needs attention sees new and different perspectives emerge.

Through new found perspective there is space to re-evaluate where you are, where you would like to be and what can be done to align the two. This evaluation in itself fuels the energy of inspiration, provided you view through the eyes of non-judgment and with the intention of keeping what is working and releasing what is not.

Holding onto outdated ideas and wishes or refusing to see the reality of a situation suffocates inspiration. Each one of us has arrived where we are based on the interaction we have had with life this far. But this does not mean we have to continue on the same path unless we choose to and if we feel that we are treading down a path that is not delivering what want, then it is time to shift direction.

Becoming aware of the need to shift is inspired by your spirit that wants to break free and start living the life you were born to live.

A fleeting moment of inspiration can be enough to initiate the energy needed to shake things up and get out of a rut or to realise that life is not mediocre, but dynamic.

TECHNIQUE

Breathe in the essence of life. Take a moment to breathe in and as you do feel your body, really feel your body. Acknowledge the capacity of your body to do all it does without you needing to think about it. That is miraculous.

Inhale again and recognize that within you is a mind that has ability beyond current comprehension. A mind that thirsts to be motivated and thrives when inspired. Inspiration revitalizes the mind and enables it to become creative, to imagine and to manifest dreams into living things. See it, feel it, have it.

Listen to the whispers of your inspiration. What do you hear? say? What do you see? Set the intention of being aware of things that inspire you. This may be found through pictures, people, places, magazines, photos, quotes, messages, scenery etc. Find something that inspires you and view it on a daily basis. Attune to feelings of inspiration. Inspiration can come from anywhere. Notice when you feel inspiration stirring. What does it relate to? Where did it come from? How does it make you feel? Is there an idea that inspires you?

Douse the voice of doubt and dissolve negativity with reassurance that what you desire is achievable.

PLEDGE FOR INSPIRATION

I hear the whispers of inspiration. This sparks my creative flow.

I am inspired with ideas ripe for manifestation. The positive pictures of my imagination are unfolding and blossoming into magnificence. I am a creative being realizing my potential.

SUMMARY

- Hear the quiet inner voice that calls to you to awaken to your potential.
- The inner voice of inspiration can be heard when mind chatter is put on mute.
- Awareness of the quiet one allows you to hear inspirational melodies.
- See barriers crumble as you embrace your inspirations and spark the creative flow.
- You are an amazingly creative being.
- Birth your ideas into reality.
- Erode stagnation by maintaining momentum.
- Persist through challenges.
- Dissolve doubt with faith and trust.
- Believe that you can and you surely will.

Inspiration is captured by a mind open to receive.

INSPIRATION

I listen to the inner whispers of my inspiration.

Inspiration gave birth to all creation. In that lays the foundations of who you are. May the voice of doubt be hushed by the realization of this truth. Awaken to your inner creativity and bestow your inspired spirit upon this Earth.

Spiritual Quest

Intention

This reflection comes as an insightful blessing

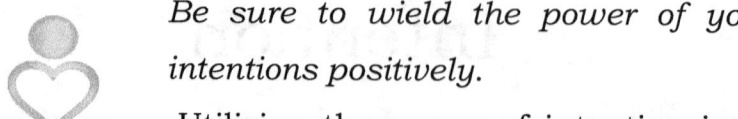

Be sure to wield the power of your intentions positively.

Utilizing the power of intention is to wield a phenomenal manifestation tool. Set intentions upon a solid foundation of positive energy. Projecting positive intention into goals, hopes and aspirations sets the scene for significant reward.

Creative visualization enhances the energy of the intention which imprints the mind with a picture of what is wanted. This allows the intention to flow outward and attract like energy. Although this may sound somewhat mystical, the fact is that positive intention capturing positive energy is the natural law of attraction.

Whatever it is you have in your life there was an energy match for it to have manifested. Meeting of a life partner, landing the ideal career position, purchasing the dream home are the rewards of setting positive and clear intentions. If intentions are washed down with doubt, delivered with a vibration of desperation or with a need attached we may find ourselves attracting something less than desirable.

For example when in search of the 'perfect

partner' we project an image outwards and the vibration of that image will seek a matching image and return it complete with any need based attachment it was sent out with. So when the 'perfect mate' turns up in our life we welcome them with open arms. However the attachments that went out with that request e.g. feelings of loneliness, isolation, rejection went out with them.

So while the relationship may start off rosy in time the partner we attracted will not be able to fulfill the underlying need because it is up to us to fulfill that within ourselves. This is the same for any intention set. This is why often we get what we want, or think we want, and ravel in the happiness only to find that shortly afterwards our happiness bubble has burst and we are on the prowl for the next thing.

If what we put out carries a negative vibe we can expect that what is returned will be aligned with negativity. This often creates more negativity and the cycle continues. Waking up to this is not an easy thing to do, but it is essential or we will continue to get much of the same.

Basically positive retrieves positive and negative retrieves negative. This does not mean to say that we will receive only positive or only negative. Life delivers both, what is important is that we have a level of awareness of what is being projected and make conscious shifts towards the positive polarity.

If you find yourself in a repetitive cycle and past history seems to repeat e.g. find yourself in similar circumstances then it is likely that there is a shadow aspect lurking and in order to circumvent repeat patterns this aspect requires attention

Being aware of this helps move the aspect, which can be detected through thoughts and feelings. As an example feeling doubtful about something can be a typical response to an new idea, there may be a range of doubts that go through your mind such as if it was that good why hasn't someone else done it? However we are often able to navigate ourselves through the doubts. But when these doubts are consuming to the point they render us helpless then action is called for.

Using various tools and techniques helps defuse the doubt held by the aspect projecting it and enables positive intention setting that is no longer clouded by doubt.

To achieve positive outcomes one needs to infuse their intentions with belief. The most effective way of harnessing belief is to make a conscious choice to align with your highest-good. Being aligned with your highest good is to be aligned with purpose, when aligned with purpose the support and opportunities that become available is profound.

This is not to say that all will be smooth sailing, all projects and life ventures have their ups and downs no matter how purpose driven they are. But those with good merit are able to withstand the obstacles and triumph.

If you feel disconnected or distracted and cannot seem to get into positive intention setting mode try the following: Imagine you are holding a lasso. You cast your rope and it catches what is hindering you. You pull towards you and see what it is. You infuse whatever it is with the colours green and pink. See love move through the rope and then let it go. The hindrance can no longer hinder you. If in the future this image returns send it love and see it disappear again. If you feel hindered by something else do the same technique.

TECHNIQUE
Setting Intentions

Write down, draw or cut out pictures of what you would like to manifest, fold it into three. Write: With the power within me I see this image manifest into my life. Light a white candle, focus and see the flame of the candle carry your intention out into the Universe and say "and it is so". Place the paper under your pillow.

Hold your intentions with positive regard. If any negative images should invade, replace them with your positive intention. Infuse every day with positive energy.

Be creative on ways to do this. Read an affirmation, read a couple of pages from a motivational book, read some inspirational quotes, do a mini-meditation, take a minute to focus on your breath, listen to ambient music that uplifts and inspires or is calming and relaxing. During the day if the energy shifts and starts to carry a negative vibration do one of the above mentioned to reset the vibration into positive mode.

PLEDGE FOR INTENTION

I keep my intentions pure and inspired with positivity as it is my intentions that provide the foundation I build my life on.

My intentions present themselves in the light I have surrounded them in.

My intentions fulfill my desire to live the life I aspire to lead.

I reap the benefits of projecting positive intention in all I do.

SUMMARY

- Know the power of your intentions.
- Setting intentions allows the Universal flow of energy into your life.
- Combine purpose with the phenomenal power of belief and witness objects of your desires manifest.
- Casting your intentions into positive visualization and projecting them forth captures the vibe of like energy.
- Be enchanted as the energy created by your intentions charismatically weaves its magic.
- Life is illuminated by the realization of dreams.

INTENTION

I co-create my reality with the law of attraction. My visions of positive intent will materialize into my life.

If we utilised the power contained within our breath, understood the gift of positive intention and conducted ourselves in accordance with the law of attraction each of us would have the capacity to shape existence into one of magnificence.

Spiritual Quest

Intuition

Your intuition was gifted upon you when you descended upon this Earth

Intuition is a gift of phenomenal insight and wisdom.

Understanding life's lessons and deriving purpose is gained by activating intuitive awareness. Trust your inner voice, it will offer wise guidance. Your intuition will help interpret the signs, messages and symbolic representations there to assist your journey.

Your intuition feeds back what it senses through inner-knowing. When you know something without doubt, that is your intuition. Those 'light-bulb' moments is your intuition communicating with you. It comes quickly like a flash and fades.

Second guessing intuition may lead to taking the longer and often more difficult route. Be careful not to override your own intuitive insight with what is said by others. If you have an inner knowing about something trust that before all else.

Intuitive awareness is the perfect companion for the intellect. Combining intuition and intellect creates a phenomenal source of power. When intuition and intellect connect there is a spark that creates the essence of wisdom. Consolidation of this partnership sees the emergence of untapped potential. Placing faith in intuitive innervations sends a message of trust. Placing trust in your intuition will reward you greatly.

Intuition is a profound tool that guides so subtly that it often goes undetected. Intuition is to sense and know without explanation. It is the visions, inner stirrings, feelings or subtle guidance that occurs before rationalization.

Sometimes it is felt as a stirring in the solar plexus area that is accompanied by a feeling of inner knowing. This may be referred to as gut instinct. Intuitive guidance can be received through visual, auditory and kinaesthetic mediums.

These mediums may present independently or as companions such as visual images accompanied by a feeling or auditory communication that comes with the formation of a concept that seems to come from a higher source of knowing. Attune to how your intuition communicates with you. If your intuition communicates via kinaesthetic channels then messages will be received through your feelings. If visual then your intuition will communicate via images. If auditory then communication will be via words that form into concepts. Although our intuition communicates through every channel, we are usually more attuned to one than the others. The one we are more attuned to is our primary source of intuitive communication. Notice messages, signs and clues that clarify your hunches. They are the most reliable source of guidance.

Intuitive development requires practice, discipline and patience. Acknowledging inner urges, recognizing gut feelings and being aware of higher thought processes increases intuitive awareness and connection. An instantaneous message that manifests in your mind is intuition. Learning to trust your intuition is the key to making it stronger.

There are many stories of people who have avoided dire consequences by listening to their inner-voice guiding them. There are also those who are blessed with 'good luck'. They just seem to be in the right place at the right time or make a decision that transforms their life. This is less about luck and more about listening to and having faith in the voice of intuition. Aligning with intuition sees new opportunities arise and potential blossom.

INTUITION

Intuition pops up. It is knowing without doubt.
Intuition comes in snippets, as flashes of insight.
Intuition can be presented as symbolic messages seen within the mind's eye or externally as a physical icon.
Intuition is communicated through messages, signs and symbols that resonates within.
Intuition is strengthened through faith.
Be present! Be aware! Tune in and trust.

TECHNIQUE

Relax and inhale deeply and then exhale. On the exhale let your shoulders drop and feel all tension leave the body. Inhale again and feel yourself being filled with calming energy that relaxes all your muscles. Your body is relaxed and your mind is calm. Repeat the word calm as you gently inhale and exhale a few times. If your mind starts to wander at any stage during the practice bring your focus back to your breathing and say the word **'*calm*'**.

Tune into the area between your eyes. This is

the intuitive centre. Intuitive insight will be communicated in different ways. There may be visual images, colours, feelings, messages, single words and clues that unravel into meaning. Feel the area between your eyes stir. Do not worry if you feel nothing. This area will awaken in time and with practice. Imagine this area moving slowly in a clockwise direction. You are awakening your intuitive channel. Picture a vibrant violet light sparkling in this area. Look deeply into the light. Transform the light into a flower. Watch as if you are watching a television screen. See how the picture forms.

Now think of a different flower and watch as it forms upon your visual screen. Clear your mind and paint a picture with your imagination. Remember this may be represented in another way as mentioned earlier. Notice any feelings that may arise as you see the pictures on your visual screen. Intuition connects you to higher aspects of self. It communicates soul purpose and provides alternative perspectives of self and others.

Seeing through the eyes of our intuitive selves facilitates empathy, understanding and wisdom. Explore the power of this centre by tuning in regularly and asking for guidance. Trust and relax. Intuitive insight becomes more accessible with practice.

PLEDGE TO ENHANCE INTUITION

My intuition is a grand treasure I trust impeccably. I tune in and receive insight, guidance and wisdom that enables me to move with grace and ease in the direction I am destined. A destiny that I create with my inner vision. The combined power of my intuition and reason gives me a reliable source of intelligence which I follow with faith.

SUMMARY

- A grand treasure offering phenomenal insight, guidance and wisdom.
- Activation of your intuitive centre allows you to derive understanding and meaning of life's lessons and their purpose.
- Your intuition is asking you to listen and have faith in your ability to trust its guidance.
- Inner knowing will guide you wisely – allow it to take you to where you need to go.
- Signs and messages will light your path.
- Your intuition needs no explanation – It senses the truth.
- You need only to trust and go with this.
- Follow your innervation with faith.

Spiritual Quest

INTUITION

*I fully awaken to the power
of my inner knowing.
I can fully trust my intuition*

Spiritual Quest

Journal

Journaling gives profound insight into your inner thoughts and feelings

A journal will become your confidant and enables you to explore inner aspects of self.

Reflecting on what has been written can be done with objectivity. From this perspective we can use logical reasoning which provides an altered viewpoint that helps enhance understanding. Journaling can help to uncover thoughts, feelings and beliefs that we are unaware of. This is part of getting to fully know thyself. Our journal becomes a mirror that reflects known and hidden aspects of self.

One such aspect is our inner saboteur. Journaling provides insight into the thoughts and feelings of our inner saboteur which enables us to see how and why this aspect does what it does. With this understanding we can use the necessary tools to assist the inner saboteur to step from the shadows and operate with new awareness. This empowers us to break free from the limitations the inner saboteur burdens us with. This applies to all aspects of self.

Aspects are created through our experiences. Personal interpretations of our experiences create thought processes, emotional associations and establish beliefs. Identifying aspects of self helps to clarify where our thoughts, feelings and beliefs have emerged. Thus we gain deeper understanding of who we are, what has influenced us, and how our interpretations have formed our beliefs.

This knowledge enables us to see where our strengths and vulnerabilities lie, why we like and dislike certain things, what has affected us positively and what has had a negative effect. Journaling provides a space for constructive thought and intuitive insight from which we engage in a holistic interaction with self.

Allow thoughts and feelings to flow onto the page. They may appear scattered at first, but once the superficial ramblings are expressed room is made for deeper expression. Here is where things get interesting and the need to protect what is being expressed from being interrupted by mind chatter is required.

Be aware not to be drawn into distractions, this is the mind trying to take control. This may lead to thoughts taking over and rewinding back to the past, projecting into the future or getting caught up in current concerns. This is unproductive and keeps us locked into superficial thought processes rather than obtaining access into the deeper recesses. To uncover what lies beneath we need to balance thought processes with intuitive awareness to gain insight and clarity of the information received.

With increased awareness it becomes easier to differentiate between mind chatter and constructive communication with aspects of self. There may be times when something begins to emerge and then disappears.

Communicating with the inner self with focused attention is something that is not done on a regular basis, thus it may take some time for flow to develop.

Establishing a regular routine to catch up with self requires conscious effort such as scheduling time in our diary to ensure time is taken for this date with self. Think of this time as being an important meeting that cannot be missed.

Hectic lifestyles make it easy to rank ourselves low on the priority scale. This serves as an injustice, as we rob ourselves of the quality time needed to become our own best friend. Creating a loyal, trusting friendship with self is one of the greatest gifts we can give ourselves and will have a positive impact in all areas of our life.

We are whole beings composed of individual aspects that have been created through interpretation of our experiences. Journaling is an effective tool that coaxes aspects of self to express themselves.

This provides us with knowledge about how we think, feel and behave. Aspects are created throughout our various stages of our development. Each aspect has perceptions, beliefs and emotions that contribute to who we believe we are. For example our child self has constructed perceptions, beliefs and feelings that operate independently to our adult self.

The same is true for our adolescent self who perceives things differently to the child self and adult self. Each of these aspects resonates differently and reacts to different triggers.

If something triggers the inner adolescent it will be the adolescent that responds which may see the emergence of adolescent type behaviour. The same is true when we witness an adult behaving like a child, the inner child has been triggered and hence there is the presentation of child-like behaviour.

Journaling provides an avenue where these

aspects can be acknowledged and any unmet needs can be attended to. From this perspective we can see that the arousal of an emotional reaction represents an unmet need that has compounded and smoldered and when triggered evokes a behavioural response.

For example, a display of anger does not deem the person is an angry person, but that an aspect of that person is reacting to an emotional trigger. They respond according to the level of development of the triggered aspect. However if the aspect is not attended to the anger will continue and that person may eventually be ruled by that aspect.

This is the case with any emotionally triggered behaviour. Effective use of a journal enables us to uncover which inner aspect is reacting and where it is coming from. We can then implement tools and techniques to help fulfil unmet needs of the aspect which will aid in its development, which aids in the development of the whole self.

TECHNIQUE

Source a journal that appeals to you.

Make some time to write in your journal. Light a candle, put on some relaxing music. Sit with your journal, pen or pencil and write down any thoughts that wander through your mind. The thoughts may be superficial to begin with, this is mind-chatter.

Sometimes we have to sort through the superficial mind-chatter until we gain access to the deeper levels of thought. When the mind-chatter quietens interesting and insightful concepts will emerge.

When these thoughts come, observe what they are composed of and from where they arise. If they hold something of substance write it down. Set the intention of being aware of your thoughts.

Carry your journal for a period to write down thoughts and associated feelings as they come. Acknowledging the inner realms of self sparks the interest of aspects that have yearned attention.

These aspects will want to communicate which may see thoughts, feelings and memories emerge at times other than when journaling. Notice what floats into your consciousness and if there are any links to what is presented. Ask yourself questions relating to the thoughts and feelings and remain aware of the answers that arise. Answers may come instantly or they may take a while to manifest.

If this is the first time you have consciously acknowledged aspects of your inner self, you may be presented with an influx of thoughts and feelings or there may be a void where nothing comes. Be patient as it may take time for a trusting relationship with self to develop.

We may be confronted with emotions that we have kept buried. Their emergence is positive as it provides an opportunity for them to be acknowledged and receive the attention required. This releases them from a suppressed state.

Once acknowledged, we see that when suppressed emotion emerges it is less daunting than we may have anticipated. Identifying an emotion and writing down anything associated with it is to acknowledge aspects of ourselves that influence us in some way.

All emotion affects us, be it positively or negatively. Suppressed emotions have negative impact and dis-empower, whereas positively expressed emotion empowers. Whatever comes to the forefront while journaling can be viewed by our own inherent inner counsellor. This is an aspect of self that can look at what is being expressed objectively, ask relevant questions to gain clarity and select appropriate tools and techniques to use for guidance and support.

Journaling provides immense support on the journey of exploration, discovery, and development of the inner self. When finished journaling write a positive reflection or affirmation such as "I am grateful that I am becoming more attuned with my inner self". Treating ourselves with kindness creates a level of comfort that encourages emotional expression and enriches the relationship we have with self.

TECHNIQUE

Make a list of questions you would like to ask yourself. Make the questions specific and then be open to receive an answer.

It may come in the form of a vision, a message, a feeling, a symbol, a word, a sound or stimulation of any of the senses.

Sample Questions

Where does this thought, belief or feeling come from?

Why do I feel the way I do about such and such?

What triggers me to behave in certain ways?

Where does the emotion I am experiencing come from?

What is the underlying fear of (state situation)?

How did this come about?

Where do my strengths lie?

How can I use my strengths to assist my weaknesses?

What are my vulnerabilities?

How can I support my vulnerabilities so I may grow?

What belief do I hold about (subject)?

Is this thought, belief or feeling aligning with what I choose for my life right now?

Remember to trust what comes up, even if the information presented is limited initially, as time moves forward more insight will be gained.

If a question is related to a particular issue or set of circumstances go slowly and gently. If discomfort emerges stop and do the breathing and grounding meditation (see back of book). If required seek assistance.

Everyone needs support at some time during their life, whether it is from a family member, a friend or a professional. We learn from every person we engage with, even if only briefly. We never know who it will be that gives a clue, a message or insight that puts another piece in our ever expanding puzzle. Understanding the inner aspects of self is part of what forms the picture of who we are and what we are here to do. This is the secret to finding the true meaning of inner-happiness.

Communicating with our inner-selves provide profound insight

PLEDGE FOR JOURNALING

I capture an honest account of my inner thoughts, beliefs and emotions through journaling. This enables me to take an objective view of how these effects me. Journaling enables me to weed out toxic influences. I can reinforce what serves me and disengage from what does not. I create positive pathways that counter any negative influence. I am entitled to happiness and will contest self-sabotage, the inner-critic and shadow aspects so they too can see the same path I see for myself and walk along side me united as one. Journaling provides insight into my strengths and vulnerabilities. I can see what is working and what needs work. I have a valuable tool that gives form to my inner-self. I find clarity.

SUMMARY

- Gives form to thoughts and feelings so they can be viewed objectively.
- Consciously unlocks what is hiding in the subconscious.
- Helps identify the different dimensions of self.
- Is a venting tool that assists self expression.

JOURNAL

*These are my private reflections
that give me personal insight to
my inner thoughts, feelings and beliefs*

Spiritual Quest

JOURNEY

When on the seeker's path be guided by your intuition, connected to your heart and coached through your logic

Every day take a step towards your desires. Explore beyond your boundaries and discover more of who you are and what you are capable of. Every experience has a lesson from which we learn.

Our journey is an adventure of wonder and intrigue. As with any great journey, there are highs and lows; trials and tribulations; moments of triumph and of defeat. Things that go askew have a way of balancing so all things become equal. Knowledge and wisdom are reliable escorts to have upon this journey of life.

Life is a precious gift as it provides us with the opportunities our soul needs to evolve. We are students on a magnificent learning journey, in which our experiences provided the grounds on which to learn.

When we reflect on any of our experiences they will be remembered as a point in time that forms part of our journey. Life is a progressive cycle of endings and beginnings. Some experiences are pleasant and some are not, some will extend longer than we would like and some end before we want them to. Sometimes we get stuck and find it difficult to move on from an experience. It is what we take from the experiences that is important and not moving on from an experience means we have not processed it and obtained the lesson contained in the experience.

There is reason for everything; it may just take time for the reason to reveal itself. So long as we maintain forward momentum we will always be positioned exactly where we need to be.

It is when we get stuck that it makes moving into the next cycle difficult. We cannot fully embrace the next cycle if we are still holding onto things from the past. It must be remembered that our experiences provide what is needed to grow.

When we are challenged by an experience it may be that the associated discomfort is the motivation needed to move us out of our comfort zone.

Growth is inevitable when one exercises the courage needed to shift out of a comfort zone. When the foundation of our comfort zone begins to shake, our attention is drawn to areas that need attention.

Our real life situation is there to awaken us to something, usually pertaining to the inner-self. If we are not fulfilling our potential and ignore subtle nudges, then it may be that we receive a significant wake up call. This is not a form of punishment, but a way towards new perspective and most likely a new path.

When we receive signs and messages that something has to change it is time to do an appraisal of life. This includes a personal appraisal to obtain feedback that will help identify strengths, personal attributes, inner resources, and the tools needed to facilitate our journey in the direction we want to go.

When we step back and take an objective view of our lives we can identify what we are holding onto from the past, any continuation of old patterns, behaviours that no longer serve and areas that require healing.

From an objective viewpoint we can evaluate, acknowledge and accept what needs to change. We are also more able to be empathetic towards ourselves and at the same time empowered to take action.

The journey of life is one full of shifts and changes. One moment we may be meandering and the next we find ourselves in the eye of a storm. Throughout our journey we will be presented with experiences of multiple kinds, some will challenge us to our limits. When at our limit we are forced to draw upon aspects of ourselves that we may not know exist.

Dynamic experiences give us learning that expands our consciousness, extends our abilities and broadens intellectual and spiritual awareness. If life is stagnant ask yourself if sitting still is the way to get the most out of life? If the answer is no then ask what you can do to start getting more fully into life. Throwing yourself into life is to be enthralled by what can be discovered.

Life is the journey of the spirit partaking in the experience of physical form. We must seek the guidance of our spirit if we are to step beyond the parameters of our individual minds.

When the mind is united with the virtues of the soul previous limitations dissolve and one expands into unrecognised potential. How can this be? When the mind is bound by ego-perspectives it is contained within those perspectives and believes that is all there is. However when the mind expands past this view the level of awareness heightens. This process continues as the layers of perception peel away to reveal the essence of who we are, which at its core is shared by all. Only the soul knows this, hence the importance of the soul/mind relationship. From mind/ego perspective we are separate.

However mind/soul perspective sees all as coming from source and hence connectedness. This is the fundamental principle that unites every living being, with this realisation the essence of love flows freely as does compassion and feelings of joy of not only knowing but feeling the truth.

This is to truly find oneself and in doing so all that divided the mind from the soul dissolves. It may just be that for the first time one experiences what it is like to be fully alive.

While on this earth it is our mission to marry mind-consciousness with soul-principles and live as heart-centred beings. The love and compassion that flows from this will heal the ego. This is what is meant by 'love thyself', a term that when interpreted by the ego is an impossible task. But when we fall in love with our essence, our inner light, it becomes natural that love and compassion will flow towards wounded aspects of self and wounded aspects of others. It becomes impossible to judge or condemn when centered upon the principles of the soul. With this comes and awareness of times when we are operating through ego. Initially this is challenging as our habits, thoughts and behaviours are ingrained. It is only through awareness of what our habits, thoughts and behaviours are that we can make conscious choices. Therein comes the need for the tools and techniques that assist us to become heart centred.

HEART CENTERING

Everyday breathe into the heart area and imagine the colours of pink and green. These colour represent the giving and receiving of love. Reconnection to the area is transformational. If there is disconnection from love there will be disharmony within one's life. For blockages in this area see writings on Love.

What separates us from our source energy in the first place? The ego aspects of self, many of which are constructed during childhood based on inaccurate assumptions made by others and by ourselves. Uncovering what they are will prove that the beliefs we hold come from someone else's opinion, based on judgement or created by criticism. We can spend years unravelling these beliefs or we can choose to exchange negative beliefs about self for positive. Welcome 'I can' into your vocabulary. If 'I can't' scratches at the door sit with it and repeat "I can't because?" "I can't because?" "I can't because?" it may take some time but a little voice will pipe up and tell you why you think you can't. When you hear this it will be like hearing a child's version of a story.

By asking questions of a silent mind, which is one free of thought, we will hear more than we have ever heard and what we hear will assist in a multiple of ways. For one thing it will become apparent that certain beliefs we have about ourselves are redundant and need to be refined to create a more helpful view.

By continuing to unravel and unveil all the mistruths we hold about ourselves we empty the belief tank. When we arrive at this point we can ask: "If I am not all those things I thought I was then who am I?" It is imperative that you await the answer without trying to answer with logic.

Logic does not know the truth of who you are, it tries to understand, but has no depth of inner knowing. If you wait patiently you will receive your answer. How do you know the answer is the truth?

When one experiences the depth of inner knowing there is no denying its validity.

Connecting to the truth of who we are, our essence, is finding yourself for the first time. In fact it may be that you did not know you were lost until YOU are found. From this comes a deeper feeling of connectedness.

Discovering the Essence as shared by a friend. I hope I give this story justice, because when my friend described it she created a magnificent picture that saw us both shed tears of joy. We were sitting in a café having one of our usual enlightening conversations when

I felt the energy shift, my friend took my hand in hers and looked me in the eye and said she wanted to share something profound with me. This is her recount: *"I was feeling somewhat overwhelmed about nothing in particular perhaps the worries that go with life. From this my thoughts began to ponder what life really is and with that who I really am. Am I my worries? Am I my doubts? Am I my sadness? Am I my thoughts? Am I my feelings? Of course the answer to these questions is No. Then if I am not these things then who I am? As*

I pondered this my mind went quiet, an unusual state of being emerged. I was free of the thought that whirled aimlessly through my head. It was like a vessel opened and through it there was a release, a letting go of being attached to the things I had clung so tightly to. With this I felt a stirring in my chest and a power surge within me. I looked into my heart and there it was! this beautiful light vibrating within, it felt so strong that it seemed to radiate outward and I felt an instant connectedness. I was awestruck! As I tuned in further my life transformed. In that instant my concerns dissolved, I saw higher purpose and gained insight into who I really was. I had total clarity. From that moment life felt different, while I still had concerns it seemed to be just part of bigger plan. Whenever feelings of being overwhelmed began to knock I just placed my focus on the essence of my real self and instantly things felt different. Since then I have become my own source of guidance".

Connecting to the essence of who we really are transforms

Overwhelm to tranquillity

Disturbance to harmony

Judgement to compassion

Loneliness becomes connectedness
Ego–based perspectives are replaced with Soulful understanding there is no better feeling that being aligned in this way.

This provides the foundation on which to formulate goals that are aligned with the path to reaching our potential. Setting the goal is part of the equation; there are other steps to assist us to achieve what we have set our minds on.

The goal is the intention, which needs the support of tools, techniques, awareness of possible resistance and the vital component, action. These are the fundamental ingredients needed to manifest goals and aspirations.

Having set your goal, explored the available tools that will assist your journey and prepared a plan of action you are now ready to act. Act you must and when you do you will be surprised at what opportunities present themselves.

But wait! what happens if at this stage the brakes go on, usually in the form of excuses, or you start and fizzle out and lose motivation? There are many reasons for this, most of which are associated with procrastination, resistance and/or a belief that you cannot do what we propose. All come from aspects and these aspects can be uncovered, explored and answers can be derived. For example if we find that our career is less that fulfilling and it is a desire to change paths this may require additional study. Study may be welcomed by some and rejected by others.

Objections towards study will be justified as excuses, but if time is taken to pry there may be an underlying belief associated with study that stems back to school. As children we were made to exchange play time for times tables.

Great for auditory learning people, but not so good for visual and kinaesthetic learners. For many this exchange was less than satisfactory. Added to this our worth was judged on our academic ability.

This flows into the next possible reason for rejection of study, that being judged in this way will trigger aspects that were dis-empowered during this stage of development and the mention of study stimulates the associated unpleasant feelings.

The way forward is to challenge and exchange the associated unpleasant feelings for ones that empower. This will make it possible to do what needs to be done to achieve the goal.

The journey of life begins the moment we are conceived and continues until our last breath. We do not come equipped with a unique life plan to follow. It is up to us to create our own plan and direct out our lives.

By setting goals that align with our aspirations we can set ourselves upon a path set for success. This is designing the blueprint of our Life Quest. Include in your blueprint the ability to be open-minded, a willingness to go with the flow and the intention to replace worry, doubt and fear with faith, hope and courage.

Worry, doubt and fear cages the mind in a self-defeating trap of negativity. This only serves to extinguish dreams, douse desires and squeeze the joy out of life. This totally opposes the quest for joy and happiness which is at the core of our dreams and desires.

Re-evaluating our thinking to ensure it is aligned with what we want for ourselves will uncover certain truths about what we think we think and what we are actually thinking. Having a dream and believing it is wistful thinking is what stops dreams manifesting into reality. To bring our dreams into the realm of reality we need to free our thoughts from worry and doubt. This can be done by implementing tools and techniques that engage, inspire and kick-start us into creative action mode.

As you journey through life keep your eyes and ears open. Being aware of what you see and hear will make visible the vast amount of guidance that will be presented to you.

Experiences will begin to hold the meaning that was once absent. There may be times when you may feel off track and wonder why a certain event or set of circumstances occurred.

Gently bring yourself back and know that even if the meaning is not identifiable at that point in time you will receive understanding. All our experiences are part of the course of our lives. Reflection will reveal what you have gained so far in your journey, all experiences have given you something from which you can derive wisdom. Ask yourself where you have gained strength? Where have you been humbled? Where your greatest moments of happiness were found? How have your perceptions developed through your experiences? How have your experiences changed certain aspects of your life? Where do you derive significance and meaning? Where are you placing your focus on the experience or the purpose? For those experiences that have been less than pleasant, assess them one at a time until you gain insight into what was gained from the experience.

If you cannot see that you gained anything then put the hat of objectivity on and continue to appraise until you find something of significance. Maybe it's as simple as being shown what not to do in a situation. If you see only loss or missed opportunity then chances are you are yet to derive the purpose of the experience and this may bring feelings of being stuck and possibly of failing.

Failure is a false perception of not achieving or succeeding in something we set out to do. There are many reasons why this may have been, none of which equate to failure. Feeling as if we have failed is more closely linked to holding onto past mistakes instead of learning from them and moving onto new opportunities. Unwrapping the layers of our experiences enables us to find the gift contained within.

Note: Each one of us is on a journey and each of us has different levels of conscious awareness. When we begin to tune into higher aspects of self we are naturally attracted to people who are also attuning to higher aspects of themselves. Find your inner essence and you will attract those who will walk in the light with you.

Doing the same thing over and over opposes growth and denies us access to our potential. Realising potential can be progressive or may be kicked into action by one major event that forces us to step up and do something beyond what we thought we were capable of.

However it comes about, part of discovering potential is by moving through things that try to oppose us. Remember that what we perceive as trying to oppose us is just that-A Perception. A perception may be a barrier in the form of "I can't" if really believed it will cripple one's potential. Whereas "I will" enables potential. Opposing forces motivate us to seek and find tools, techniques and solutions that aid our journey.

Every tool we add to our inner-resource kit becomes a life skill that will assist our development. The bigger the tool-kit the less we are challenged by challenges. Recoiling from challenges or missing what they teach is to overlook something of significant value. Approach a challenge with a "what can I learn from this" attitude reduces the tension and increases determination. Challenge makes us grow. NEVER shy away from opposition as it may be the conduit to finding your greatness. Reflect on past challenges, did you emerge stronger and more resilient? Did it teach you how to pull upon inner resources and find ways of doing things that you did not know you were capable of? If a challenge turns into a struggle it is time to take an objective overview and identify what needs to be done to shrug yourself free of struggle and begin reaping the benefits of what challenges you.

Challenge = learning= growth=realising potential Appraising self from an objective view point enables us to uncover beliefs that keep us attached to an outdated version of ourselves. If we are holding onto a vision of self that has a 'can't do' attitude then that vision can be exchanged for a 'can do' attitude. What we think we can and can't do have been created by beliefs we have formed about ourselves.

Once the seed of belief has been planted our thoughts will reinforce that belief until we accept it as being true. Beliefs can be changed by modifying our thoughts to reflect the new belief we do want to have. This is how positive thinking and the repetitive use of affirmations work.

By consciously amending our thoughts we realign what we think about ourselves to reflect the new vision. Revamping thoughts that have existed for a long time takes time and can be challenging as old thought patterns have embedded themselves into the subconscious.

A repetitive thought takes the same pathway each and every time, trying to bypass or shift this pathway into a direction will cause objection and resistance. This is the aspect holding on and defending its belief. KEEP PERSISTING and keep restructuring thoughts to reflect positivity.

Thoughts reinforced the belief in the first place which means they have the capacity to reverse the belief. One day positivity will triumph. Hallelujah! as that is testament that we have the power to rearrange our thinking to reflect whatever it is we like.

Even if in the future an old belief tries to emerge our thoughts will automatically restructure themselves to counter that belief as it no longer aligns with the new vision of self. When this occurs congratulations is warranted as you have successfully transformed an old thought pattern and an old belief about self into a new one.

You now have a method that can be implemented any time thoughts try to revert back to old ways of thinking. And so the journey continues in the light of positivity. Oh what a beautiful existence.

EXPLORE! DISCOVER! EVOLVE!

Bringing a goal to life so it inspires and motivates requires action! Be Dynamic-use vivid visual images that evoke positive feelings! Reinforcement- to firmly embed the picture of your intentions in your subconscious! Engage-your dream every day! See all it contains and feel the good feelings it inspires. Affirmations-embed positive messages and negate negativity! Motivation-keep committed to your self-created abundance and personal empowerment! The only person who can make your success a reality is YOU!

Take a moment to answer these questions honestly.

How satisfied are you with your current direction in life?

Do you have a clear picture of your wants, wishes and desires? What do you enjoy doing?

What would you like to be doing in life right now?

How do you currently spend your time?

How are you acknowledging your qualities, strengths and attributes?

If you had a magic wand what would you wish for?

GOAL SETTING FOR SELF, PURPOSE AND LIFESTYLE

Goal Setting for Self

Focusing on a specific goal to do with self may relate to physical, emotional or spiritual aspects of self.

For example, if the goal is to improve your level of fitness, then saying you want to become physically fit won't do much, nor will going to the gym a couple of times or watching what you eat for a couple of days. Increasing your level of fitness will require a commitment and not just on the physical level.

Getting fit means nothing to the subconscious- it yawns and remembers all the other attempts, the conscious mind will push it forward for a bit, but without sincere belief and commitment from the subconscious the attempt to be fit will be in vain.

What will motivate the subconscious so it accepts the new image of a fitter, healthier you requires a different approach. That is, the fitness needs to be presented visually and followed up by reaffirming affirmations that negate any negative inner-dialogue.

There may be some emotional maintenance needed to attend to any aspect that may oppose a healthy self-image. The use of creative visualisation and journaling will help to support a positive image of self. While becoming physically fit makes us feel good it can begin to feel somewhat shallow if it becomes a central focus.

Attending to our physical fitness is part of what contributes to our overall well-being and so we may begin to feel discontent and unfulfilled. This is because our physical needs are just one part of the mind, body, soul trio. And so the journey continues as other aspects of self call for our attention and the goal setting process begins again.

Goal Setting for Purpose

Look at what you want to do aligned with career advancement, study opportunities and work involvement. Look at what interests you?

What would you like to do every day?
What would you like to do every day and get paid for?
Are you passionate about something?
If you could design your dream job what would it look like?
What would have you getting out of bed early just so you could get more hours at what you love doing?
What do you love doing so much that getting money for it would be a bonus?
Is there something that, if you allowed yourself, you could admit to being good at?
Does your passion lie with people, animals, the environment, building, designing, networking?
Reflect on how you were as a child and what you enjoyed doing.
What was your nature like as a child?
What qualities can you call yours?
Acknowledging qualities and strengths helps find clues to what we can be doing. Our inherent abilities, talents and qualities provide the clues we need to find our purpose. If you are a creative person, then a career that allows you to explore and develop your creativity would be more suited

than a job that is structured and systems based. If you are a systems person then being in a role that is unstructured and requires artistic flair may not be the way to find your potential.

Remember to acknowledge achievements along the way, no matter how small you may deem them.

Goal Setting for Lifestyle

What would you like as part of your lifestyle? Would you like to travel, drive a nice car, live in your dream home? Would you like your lifestyle to be fast-paced and driven or calm and relaxed? What is your ideal environment? Would you prefer to live by the water, in the countryside or in the city? If you could live anywhere in the world where would it be? If you are unable to move from where you are but would like a lifestyle offered elsewhere, what could you do to incorporate similar aspects of the desired lifestyle into your life now?

The Goal Setting process.

INTENTION: Imagine it. Clearly define what your objective is.

PLAN: To succeed. What do you need to do? How

will you do it? When will you start?

TOOLS: What tools and techniques do you need to assist you? Continue to be inspired through the use of affirmations, self-encouragement and motivation.

ACTION: Every day do something towards your goal. Commitment, continuity and consistency are essential ingredients. Review your goals and make necessary adjustments.

Essential tools for your journey:
- Openness
- Willingness
- Awareness
- Positivity

TECHNIQUE

Introducing the art of Dreamscaping...

Dreamscaping is to create a physical representation of your internal vision. This helps activate hopes, desires and dreams. When you

Dreamscape you become the architects that create the blueprint of your life. Using visual, auditory and kinaesthetic stimulation you can plant the seed of your aspirations into the subconscious and then consciously anchor and reinforce your aspirations in fun, exciting and motivating ways. This is how to communicate using the language understood by the subconscious.

Begin by putting on some relaxing music. On the top of a blank piece of paper write in large letters DREAMSCAPE. The idea is to make your dreamscape dynamic using pictures, affirmations and inspirational quotes.

Just as we would build and decorate a house according to our personal tastes and choices the same is true when it comes to designing a dreamscape.

It is designed to reflect hopes, dreams and desires for self, purpose and lifestyle. These things are then reinforced so your subconscious can grasp what is wanted.

Reinforcing is done through self-encouragement and the use of affirmations that emphasize positivity and negate fear, worry and doubt. To inspire and motivate, your dreamscape should be kept where you will see it often. Your dreamscape is your personalised self-motivating tool that will assist you to realise the abundant, empowered and inspired person that you are. When used to its fullest potential a dreamscape can fulfil the promise of all it contains. Be realistic, positive, active and acknowledge opportunities that come your way.

May your journey enrich and reward you and may the choices you make be those that assist you to realise your potential.

Get inspired, get creative and start Dreamscaping your desires into reality.

Note: During your journey there are a few things to be aware of as they can hinder progress if allowed. These are:

Procrastination- Procrastination is the opposite to action. Goals need to be acted on with enthusiasm. Procrastination squashes enthusiasm through excuses and rationalisation of why we can't do what we want to. Statements that contain 'if', 'but' and 'when' are procrastinations.

The reality is that all procrastination will do is take us years down the track without having done anything about the project, the job, the study, the relationship, the family, the business or whatever we dreamt of starting. Waking up from procrastination may come as a shock when we realise how much time has lapsed. Time keeps it own agenda and does not wait for anyone. Each of us are allocated a certain amount of time on this earth, trying to increase that amount is not possible. Time cannot be bought and cannot be made, it is here and then it is gone. Hence the need to utilise time wisely and constructively. Procrastination will see dreams absorbed by the sands of time. The remedy is to get ACTIVATED.

Excuses-Excuses can get us out of anything if we let them. Even the things we really want to do like creating the best life we can.

Unfortunately, nothing eventuates from making excuses. If we continue to make excuses they may morph into self-fulfilling prophecies. Who would choose to live a life full of excuses you may ask, but many of us do because excuses can be seen as actual reasons for not being able to do what we want.

Excuses get in the way of the real reason for not taking the plunge and that can be a downfall. Additionally, it can become easy to make excuses without thought. Stopping before making an excuse provides some space to think of the reason for wanting to make the excuse in the first place. This helps to discover where resistance lies and empowers us to act rather than fall victim to excuses in the future. To prevent an excuse turning into regret seek the real reason behind the excuse, be honest with yourself and challenge yourself to step through the excuse and into action mode. Making something happen in exchange for an excuse takes courage and commitment, the benefits will be immensely rewarding.

Sabotage-Admitting defeat can be a protection mechanism that saves us from having to admit failure if we try and not succeed.

If thoughts of failure start to encroach on hopes for success we will start to see resistance move into the picture. Our visions of success may be clouded by foreseeing adverse outcomes. This may be intuition and it would pay to listen to this, but only if it is true intuitive insight. How do we know if it is intuitive? Intuition will provide insight into other possible avenues to explore.

Whereas defeatism will make you throw away your dream and resume your place in your comfort zone fully equipped with excuses as to why your dream didn't eventuate. This is self-sabotage and it can become perpetual. First we sabotage ourselves, admit defeat and then justify why things didn't work out.

This is the subconscious at work and, if allowed, it will drive a wedge between what you want and what actually eventuates.

We may be able to falsely justify to ourselves that it is ok just to wonder and wish, but underneath lurks the stench of regret. If this does not stimulate feelings of elation then review is called for.

We can only gain if we give it a go. Giving our dream our best shot is to aim and adjust until we get the goal. Check your intentions. What action have you taken? What is working? What needs to be implemented? How are you keeping yourself inspired and motivated?

The inner-saboteur can sneak in with thoughts that jeopardise motivation and snuff our inspiration, without us realising it. Hence the importance of checking in to see what our thoughts are telling us and the need to ensure we revitalise our motivation on a regular basis.

Fear- Fear poses in many guises and as such is often not recognised for what it is. Fear camouflages itself as procrastination, excuses, sabotage and defeatism. All fear has an underlying cause which varies according to the individual. Some common fears are fear of change, fear of loss, fear of difference, fear of the unknown, fear of failure, fear of success, fear of exposure and the list continues.

Fear is evoked when the known is threatened by the unknown. Some see fear as a challenge and don't hesitate to look it in the eye and surge forward. Others will feel threatened by fear and succumb.

Fear is crafty and will present itself in ways that appear rational and justifiable. inner monologue such as "You can't because you have never done that before". "Other people know better than you". "You have too many other commitments". "It will be too hard for you". "You will have to give up such and such". "What will happen?" "How do you know it will work?" "It won't work!" And on it goes. One of fear's favourites is: "better not to try than to try and fail".

When the mind gets caught in a negative whirlwind of thoughts like these it perpetuates fear. One of two things will happen at this stage. We can become immobilised and stay put or be courageous enough to persevere through this line of defence. The next line of defence may be more confronting as the fearful aspect will get personal.

You may be confronted by the inner-intimidator, inner-critic, inner-saboteur, that say things such as "who do you think you are?" "you're hopeless!", "you're kidding yourself!", "who would listen to you?", "you're useless, worthless etc." "you just don't have what it takes", "you are stupid", "even thinking that makes it clear how daft you are", "if it was possible, don't you think someone better than you would have thought of it by now?"

On goes the berating, belittling and criticizing in an attempt to bully you into submission. A rescue remedy is needed and quickly. What is fear afraid of? Fear is afraid that you will expose the core reason for its existence.

Fear is an aspect that has taken on the important job of keeping us safe from being hurt and now redundancy threatens. If we treat fear like the enemy when it believes it is working hard to keep us safe it will become disgruntled. While this may be a bizarre way of referring to fear, giving it an identity makes its purpose known and helps counter the attack it is preparing to launch. Fear can be a formidable opponent when challenged.

Treating fear as an ally rather than an enemy is the way through the fear barrier. Here we use positive inner-dialogue to counteract negative inner-dialogue. Having a two way conversation with ourselves, heard in our thinking voice, is a healthy way to calm thoughts and find perspective. This is making a conscious effort to create a positive space within.

Revealing where the fear lies helps us to see what it is protecting us from. We can then address fear and coach it forward. There is liberation in admitting to feeling like a hostage of fear, most of us have something that strikes the cord of fear.

Addressing fear is part of what it takes to reach our potential. If fear knocks be brave open the door and say "thank you for letting me know you are there and for trying to keep me safe, but I can do this". If fear flares be courageous and ask that it takes a back seat. Seek what underlies the objections and attend to any malicious inner-dialogue.

Fear can present itself as anxiety, anguish or anger. It can make us shake, sweat, feel nauseous and make our heart rate go up. When fear is felt take charge in a calm and firm manner. Close your eyes to reduce incoming stimulus, breathe deeply to flick your switch into higher thought. Give yourself a hug while focusing on being present and connected to your body. When calm ask: "what am

I fearful of?" Pause and wait for an answer. This may come as a feeling, a vision and/or a statement from your inner-dialogue. When the source of the fear is unveiled show compassion and understanding. Explore ways of overcoming the fear which will likely be associated with something from the past or pre-empting a possible future outcome. Remind yourself that the past is a memory and the future is yet to be determined.

You are now choosing to take the wheel and steer your future where you want it to go. Along the way you are gathering the resources needed to assist your personal growth.

If fear continues to rattle you, acknowledge it but do not succumb to it. Keep going. As you prove that you can do as you planned fear will subside. The greatest antidote to fear is success.

Start each day with a spark of enthusiasm and prepare yourself to explore and discover. Shrug off mishaps, knowing that you will learn something from it and choose differently next time. Focus on stirring the excitement of obtaining new knowledge and insight. You are on the seeker's path.

PLEDGE FOR YOUR JOURNEY

Life is a precious gift. We choose life as it provides the opportunities our soul needs to evolve and evolve we must. It is the way of the Universe. Complete with ups and downs, twists and turns, trials and tribulations. My experiences provide the grounds on I learn and gain wisdom. When I reflect on any of my experiences I remember them as points in time that form part of my journey. I choose to take the lesson of the experience and leave the rest where it belongs. Life is a progressive cycle of endings and beginnings. I am a student on a magnificent learning journey and a teacher who passes on the knowledge and wisdom gained.

SUMMARY

- Always move forward.
- You are preparing to explore beyond what you know and discover more.
- The deeper you journey the more you learn and realise there is to know.
- When you look back to where you came from you realise just how far you have come and much you have learned.

- Excitement stirs as you welcome new knowledge and insight.
- Allow your heart and intuition to guide your journey so you may learn and grow through love and light.

JOURNEY

I step onto the seeker's path with an open mind and willingness to derive meaning and purpose of all this journey presents.

Our spirituality plays an important role in the journey of life. Spirituality is not a set of beliefs, it is a way of life. Living through the virtues of kindness, compassion, gratitude and authenticity is to live in alignment with your spiritual-self. Enhancing the connection with this aspect of self can be achieved through meditation, visualisation, affirmation and readings that facilitate self-awareness.

Spiritual Quest

Karma

Karma is a teacher. It teaches us to be responsible, to be heart centered and to be kind to all living beings

Karma sustains universal equilibrium through the directive of cause and effect.

That which is done will create an experience of similar nature. The purpose of your soul is to evolve by obtaining wisdom from experience. Experience is derived through the events and circumstances of our lives.

Everything we encounter provides us with the opportunity to choose. We inherently know the merit in our choices. Attached to those choices are karmic ramifications. If our intention is to align with the best possible outcome then we are selecting from the higher aspects of ourselves.

If our choices are made through shadow aspects then we can expect to encounter the consequences of such. There is not a jury of judges overseeing our deeds and deeming them right or wrong.

Our choices attract natural consequences governed by universal principles that assist in the development of human consciousness.

What we project will be returned. If we project positive vibes and positive intent that is what will be returned. If we project negative vibes that is what will be returned. Negative output is generated by aspects of our ego. They are shadowy in nature, less aware and do not hold the same perspective as the soul.

The ego is fearful as it has limited perception of all that life entails, it is attracted to instant gratification, has a need for control and is narrow in its view points. However it shares space with our soul and as such can be influenced positively by soul virtues. The key is to be open-minded, aware of ego expression and provide guidance so it can step free of its limitations.

The ego and the soul have different agendas. The ego is self-centered and limited, whereas the soul is purpose-focused and limitless. The different expressions of these aspects can sometimes be felt as a battle of will where the ego wants to restrict and the soul wants to expand.

Being aware of this enhances our connection with the light of our soul, even when being dominated by ego aspects. Soul guidance will provide awareness, clarity and inner knowing. It is attuned with our highest good and will provide insight into our experiences.

The ego will dictate, confuse and reflect negatively

on experiences. It will use this to manipulate and keep one bound to limitations. While the picture presented of the ego is less than perfect it is a necessary part of our being as it casts the shadow that enables choice and directs us to aspects that are in need of attention. It keeps us grounded and helps keep us safe. It is only when it becomes overzealous that complications arise.

Even so we learn much through the ego, it is one of the finest teachers, provided we derive meaning from its lessons. It can also fuel us with immense drive that enables us to strive forth, put ourselves out there and do what we are here to do.

When the ego works in tandem with our higher self we have an enhanced belief in self, are motivated to achieve, can recognize our strengths and be vigilant about our well-being. It is when we disconnect from soul qualities and become ego-bound that we create karma that is best avoided.

If we judge another harshly, we can be assured that others will be judging us. Additionally we can expect to be presented with an experience similar to what we are judging. Judging others displays a lack of empathy. We do not know what the lives of others contain or the memories they have.

Until we can arrive at a point of non-judgment where we can honestly embrace a 'live and let live' attitude then we will continue to bring to us the very things we are judging. The experience will be personalized to align with what is required for personal development.

Being consciously aware helps us to see beyond the presenting issue and register the merit in the lesson. Karma has the uncanny ability of always getting it right. Whether aware of it or not we live our karma every day. Careful scanning of thoughts, feelings and general attitude towards life past and present will provide insight into this.

We are not the puppets of karma, but rather karma is a loyal servant retrieving for us what we have requested through our thoughts, actions and deeds. There is more to life than merely existing and attending to our daily routine.

We are here to awaken to the deeper meaning of our experiences and to realise that the life we live is a reflection of the choices made based upon the level of conscious awareness.

Lack of awareness will contribute to the accumulation of negative karma. This being in opposition of our soul's purpose, which seeks balance and harmony through the virtues of love, compassion and wisdom.

An awakened state is to consciously choose to be authentic. This will create a natural energy exchange and attract like sincerity. We may not always get it right, but setting positive intention is a step towards enhanced awareness.

Our choices will align naturally with our intentions and as they do we find that the departure of old will enable the new. This may feel surreal for a period, especially when we are ready to let go of things held dear. But as the outcomes of changes made are revealed it will be evident that everything is as it is meant to be.

There may be times when we need to call upon your wise inner-counsel for guidance. This will provide insight into possible karmic ramifications of decisions and choices that are being made.

Remember to stop, think and reflect rather than react on random impulse and emotional triggers. Inevitably we will continue to be presented with the opportunities needed to shed past karma. This is best done through conscious awareness and choice to empower self and to empower others through the soul virtues that encapsulate the light aspects of our being.

Be aware of where your thoughts are taking you, if they are being critical of the way another person is living their life or of the actions of others, this will create unwanted karma. Gossip and speaking about others in negative ways will attract unwanted karma.

We are here to support and assist each other not pass unhelpful opinions. Doing this opposes the soul-principles of being kind and compassionate to others. If you wouldn't say something to someone in person then it is best to withhold saying it when not in their presence. Unless it is going to help in some way.

Observe a conversation before launching in. This will provide insight into where the participants of the conversation are positioned. Take a breath and be mindful of what you can contribute to the conversation that will assist it forth positively or end it so to extinguish any toxicity from spilling outwards.

One morning I was sitting in a cafe doing some writing when I became aware of the conversation at the next table. The toxic energy spewing out from this conversation was polluting the air and energy, which we were all sharing. I closed my eyes and sent the participants a swirl of loving energy. There are two ways this energy could have been received.

1. *the conversation could have transformed into one of positivity.*
2. *as was what happened in this instance - the participants went quiet for a moment and departed. One participant acknowledged me briefly on the way out.*

Of course my intention was not to have them leave, I would have been thrilled if their conversation shifted into positive mode and they stayed, however the energy I sent did not resonate and when that happens it makes us feel uncomfortable and so we remove ourselves from the energy. This is relevant when in the presence of positive or negative energy.

Everyone feels energy and the vibe it carries. To test the power of wielding energy take a deep breath in through the nose and then exhale out through the mouth, do this a couple of times or until you feel in-sync with your breathing. Then focus on breathing into your heart area, imagine this area is full of pink and green energy or light.

Then imagine sending it to someone in close proximity. You will receive some form of acknowledgment. Usually a smile or some other kind gesture.

Karma helps guide choices. Inherently we know their merit in our choices and what virtues they are aligned with.

When making a choice ask yourself if the choice is aligned with your highest good, if it aligns with your hopes and aspirations. How does your choice feel? What does it look like? What are your reasons for making this choice? Are your reasons sound or do they need re-evaluation? If others are involved how will it affect them? Are there any reservations about your choice and if so what are they? What are the possible karmic ramifications of your choice? Be honest with yourself when answering these questions. Let niggles of doubt surface so they can be evaluated. Most importantly listen, see and feel your intuitive guidance before making your choice.

Karma Release Visualization

 Take a deep breath in through your nose and then exhale out through your mouth.

Take another deep breath and then exhale.

See beautiful white light surround you.

You know you are safe and protected and anything that you see you see as an observer. Like viewing a movie-screen.

Breathe into any emotions that might come up and remember that this is a replay and it is not actually happening.

You see yourself walking along a secluded beach, the sand is soft and warm under your bare feet.

As you walk you notice someone standing at the water's edge. Or you might be seeing a scene from the past. From long ago.

As you approach, you notice a cord linking you to this person or scene.

You stay for a while to gain meaning and understanding from what you see, hear or feel.

There may be a message that provides insight into something relating to your current day life.

When you feel that you have spent adequate time here you thank the person or the scene for the knowledge and experience gained.

You sense something in your hand, you look down and see that you hold a karma cutting device. You take the device and gently cut the cord connecting you to the person or scene, knowing that this will release you and all those involved.

As the cord is released you have a sense of relief. You send love from your heart centre. You might see the energy of love as pink or green or any colour that resonates with you. As you send this energy you see that the connection has been resolved and no longer affects any part of your current life. Healing has been done.

Continue this exercise until all karmic ties are resolved. Take your time to resolve karmic ties at a pace you feel comfortable with. Remember to continue your journey with kind thoughts and right action.

Allow emotions to surface, but do not become attached as they are from another time and no longer have control over you. Just watch and see how the emotion connects you to a past event, deed or situation.

Disconnecting the emotional link will free you from its clutches. Releasing yourself from the emotional aspect of the past allows you to see from a higher perspective.

From higher perspective you obtain reason and meaning of the past event, situation or deed. Understanding the lesson or reason for an experience is part of how one balances their karma. It provides insight into choices made.

You are now aligning your choices so that you may reap the benefits of what these choices offer.

PLEDGE FOR KARMIC UNDERSTANDING

The purpose of my soul is to learn. My interactions, thoughts and life choices create karma. I choose to align my karma with my soul's journey. I choose to align with the virtues of kindness, acceptance, trust and faith. These life influencing principles will clear past karma and sow the seeds of a fortunate future. I am the creator of all that pertains to me. I choose to walk in the light and attune to higher vibrations. This is the key to my ongoing happiness.

SUMMARY

- Every deed, every word, every thought will recreate itself somewhere, somehow. This is a universal principle that orchestrates like experiences so we may learn the lessons of our ways.
- Karma is a perspective that arranges itself until we derive meaning from the messages delivered. If we did not understand one way then we will be given an alternative and so it goes on.
- All karma will be balanced. Be it instantaneous or over time.
- Shedding past karma revitalizes the mind, the body and the soul.
- Light your karmic path by aligning with positive soul qualities and be free to live the life you we meant to.

Spiritual Quest

KARMA

I choose to create positive karma through thoughts, feelings and deeds that are positively aligned with the virtues of love and peace.

As fellow beings we are indebted to assist each other, if not actively, then with the courtesy of having a 'live and let live' attitude. We are fellow beings with different life lessons. Judgment of those lessons makes the journey harder for the judged and those who are judging. The consequences of such will be dealt with through the karmic law of cause and effect. Not as punishment, but as a natural occurrence.

Spiritual Quest

Love

I am free to love myself unconditionally

 Discover the beauty contained in the essence of unconditional love. It is the most powerful source of energy and comes from within oneself. The essence of love dissolves expectations and generates positive perceptions.

Love has many dimensions. There is the romantic love shared between partners, there is love shared between family members, there is the love shared between close friends and there is love of self. Self-love develops from the relationship we establish with our inner-self. There are any aspects of the inner-self, some of which have negatively associated images of who we are and what we do.

One such aspect is the inner-critic. The inner-critic is an aspect that can be identified by thoughts that berate, put down, reflect disappointment or demoralize.

The inner-critic gathers evidence that supports a negative view of self. This can be crippling if allowed to go unchecked. Although the consequence of tuning into the negative banter of the inner-critic is detrimental, the inner-critic does not operate with malicious intent.

The intention of the inner-critic is to protect

from disappointment, to avoid the devastation associated with failure and in a convoluted way tries to motivate us to do better. From this perspective we can understand that even those aspects that appear to loath us are, from their perspective, doing what is in our best interest.

This can be likened to the hyper-critical parent, who thinks that in some way their criticism will help us do better, makes us try harder and be the best we can be.

Just like the hyper-critical parent our inner-critic needs assistance to help it understand that there are more positive ways to inspire and motivate.

It pays to remember that the inner-critic is just one of the aspects misguided in its approach. However with growing awareness we can identify when unhelpful aspects are active and provide the appropriate techniques that will support and redirect perspectives in ways that encourage a positive view of self. The view we have of ourselves is constructed through our self-talk. Being aware of how we talk to ourselves requires us to become observers of our thoughts.

Setting the scene to evoke a response from an

aspect that opposes your good intentions. Begin by stating a positive affirmation about self and then listen to what comes back. Using the inner-critic as an example, if it hears "I am free to love myself unconditionally" it cannot accept this as it has never known unconditional love and therefore does not believe it is possible.

To defend its position and reinforce what it thinks to be true it will chime in with what it believes is evidence and will give reasons why it believes it is unlovable.

Reading this may spark a twang of empathy for the inner-critic and its belief that it is unlovable. And it is empathy and compassion that this aspect and all aspects that hold a dim view need.

A point to remember here it that they are aspects, which means that they do not account for the whole of self, but they do have strong opinions and reflect areas that are in need of attention.

These opinions hold us captive and it is not until awareness dawns, which is part of developing the inner-self, that we can begin the process of transforming negative inner-dialogue into positive and when we do we free ourselves from being the prisoners of self-sabotaging internal programming.

And although perseverance and patience will be required when transforming inner-dialogue it will be immensely gratifying when you reap the rewards of having a positive relationship with self, which inevitably will extend to relationships with others.

Learning to focus on, hear and feel the kind loving aspects of self is vital.

Often the booming voice of the inner-critic or other aspects of self is heard above the gentle tones of the meeker aspects. Turning up the volume of the aspects that encourage, are kind and supportive makes them easier to hear and hushes less helpful inner-dialogue.

Every day say at least one good thing about yourself. By finding encouraging ways to embrace ourselves with love we are finding ways of fulfilling our needs. If we allow it, love will guide us to reach beyond our emotional reactions and into a space of gratitude and compassion.

Gratitude and compassion ignite our hearts with positive vibration that flows from within and radiates outwards. Our experiences evolve when interpreted through the eyes of love. Self-love aligns us with our potential, keeps our intentions pure and allows us to give graciously. Giving graciously from our hearts attracts like generosity and kindness.

Focus on the simple things that can be enjoyed in life. Think kind thoughts & speak kind words. Show empathy and compassion for yourself and others. Dissolve judgmental thoughts towards yourself and toward others.

We all carry memories and some of those memories can follow us and interfere with our ability to connect with the self-love we need.

Centre yourself in the present to derive understanding from experiences and emotions as they occur. Breathe into emotion as it arises and ask what triggered it? What needs to be attended to? Have I felt like this before? Just allow the answers to emerge. If no is the answer that comes, just give it some time and be mindful of thoughts, feelings, images or messages that arise in relation to the questions you ask.

If memories of past hurt emerge they are seeking healing. This can be achieved by infusing these memories with empathy and compassion. Inner peace can then be found by sending love to those who have hurt us and moving on. This severs the connection to the past pain.

Using the power of love to heal releases us from the emotions that trap us in non-serving cycles. Freedom from non-serving emotion removes what blocks our connection to self-love.

Re-connecting with our inner loving essence produces a harmonious pulsation that fills us with feelings of gratitude, tenderness and warmth. These feelings radiate outward and touch others and as they do our world projects those feelings back. Seeing through the eyes of love allows us to accept, allow and to be.

TECHNIQUE

 Take a minute to do an affirmation. Remain aware of any thoughts that follow the affirmation. Trying to input an affirmation without hearing objections denies the chance to learn about different aspects and why they exist.

Listening to the retorts of certain aspects awakens us to beliefs we have about ourselves and enables the release and the reconstruction of a new, more positive belief about self.

For example the affirmation "I am free to love myself unconditionally" will evoke a response. By taking note of the response we can uncover what prevents access to believing that loving oneself unconditionally is possible.

We can then embrace this aspect and assist it to release the negative belief and establish a positive belief. The exchange of negative self-talk for positive self-talk facilitates self-love.

A healthy inner monologue reflects beauty and enables us to see the best in ourselves and others. This lifts our vibration.

Try saying either to yourself or aloud

"I am free to love myself unconditionally!"
"I am free to love myself unconditionally!"
"I am free to love myself unconditionally!"

Stop and listen in silence. Do you hear an inner voice embracing or rejecting what you say?

If there is an objection you have uncovered an aspect that has an opposing belief. At the root of this aspect lies hurt of some sort. This aspect requires the love that it has rejected or has been denied.

The voice of the inner aspects that reflect negativity can be detected by being aware. Be aware of thoughts that put down demoralize or are degrading and of negative self-talk that is detrimental.

Realign

Focus your attention on your heart centre and imagine pink energy flowing in this area. This is pure loving energy. Rub your hands together, feel the pink energy from your heart centre flow down into your hands. Know that this loving energy has amazing healing power. Wherever you place your hands the healing energy flows. Put your healing hands anywhere on your body and feel the power of your love flow into the area. Physical and emotional disharmony can be eased when infused with your love. Connect and nurture by honouring yourself with your own divine loving essence.

Love has no boundaries, it has the capacity to give to all.

PLEDGE FOR SELF-LOVE

Self-love enables me to acknowledge my flaws and embrace them with the love they have been denied. Through self-love I instill confidence in myself. This is being the best me I can be. I think loving thoughts and act in loving ways towards myself. My inner love for self radiates out and attracts more love into my life.

SUMMARY

- Discover the beauty contained in the essence of unconditional love.
- Love lives on even in the mists of turmoil.
- Love sees through the eyes of compassion and empathy.
- Love dissolves negativity and generates positive perceptions.
- Grant yourself the gift of self-love. Accept and cherish all of you.
- Love sees potential, even if it is hiding.
- Purity of heart equates to pure intent.
- Infuse your life with love so you can expand beyond emotional reactions and see with compassion and empathy.
- Giving graciously attracts like generosity, kindness and graciousness.
- Let the power of love align you with your potential and discover all that you are. Keep your intentions pure.

LOVE

*I seek that which empowers my
mind, my body and my spirit.
I choose to be guided by
love, empathy and compassion.*

Infuse your life with love so you can expand beyond emotional reactions and see with compassion and empathy towards yourself and others. Love is the essence that maintains balance, even in the mists of turmoil. Grant yourself the gift of self-love and see positive perceptions evolve.

Spiritual Quest

Miracle

Miracles occur every day. They remind us that a realm beyond this exists

 *The physical body is home to the soul. The purpose of such an arrangement is for the soul to experience life and all that involves.*

Miraculous discoveries will be made through your own intuitive interpretation of signs, symbols and messages that are presented to you. Feathers, pebbles, coins, flowers and other tokens may be presented unexpectedly.

Experiencing the manifestation of such is to revitalize trust and re-establish faith in the non-physical realms of existence.

Miracles are an everyday occurrence. They remind us that when we transcend our physicality and evoke our energetic bodies we boost our vibration. Boosting our vibration enables us to move beyond the boundaries of the physical realm and into the realm of energy.

This is where miracles occur. We bear witness to this when the impossible transforms and becomes possible.

Ultimately we are connecting to the higher aspects of self, which also enhances our ability to connect with the higher frequencies of others. Such as in the case of healing miracles, which is when our light bodies connect with the light body of the sick. This is to transcend the physical nature of the illness and the physical attachments and direct the healing where it is needed to resolve the energetic imbalance. There are numerous ways to achieve this, including prayer, which is to evoke the energetic realms through positive intention.

Belief in a higher power enhances the energetic flow. Belief vibrates at a high frequency which connects us with the vibrations of higher realms of existence. Whether or not we believe in such does not influence the manifestation of a miracle.

When we rise beyond doubt and fear we create an opening that gives us access to hope. Through hope we find faith. Faith embraces vulnerabilities and gives strength.

When empowered by strength we awaken to possibility. This shift reconstructs energy and transforms wishes into reality. Being witness to the manifestation of a miracle is amazing.
Orchestrating one is enlightening.

Changing thought patterns helps to shift non-serving emotions. It is important to acknowledge what is being felt as this pinpoints the perspective of an aspect that is holding onto something. This could be linked to something that was said or done in the past and unless resolved will continue to emit a vibration of negativity. This obscures the ability to see that beyond what was said or done is valuable learning.

Behind every word spoken or deed done is perception. Perception is the way an individual assesses what they see, hear and feel. This is what makes us unique as no two people will perceive things exactly the same. Understanding this broadens awareness and the concept of individual response, which is always based on personal thoughts and feelings.

Example of how perceptions can be created without conscious awareness and how these perceptions remain. Imagine a child playing happily with some toys in a store while the mother was browsing the racks.

When the mother had finished browsing she turned her attention to the child, who was doing what was natural to a child-using imaginative play. The mother, only seeing the toys over the floor, begins to growl at the child saying that it was unacceptable to leave the toys over on the floor and that the child was naughty. Instantly the child withdraws and her vibration falls rapidly. The child becomes a shell of the former happy person he/she was moments before. The child starts packing up the toys.

The mother berates the child for being messy, but does nothing to help. The child went from seeing the miracle of bringing the toys alive with his/her imagination to being upset. This does not get expressed at that point in time, but remains locked in the memory.

There is no fault here the mother was reacting to her own thoughts and feelings about seeing toys on the floor, maybe they were due at an appointment, there is a gamut of reasons for her reaction. Any of which made it ok to react in that manner at that time. I don't think there is a person alive who hasn't reacted without thinking about the affect they have on another.

From an onlooker's perspective it would appear the child was entertaining herself while her mother browsed. Another onlooker may agree with the mother and another onlooker may have a different perspective altogether.

All perspectives are based on personal interpretation. If this was the mother's normal way of communicating with the child it would not be surprising if the child developed an aspect that carries a negative perception of self eg. being naughty for using her imagination and exploring her creativity.

This is just one possible example of what could be conjured in the delicate psyche of a child. Maybe enough for the child to shut down his/her creative imagination and it will remain shut until it is unlocked. As an adult that child may be blocked believing they are incapable of creative visualisation and creative expression. This can be unlocked by releasing the emotional hurt attached to the aspect that believes this of themselves and when that occurs something miraculous happens. An unseen limitation is dissolved. New light shines and what was deemed impossible becomes possible.

Seeing beyond the veil of physical existence into the realm of the divine is an intriguing adventure. Ask for messages and signs. Create your own sacred space in which to explore your inner realms. This provides insight into energetic workings. Use this time to get an idea of how energy feels. Think of something that makes you feel happy. This is a transmission of energy. As this energy carries a positive vibration it uplifts. Now think of something that makes you feel annoyed. The energy of this feeling carries a different vibration, the response felt in the mind and body is opposite to the uplifting feelings of happiness.

The transmission of energy through thoughts is a constant occurrence. So are the feelings that the thoughts evoke. If this is not balanced or reflects negatively then it could be that a big part of the day is spent in the clutches of negative energy transmission. This mostly occurs without conscious awareness, hence the emphasis on enhancing awareness.

Being aware of the thoughts and feelings that occur during the day enables you to consciously align them with what you are hoping to achieve. When the sun shines through clouded thoughts clarity is received, this is the moment to grasp the miracle of the moment. The more moments acknowledged the more miracles manifest.

TECHNIQUE
Feeling Miraculous

Imagine a scenario or reflect on a memory that brings great happiness. If this is difficult look at a digital or physical picture of a scene that conjures feelings of joy. When you have your picture in mind place yourself at the centre of your image. See yourself fully enjoying whatever it is you are doing. Hone in on the blissful feelings you are experiencing right at that moment. Transfer this feeling into other aspects of your life. You are creating a dreamscape where you can create feelings of bliss through the images of your mind. Our inner being thirsts for a dose of the happy chemicals that are released when it feels joy. Prescribe this formula daily and from us will emanate a lightness of being. So potent is the effect of this daily formula that we become acutely sensitive and instantly recognize negativity through our feelings. As this does not boost our intake of happy chemicals it becomes easier to consciously shift ourselves into a better space emotionally. This is to tap into our emotional tool kit and utilize our internal resources to train our neural pathways to respond in ways we want them to. When we recruit ourselves as an innovative and inspiring leader of our mind, it becomes happily employed as our faithful and loyal assistant. United in this way is to be co-creators of our greatness, the outcome of which is positively miraculous.

PLEDGE TO EMBRACE MIRACLES

I boost my vibration into the realm of energetic magnetism where energy transcends matter and becomes the creator of miracles. All things are possible. I release beliefs that identifies closely with the density of physicality. Miracles exist on an alternative plane that I have access to through my good intentions and positive energy. I am a co-creator of miracles.

May miracles become a part of your every day, for they are all around you.

SUMMARY

- This is your mystical calling card asking that you to connect with your inner being, your highest self.
- Acknowledging ourselves as energetic beings in physical bodies enhances our connection with Universal energy.
- We can utilize energy in ways beyond what we know we are capable of.
- Miraculous discoveries will be made through your own intuitive interpretation of signs, symbols and messages that are presented to you.
- Watch as a new world emerges, the manifestation of such will revitalize trust and re-establish faith in the realm of energetic connection.

Spiritual Quest

MIRACLE

*I see beyond the veil of physical density and into the energetic realm of divine existence.
I am safe to expand my conscious awareness.
I am guided by love.*

It is a bizarre thing to expect magical solutions to our problems without believing it possible. Believe in the magic and see the manifestation of solutions beyond what was thought possible. Now that is miraculous.

Spiritual Quest

Past, Present, Future

Although viewed as linear, past, present and future are consolidated dimensions of each other

*The past and future collide at the point in the present moment, which is representative of all that has been and all that is.*

All past experiences have contributed to the present and all present experiences will contribute to the future. This has contributed to the you, you identify with today.

Although presented in a linear fashion, the past, present and future are reflections of each other and occur simultaneously in what is occurring right now. How you interact with the present is based upon perceptions formed in the past and the perspective taken in this moment will affect what happens in the future.

Consolidating the past and future into the present provides the opportunity to assess what has been following us from the past. There will be an assortment of things that we have held onto.

Some things we will want to keep as they are aligned with our path and some will need releasing as they do not align. By discarding the debris of the past we make room for better things to enter our lives. Holding onto the fragments of the past will see them infiltrate what is happening right now; this sets the fate of the future. What is happening in the current moment transfers into the next through our thoughts and our actions.

Being aware of thoughts enables us to make choices that are aligned with what we want in the future. The future springs from what we are thinking and doing right now. Hence the importance of what we inject into that moment.

Conscious awareness enables us to choose what we inject, be it positive or negative. If we think we are projecting positivity, but are thinking in negative ways then those thoughts will have a negative effect as they are attached to a belief that opposes what we are trying to achieve.

Taking a course to improve career options (positive) while denigrating one's own ability or believing that all the jobs in that field are taken or go to better, smarter, more capable people puts opposing forces in operation.

What we tell ourselves is our truth and has significant power over us. Determining which personal beliefs are holding us back requires a belief assessment. Being aware of the inner beliefs enables the ability to see how those beliefs affect choices. Our choices create what becomes the life we live, which means we must be cognizant of the contents of our thoughts and the beliefs behind them. This enables us to reconfigure negative thoughts and to be aware of the beliefs that oppose what we are trying to achieve.

We are then equipped to counteract self-sacrificing beliefs using any of the many tools and techniques one acquires throughout the journey of self-discovery. With this in mind we can set the intention of creating each moment on a foundation of positivity.

Being present requires conscious effort to switch our mind from auto pilot and become aware of how we are interacting at that point in time. This is to be aware of thoughts and feelings and how they are shaping impressions of what is occurring in that moment.

When we are functioning on auto pilot our thoughts determine our direction, wherever they go we shall follow, making us wandering nomads of the mind; the outcome is the evaporation of precious moments.

What we end up with is snippets of time gone by. If today we are thinking about tomorrow or about yesterday we are disconnected from what is actually happening. So many precious moments are missed in anticipation of what might be or of what was. For example, planning a special occasion can become so intense that the pleasure of the journey leading up to the occasion is dulled.

The monumental celebration is over in a blink of an eye. If every moment pertaining to the monumental celebration was cherished the experience would be a wonderful journey of memorable moments.

The mind is so busy running around in a web of thoughts that it doesn't have time to stop and appreciate the beauty of being present. Taking a break from the thought-churning cogs is to capture a moment of pure bliss.

The senses awaken to see, hear and feel that moment. When a moment is untouched by the past or distracted by thoughts of the future, a space opens. This is where mind and soul merge into that moment.

Breathing into this space is to experience serenity. If a thought or a feeling enters this space it will be viewed with detachment, non-judgment and from higher perspective. It is in this space that we gain insight into our inner selves and if something unpleasant emerges it can be freely expressed without the interference of judgmental and critical thoughts that suppress or deny what needs acknowledge.

Continuing to bring unsatisfactory parts of the past into our thoughts continues the story of what was. This story becomes the basis of our life and link to everything we do, even to the point that we define ourselves by what happened.

The past continues to be lived over and over again. We can become so lost in our story that there is no clear definition of what part of our lives is the story and what forms our current life.

The by-line of the story will be applied to other areas of our life, including relationships, lifestyle, viewpoints and how we think and feel about ourselves. At some point in time we may awaken and realize that we no longer want to keep re-hashing the same story.

This is the time when we begin to accept that what has happened has happened and that we can consciously set down the story as we would a book that has come to an end and thus empower ourselves to re-create what we want for ourselves now and in the future. This is to re-write your own story. Starting from today, with you as the main character. Think about who and what you would like in your story.

Becoming consciously aware of the thoughts that run through our mind and, importantly where they take us, requires practice. Plan to implement thought awareness throughout the day. The act of intention has a profound effect.

Try to take a few moments each day to consciously stay in the moment. If thoughts of the past or the future come allow them to float by, like a cloud drifting across the sky. Take note of the thoughts that are trying to attract your attention; also notice associated feelings.

If an unpleasant feeling emerges find the space where moment, mind and soul meet and breathe into this space to prepare the void needed for the feeling to flow through freely.

If past memories are a distraction or if thoughts of the future encroach on the space, acknowledge them and then let go with the intention to reflect further when the space is cleared to do so.

Attending to the needs of your inner self in a calm and relaxed state prevents being bombarded by thoughts and feelings that become entwined in one another. Thoughts will try different tactics to pull you from the centre of the moment; with practice it will become easier to focus thoughts and create the space needed to find inner peace and harmony.

Being present puts you in a position to sculpt your life as you choose. You may notice that some of the thoughts and feelings that float into your space are not aligned with your goals and desires. They will block your path until dealt with. This is done when anchored in the moment in the space where mind and soul meet. Here is where two perspectives are observed, the mind perceives the details the soul perceives the meaning. Together they will guide you through.

When we are consciously aware of what is happening in the moment of now, we have the power of choice. However, if we allow that moment to be stolen by unnecessary thought we have wasted valuable time and precious energy.

Thought spiraling costs an immense amount of energy and has no value. Would you knowingly invest in something that is meaningless and of no value? Probably not, however we continue to invest in meaningless thought that has no value and serves no purpose? Rather than being caught in the thought grinding cogs try being centered in the present moment. This creates a space where mind and soul merge, what arises from this are feelings of euphoria.

Stop whatever you are doing, take a few deep breaths and focus on something in nature. Really see what you are looking at, marvel at the colours and definition. Ponder the existence of what you see, this is living proof that miracles occur.

Every living thing is a miracle. Take some time to be present with your thoughts and feelings about the following statement: Every living thing is the manifestation of a miracle.

Take a moment every day to be present with nature, ponder the existence of what you see and recognise the miracle you are observing. A bird, a tree, a plant, an ant or a bee carry the essence of a miracle.

When you have achieved appreciation of the manifestation of nature's miracles bring your focus towards yourself and ponder your miraculous existence. Bringing your awareness to the point of your existence expands perception of self and provides transformational insight. Such conscious awareness empowers us to choose the position of our focus, which is to choose what we inject into each moment, be it positive or negative.

By infusing positivity into each moment we are laying a sound foundation on which to build our future. Making these positive moments memorable is to be present.

Being present is to be mindful of what we are doing. When having a conversation clear your thoughts and focus on what the other person is saying. All too often conversations are filled with active thinking about what one wants to say rather than actively listening to what is being said.

Actively listening is to derive understanding and meaning of the message behind what is being spoken. This is mindful communication and it is transformational.

Being mindful is to be aware of our surroundings, of the people in our surroundings, of our thoughts and how they are affecting our feelings.

Being present means to sit with feelings as they arise, without fading into the past or projecting into the future. Sitting with our feelings, even if they reach a point of being uncomfortable, will see them peak and then reduce. They may return, but their intensity will reduce with time. This is to allow natural expression of our feelings without suppressing, denying or escaping by busying ourselves physically or through meaningless thought.

Being mindful captures the moment that would have otherwise escaped our attention and that moment may be one we want to commit to memory.

Taking notice is to stop our thoughts from churning over the past or running forward into the future so we can create our experiences to become those we want to reflect on when they become our memories.

> *Focus feelings of joy into the present moment and see energetic forces align and form the manifestation of miracles.*

PLEDGE FOR PAST, PRESENT & FUTURE

 I return to the essence of me. This is being free of preconceptions formed in the past and anticipated future expectations. I am one with the present, the only real moment where I am the co-creator with the universal energy that flows within and without. By being present I choose my thoughts and in doing so my feelings will reflect this. I sit with uncomfortable emotion to seek deeper meaning. I acknowledge my emotion belongs to the past, which is a memory or the future which is a presumption. Neither of which are part of right now. Magic is made in the moment and I choose to create the magic. Right now I have the chance to configure the energy on which I build my life.

SUMMARY

- All that has occurred in the past contributes to where you are and who you have become.
- What you desire for the future governs your current actions.
- Consolidating the past and future into the present gives you the opportunity to release what no longer serves.
- Each moment can be prepared to align harmoniously with the next.

- Being in the present allows you to adjust your thoughts to align with what you want.

PAST, PRESENT, FUTURE

Now is the only moment that exists.
I align myself with all that is present in the here and now.

Spiritual Quest

Perception

Our experiences are based upon our perceptions

 *Interpretations of our experiences are based upon our perception.* The way in which we view the world, which is a perception, is formed very early in our life. Perceptions and beliefs reinforce each other. Our perceptions form our beliefs and our beliefs reinforce our perception. Perceptions change as we learn and discover different ways of looking at things, but some hold firm and will remain unless challenged.

Extending beyond our own perceptions and allowing ourselves to see from a different perspective offers much insight into why people and things are the way they are.

We can learn to appreciate that everybody perceives the world differently and that reality is different for everyone. This in itself helps to reduce the tendency to take the behaviour of others personally, as all behaviour is based upon how someone perceives what is happening at that point in time. And there are a lot of factors that contribute to what is being perceived.

Being aware of this expands ones perception in relation to others; this awareness will awaken one to a new and different reality in the realm of human interaction with others and with oneself.

Perception forms our personal view of the world. Our perception is as unique as we are. No two people will perceive exactly the same. This uniqueness depicts us different and yet we have common purpose.

We are here to live, to learn and to evolve. Evolution requires that we adapt in ways that enable us live in harmony with our environment and with each other. To do this we must expand beyond linear perspectives.

Expanding our viewpoint enables us to see different perspectives and as we do a bigger picture of life and its components emerges.

By evaluating personal perspective we can see how our view points are created. Everything we do is based upon the interpretation of what we are experiencing.

The experience is being evaluated through the senses of what is being felt, heard and seen. These senses triggers reactions and if there is sensitivity then those reactions can be intense. Stress is another factor that reduces tolerance levels. This begs the question: Does a person, whether ourselves or someone else, behaving in a way deemed unacceptable need to be judged or is there a need for support so that appropriate coping strategies can be sort?

Everyone operates from different perspectives which include all the things that have happened in our lives. This is not to say that we must agree with the actions of others. But it is easier to accept that we are all products of what is contained in our history and memories. We also begin to see how our perceptions have shaped our own reality.

Reflection assists in the expansion of our conscious awareness. This is essential if we are to gain access to higher levels of intelligence. Intelligence that moves beyond the mind's ability to think and into a new dimension of thought processes.

That which lifts the lid off conservative, programmed thinking and pushes out into lesser known realms are within our reach but will remain undetectable until we open our mind to perceive such.

While we continue to identify to closely to our physical world, allow thoughts to process us rather than us processing our thoughts and operate as emotional escapees instead of practising emotional awareness and honesty, we will be confined to this realm of perception and conform to the reality this presents. If life continues to be lived by rote then it will continue to feel mundane and mechanical. We must give ourselves permission to awaken from the rut and break free, as this is the key to discovering all that is available.

Cutting loose from the grind enables us to detect deeper aspects of ourselves and gain soul perspective. Our perception will determine whether we are neglecting or nourishing our soul. Perceiving only the physicality of our being is to neglect the soul.

Whereas perceiving the energetic aspects of our being nourishes our soul and grants access to the dynamic world of energy. The energetic realm is that which elicits the magic.

Our evolution depends on us awakening and expanding our consciousness and thus expanding our perception of life and all it pertains. Our inner being will rejoice that we have made this discovery and through its excitement and enthusiasm we will receive an invigorated sense of self that will present as a surge of inspiring insights and aspirations.

Evaluating your perception. Be mindful of your

thoughts and feelings and how they make you react to things in certain ways. Be mindful of judgments. Be mindful of actions. Be mindful of interactions. BE MINDFUL. Try practicing this as often as you can. Being mindful shows us how distracted we can become.

A large percentage of our day is spent on automatic mode, where we roll from one automatic thought to the next without any conscious awareness of what our thoughts are telling us and where they are taking us.

These automatic thoughts are reinforcing our perceptions and our perceptions are strengthening the thought patterns. Becoming consciously aware requires focus.

By detecting when we are on 'auto pilot' mode we can see how robotic our approach to life can be. Doing the same things over and over without realising it.

When we swing our focus towards our thoughts we empower ourselves as we can choose to align thoughts positively and expand linear thought patterns laterally. This awareness helps us switch from auto pilot to being the executive of our thoughts. This is to take charge of what rolls through our mind.

We start running the show and can direct it in any direction we choose. If we want our desires and aspirations to be more than just dreams we must align our perceptions appropriately.

TECHNIQUE

Imagine your thoughts dancing above your head. What are they saying? If your thoughts are not what you would like to hear someone say to you or about you then change them.

Our thoughts are our mantras and if they don't benefit us then they need to be revamped. This requires awareness so we can consciously shift our perception about self and about others. If you haven't got something positive or constructive to say to yourself then refrain from saying it.

Give yourself a break and lighten up on yourself. We all make mistakes, deal with it using the appropriate technique and move on. To continue with the same perspective will retain the current way of doing things and this is how we get stuck. Coming to a stuck point requires reflection to resolve the internal conflict; anything that is not flowing is in conflict.

Decipher the internal conflict by asking yourself questions such as:

How can I construct a more positive view?

Is there another way I can think about this?

Is my view from an open or closed perspective?

In the bigger picture of who I am, how much emphasis do I need to place here?

Ask questions relevant to the problem and then try expanding your viewpoint. Look beyond the problem or issue until broader perspective is gained.

PLEDGE FOR PERCEPTION

My perceptions form my view of the world. If I don't like what I see I seek to find the root of the perception creating this view and shift it. I confront my beliefs and release those which keep me attached to out-dated scripts. I replace those scripts with new ones that show me a world I wish to live in. This starts within. By making my life the one I want to lead, I see things in a positive light. My perception makes things appear as they are to me. A shift of out-dated perceptions changes things for the better. I look, I observe, I see.

SUMMARY

- As perception expands so does our point of view.
- Perception will hold firm unless challenged.
- Beliefs form perceptions and perceptions reinforce beliefs.
- Perceptions shape our existence, the reality of a closed-minded perspective is insular, whereas an open-minded perspective will create a reality that is expansive.

- Expanding perception beyond a narrow view point will see reality transform beyond what could previously be conceived.

PERCEPTION

I align my perceptions in accordance with how I want to live my reality

Spiritual Quest

Purpose

My purpose inspires me to do as I am destined

Each and every one of us has purpose.

There is a part within that holds our purpose in sight. It is that which inspires through aspirations, impressions and ideas.

You know your purpose is calling when you become consciously aware of a stirring, an inner knowing that there is more. Focus your attention to gain insight and guidance.

Follow your instincts and trust your intuition. Intuitively you will know that you have tuned in and are discovering your purpose. You know you are answering your call when feelings of contentment and fulfillment arise from following your heart. Living life with purpose brings happiness.

When living purposefully, there is a sense of satisfaction in what we are doing. Even if what we are doing brings challenges there is an inner knowing that everything we encounter contributes in some way to our purpose.

Purpose will call us at some time during our life. This may be felt as a conscious awareness of what we need to do or it may be a series of events that align us with our purpose. Or there may be feelings of restlessness and dissatisfaction in what we are doing and that is the driver that shifts us.

In whatever way we are summoned by purpose it is a call that is worthy of attention. It is our choice whether we answer or ignore the call. To ignore does not dismiss our purpose. It will continue to attract our attention in creative ways.

Answering the call may feel like taking a leap of faith, but that leap will open up to a myriad of possibilities. Sometimes we are aligning with our purpose without recognizing it. This is why it is important to reflect and find the purpose of what we are doing.

No matter how humble or how grand, purpose is uniquely aligned to what we are here to do in this life. The path of purpose may have multiple destinations, each one providing information and knowledge in relation to what we do and do not want to do.

Be guided by your intuition and trust your instincts. Intuitively you will know what your purpose looks like. Tune in and discover.

Purpose can be found in the most unlikely places and there may not be a direct path leading to it. Sometimes there are many perceived 'setbacks' before purpose is discovered. However, behind every perceived set-back is success that comes in the form of wisdom gained, resilience built and skills obtained. These are the very skills needed to fulfil your purpose.

Sometimes purpose is stumbled upon while trying to find something else. For example, if the purpose is measured in materialistic value e.g. materialistic gain, then feelings of discontent are inevitable.

Sometimes it is when we hit rock bottom that we receive a flash of insight that awakens us to the light of purpose flickering within. So don't despair if your purpose is not immediately identifiable. It will appear somehow, it may already be but hasn't been acknowledged as such, but when recognized it will bring with it a sense of liberation.

Purpose extends into the unknown making us ponder why we are here and what it is that we are here to do. Personal purpose is something that resonates so strongly that one may make great sacrifice to follow what they feel is their calling in life.

Nothing compares to the feelings generated when we discover our purpose. Life direction floods with passion as we answer the call of our deepest desire. Awakening to who we are and why we are here may arise as if being lifted upon a wave of realization or it may be that we awaken in increments through the journey of self-discovery. As we hone in on natural or learned talents we find that we route ourselves on the path of our purpose.

Purpose is discovering how you can contribute to making the world a better place and doing it. This may be at micro or macro levels, but whatever it is it will have a positive effect that contributes to the collective.

I believe my purpose is to write this book. It is something I have had ticking away in the back of my mind, but did not know where to start or what to put in it. One day I sat down with a notebook and wrote down some words.

Those words transformed into more words and it continued to grow until I had written pages and pages; not in that one sitting, but over the years it has taken.

The words flowed and I became attached to my project and have dedicated excessive amounts of time and energy to writing it. It has been effortless as I am inspired and driven by something deep within that keeps me going. There was no agenda, I just wrote.

Often my writing would be interrupted by a visualization linked to what I was writing. I would go on the visual journey and then write about it. I sometimes wondered how I would know what to write next, but the words just kept flowing.

There have been some frustrations along the way like when it wasn't finished when I thought it 'should' be and each time I thought it was coming to a close the book kept expanding with no end in sight.

I kept going, knowing that there was no way I could stop having come so far. I hope someone; somewhere gets something from what is written. I know I have. I am, however, not attached to the outcome as I have followed my inner guidance to do what I believe I was meant to.

I now have to let it go knowing that I have fulfilled my purpose at this point in time and what will be will be. Those words are personally liberating as they set me free to allow the flow of the universe to take this book where it is meant to go.

The ego will always be there to remind us of

what we don't have and that someone else has more and that what you are doing has no worth and on it goes. However if purpose is measured in soul-based qualities perception will change and one of two things can happen.

1) is that there will be recognition of the purposeful things you do. This may be offering a kind word to someone in need, or smile at someone who looks sad, or thinking to do kind things for others such as packing lunch for a child who would otherwise go without.

2) Your attention will be drawn to what you can do to align with soul qualities. The journey is not about what can be gained along the way but what can be given; the gain will come as a result of what is given.

When what is being measured changes and value is no longer based on asset accumulation but on what we hold in our hearts, then life as we know it transforms. When the essence of love, humanity and gratitude is shared with others we have achieved something of ultimate value, and when seen in this light we begin to uncover the purpose of our existence, which is to be consciously aware beings that serve in ways that help humanity evolve.

PLEDGE TO ALIGN WITH PURPOSE

I acknowledge my personal attributes as they are the gifts that enable me to fulfill the role of my purpose.

I listen and respond to my calling as this is direct communication from my inner being, which holds the key to my purpose. Answering my inner calling is a decisive step on the path aligned with my destiny.

Our mission is uncover the seed of our purpose and follow it with faith.

SUMMARY

- There is a part within that holds your purpose in sight. It inspires through aspirations, impressions and ideas.
- Reflect within and find the insight and guidance needed to discover your purpose.
- Key clues are given in the form of strengths and qualities. Recognizing what these are is not vanity, it is essential.
- No matter how humble or grand, living a purpose filled life brings great happiness.
- Purpose calls through feelings of restlessness and dissatisfaction with superficiality and the need to awaken to something more.
- Purpose is an inner yearning that beckons and refuses to be ignored.
- Feelings of contentment and fulfilment that arise when you are following your heart suggest purpose has been found.
- Unexpected opportunities and unexpected setbacks often set purpose in motion.

Spiritual Quest

PURPOSE

I am aware of opportunities that align with my purpose and potential. I travel with divine guidance and intuitively know my path is filled with love and light.

Success starts today. Make every day count. If you don't like what you see change it. Focus on the feelings you think your success will bring and reflect on how to create those feelings right now.

Spiritual Quest

Reflection

Reflection allows you access to your inner guidance

Access to the deeper recesses of the mind is obtained through reflection.

A calm mind produces clear thought and stabilizes the emotions, which enhances the connection with the higher self, inner intelligence and guidance. This helps to dissolve confusion and dispel uncertainty and gives rise to insight and clarity. Through clarity solutions are found and can be implemented with confidence.

The lessons contained in every experience are identified through reflection. Being liberated with such knowledge shows that whatever life delivers holds meaning and purpose.

Deriving deeper meaning of experiences is to gain additional insight into who we are, why we are here and how to go about constructing meaningful interactions and experiences that will assist growth and development.

Reflection lifts the veil to reveal what has been gained from the major life experiences. This could include finding inner strength, courage, empowerment, inspiration, independence and much more. Although the experience/s that enable the attainment of these qualities may not have been pleasant they provided the necessary lessons from which to learn. There is no need to be attached to an experience once awareness of what the experience provided has been understood.

Letting go is imperative or it is likely that the experience will taint current and future experiences due to apprehension and uncertainty associated with the past.

Repeat experiences are an example of how the past can taint the present. This can result in the inclination to proceed into the future with trepidation and thus be deprived of wonderful new experiences.

Through reflection the mind becomes silent, this is the time when thoughts are resting and intuitive insight awakens. Reflection enables the processing of events and evaluation of situations. Questions can be asked and answers found.

During reflection there is no need to judge or analyze. The aim is to remain neutral and allow the process to occur naturally.

A reflection note-book to record thoughts and feelings after the reflective practice is helpful to obtain further clarity and as a reference for the future. Begin by reflecting upon an experience that you wish to derive understanding. Allow your thoughts and emotions to flow without becoming attached to them.

Watch, feel, listen as your mind recalls and presents the details. Notice any feelings or emotions that arise. If bitterness, resentment or any other unpleasant emotion is detected breathe into the heart area and ask to see through eyes of compassion. Ask to gain a perspective that will assist to release an adverse emotional connection to any experience. Be open to releasing anything that no longer serves you.

Non-serving emotion connected to the past will continue to exert a negative effect in associated areas of life. For example resentment or distrust may be connected to a past relationship. This past hurt may cause reluctance to enter into another relationship or disrupt relationships that are established.

The way forward is to heal the emotion and in doing so heal the aspect that associates relationships to being hurt. Reflection provides the space to gain perspective and ascertain what lies at the core of an experience. Nothing is in vain, there is a reason for everything and through reflection that reason can be understood.

TECHNIQUE

Reflect and Release

Reflect on an experience that you are emotionally bound to. Explore where the emotion is felt in your body. Imagine a cord linking the emotion and the experience. Untie the cord and see the experience separating from the emotion. Imagine a golden light going to the emotion.

See the area open and the emotion, be it something you can feel, hear, see or sense, being healed by the golden light. The golden light fills the area with its light.

When the golden light has been absorbed you know that you are no longer emotionally tied to the experience. This experience has empowered you with strength, wisdom and the ability to make future choices with faith.

Connecting to the wise guide within through reflection is to access soul wisdom, which is to consider the depth of learning and how it is derived. This aspect uncovers the core component without assumption or judgement. When there is certainty in knowing why something happened the details are no longer relevant and it can be let go.

When we free ourselves from what burdens us the soul is released and through the experience it is enriched with new knowledge. The liberation felt is to be touched by a miracle.

PLEDGE FOR REFLECTION

Inner reflection provides a calm space from which to derive clarity and insight. My inner reflections clear my mind giving me an objective overview of my emotions and the circumstances of my life past, present and future. Through reflection I connect with higher aspects of self. Meaning and understanding replace confusion and uncertainty. I am blessed with new knowledge and understanding. My mind is calm. I am calm. All is calm in my world.

SUMMARY

- Clarity materializes through insight.
- Questions are answered, answers are understood.
- Reflection reveals the meaning and purpose of experiences.
- Realization is derived from clear thought and calmness of mind.
- Take time to connect with this profound self-intelligence.
- Reflection is the conduit to opening the channel to deeper understanding of situations, issues, emotions, thoughts and feelings.
- Freedom is found in knowing that experiences are not random occurrences but hold meaning and purpose. This is the gift of realization, discovered through clear thought and calmness of mind.

Spiritual Quest

REFLECTION

By calming my thoughts I receive clarity of mind.

Reflection gives insight on how thoughts, feelings and emotions influences life and how life is influenced by thoughts, feelings and emotions.

Spiritual Quest

Reframe

I reframe my internal dialogue to reflect positivity

STOP! OBSERVE! REFRAME!

Our internal dialogue is the inner voice that chats away as we go about our daily business. It is what we identify as being us, our own voice.

Being aware of what the internal dialogue, our inner voice, is saying is imperative as what is being said becomes a mantra. If this mantra is a constant banter of negativity then we are feeding ourselves thoughts that are toxic to every part of our being.

This is equivalent to feeding our body mouldy, bacteria-infested food. We just wouldn't do it. And yet we will often pollute our minds with disruptive, destructive thoughts.

The thoughts we ingest through our inner monologue impacts on every aspect of our life and our well-being.

If we are ingesting critical, judgemental and self-defeating thoughts then this will be the opinion we will have of ourselves and we will see the manifestation of outcomes based on these assumptions.

What this inner voice tells us we believe. If what we are hearing is self-defeating and goes unchallenged we will eventually accept and believe what is being said. What we think and feel about ourselves and others reflects the health of our internal inner monologue.

Often we are not aware of what we tell ourselves as we are so accustomed to hearing our inner voice that we literally tune out and are not conscious of what it is saying. However our subconscious is fully aware of what is being said and takes it as being gospel.

Becoming aware of this inner voice allows us to hear and reframe when necessary. Belittling and criticizing ourselves serves no purpose and prevents us from believing in ourselves. Our inner monologue can either assist or hinder us.

The inner voice is how we hear inner aspects of self. If there is a repetitive voice of negativity, this is self limiting and requires immediate attention as it is an aspect that requires attention.

Trying to ignore an aspect that requires attention will prove futile. It will get our attention somehow as it will be affecting some area of our life and will continue to do so until we have resolved the issue and effectively attended to an inner need. If any one aspect begins to demand, intimidate or influence us in ways that oppose what we want for ourselves it is time to take action.

Observing self-talk requires conscious awareness to determine what is being said internally to self. It can be surprising how we speak to ourselves on a regular basis.

Our inner-dialogue reflects aspects of self such aspects include the inner child, the inner critic and the saboteur. Through conscious awareness we can readjust self talk and reframe negative into positive.

Reframing inner monologue begins by exchanging self-defeating inner monologue to self-encouraging dialogue. This requires conscious effort to shift the direction of thoughts. This can be supported through the use of positive affirmations. This may feel foreign at first, but with repetition the exchange will become instantaneous.

Identifying thoughts and reframing them in positive ways makes us the masters of our minds. To be the master of the mind, we must cease being servants to non-serving inner monologue.

Master or servant depends on the level of conscious awareness. The more aware we are of our self talk the more empowered we are to direct our thoughts in positive and beneficial ways. It is also important to watch what we think about others, if we think negatively about someone then we are feeding ourselves negative energy. This will turn around on itself and cloud our ability to think positive thoughts about ourselves.

Be it positive or negative our thoughts are creators and what we manifest is a representation of where our thoughts are directed.

If what is being received is not ideal then it is time to change the tape of the internal dialogue. Benefits will be seen instantly.

Maintaining awareness of where your thoughts are and how they are affecting your emotions requires diligence. The ability to shift thoughts so they align with our heart and soul is a naturally evolving process that will become easier with practice.

Tune into your inner monologue. How does it speak to you? Does your inner monologue encourage and support or degrade and discourage? Whether it is positive or negative what you hear over and over is accepted as being true. Repetitive dialogue becomes a belief.

If you would not tolerate someone else speaking to

you in the way you speak to yourself then reframe what you are saying. It is detrimental to your well-being to belittle or speak to yourself unkindly. Observing thought patterns ensures we are coaching ourselves positively. This requires vigilance to ensure we do not fall back into old patterns of thinking.

TECHNIQUE
Self Reflection

Make a list of your qualities. If you struggle to identify qualities ask yourself what others might see as qualities of yours.

Focus on your qualities for a while and watch how your thoughts react. Do they agree or do they oppose? How do your thoughts do this?

These same thoughts are what run through your mind regularly. This can be debilitating if heard often enough and can douse inspiration as you begin to believe that faults outweigh qualities.

Balance is needed, whereby we hold our qualities in high esteem and view our flaws as developing aspects. Being complimentary towards oneself is not being conceited, but establishing a positive relationship with self. This will transfer into other areas of life and as it does our life will improve in wonder-filled ways.

Create your virtues. Think of some virtues that you appreciate or admire. Make these your mantras. Hearing mantras that reflect good virtues infuse us with positivity and enable us to accept this as being true for ourselves.

PLEDGE FOR REFRAMING

I hear my internal dialogue and ensure that what it says is to my liking. I infuse my mind with positive dialogue about myself. The affirmations I use are those aligned with my goals. Noticing my thoughts makes me aware of old tapes and scripts that play over. I choose to exchange these for new, fresh recordings that enable me to realise my potential. My inner monologue supports me with kind words of encouragement and empowers me with "I can" statements. I am an empowered being, my essence is that of love and I deserve to live the life I am here to live.

SUMMARY

- The internal dialogue is our own internal voice.
- It is the voice of our thoughts; it offers advice and runs a commentary on all our encounters and experiences.
- The inner monologue gives a voice to the perspectives and beliefs of the various aspects of self. These aspects reflect positive and negative points of view.
- There are aspects that are aligned with soul qualities and those that identify more closely with ego perspectives.
- Being aware when an aspect is echoing negativity enables one to reframe detrimental inner monologue and to reflect positivity.

Spiritual Quest

REFRAME

I am dedicated to thought awareness and as such am the master of my mind and my destiny.

Spiritual Quest

Seed Of Light

My path is lit to show the lessons
I learn through my mind,
my body and my soul

Within all of us is the seed of light

 *Our being is multi-layered, composed of the mind, the body and the soul.*

Each aspect affects and responds to the other aspects. When we become too focused on any one of these aspects we will receive subtle reminders that the others exist.

This is felt in a variety of ways. Be it physical, emotional or spiritual. Physical ailments have emotional undercurrents and our emotional undercurrents are connected to the mental picture of our minds and to the need for spiritual connection and nourishment.

Our soul learns through the experiences of our mind and body. Every experience provides soul learning. These are our life lessons. Each gives us the opportunity to learn through the light or shadow aspects of our nature.

Through sickness we may learn compassion, which reflects soul perspective or illness may evoke the inner-victim which is a shadow aspect that will focus upon the negative parts of the experience. Through loss we may learn acceptance, soul perspective, or we may become resentful, shadow aspect. Through hardship we may learn gratitude, soul perspective, or we may become miserly, shadow aspect.

Through wealth we may learn generosity, soul perspective, or we may become greedy, shadow aspect.

Soul lessons present themselves throughout the duration of our life. Everything that happens is for us to learn and grow.

If we feel unworthy then we will be given experiences that will provide us opportunities to reflect on thoughts and feelings of unworthiness and do what is necessary to transcend them.

The way to learn the soul lesson of worthiness is to be consciously aware of what is occurring and seek meaning. It is to consider where feelings of unworthiness come from and what can be done to change this belief. This is using the mind to orchestrate change, the body will action what the mind proposes and your soul will guide in ways that will assist the endeavour.

Life is a journey of exploration and discovery. Sometimes we cruise and things go smoothly and sometimes they don't. Wrestling with ourselves when things aren't going as we hoped reduces our capacity to identify the pearl of wisdom contained within the experience. This is travelling the hard way, which is in contrast to the way we travel when we dissolve internal defenses, which assists our journey by reducing our resistance and building our resilience. Inevitably this is the path that will provide the best possible outcomes.

There is no right or wrong way to learn, it is purely a matter of choice. Choice determines the way we experience life. Of course, we cannot control everything that happens and often we do not get a choice of what does happen, but we can choose how we respond and the actions we take.

We can also decide if we interact with what happens through the lightness of our soul or the density of our shadow. The trick is in knowing the different aspects of self, which requires awareness, persistence and patience. Awareness, persistence and patience are key elements that we need to apply in all aspects of life.

When we learn through soul perspective we are nurturing our inner-light. It is our inner-light that will light our path and guide us forth with greater awareness and purpose.

TECHNIQUE
The Seed of Light

Visualize yourself standing with your arms spread out to the side, legs slightly apart. Move your awareness into your heart centre. See a small clear crystal sitting in the centre.

Great power is held within this crystal-seed. A tiny spec of light begins to emanate from the seed. It becomes brighter and brighter, radiating outwards in four directions, front, back and both sides.

The tip of the lights forms a sphere which is slightly open. This point focuses on and drains any negative energy from your body. See it drain outwards, float up and disappear into the ethers to be healed.

The tip of light now moves together forming a brilliant crystal-tipped star, which settles nicely in your heart centre.

Now move your awareness into your throat area. As you focus here you feel all negative energy being removed from this area. You can express yourself with ease.

Now move your awareness into your solar plexus, the area near your naval. As you focus here you feel all negative energy being removed from this area. You can derive insight into your feelings and emotions.

Now move your awareness into your sacral area, the area just below your navel. As you focus here you feel all negative energy being removed from this area. You are an inspired being free to create whatever it is you desire.

Now move your awareness into your base, the area of your perineum. As you focus here you feel all negative energy being removed from this area. You are safe and grounded, this is a solid foundation on which you can build your hopes and dream on.

Now move your awareness into the area between your eyes, your third eye. As you focus here you feel all negative energy being removed from this area. You can trust your intuition to guide you wisely.

Move your awareness to the top of your head. The jewel of the crown. See the seed of light radiate outwards to become a tip about 30cm above your head. From here the light moves outwards about 30cm from your body and moves down to encompass all of your body, creating a point about 30cm below your feet. This is your crystal-seed of light, there to protect, connect and illuminate.

Soul Qualities

*Gratitude   *Humility   *Joy   *Kindness
*Acceptance *Compassion   * Faith   * Trust
*Self-worth   *Love

Shadow Aspects

*Guilt   *Shame   *Anger   *Greed
*Judgment
*Hate   *Criticism   *Envy   * Unworthiness

Contained in every moment is the choice to align with soul qualities and practice kindness and compassion which is to live with a joyful heart. Or we can choose to align with shadow aspect perspectives and feel the associated discomfort.

This choice denies access to the euphoria associated with soul focused principles. Namaste is a sanskrit word which translates to The Spirit within me acknowledges the Spirit within you. Greeting every living being in this way is to allow spirit into our lives, which opens the space needed to live life to its fullest potential. **Namaste!!**

- Our inner light holds the key to our purpose and potential.
- Connecting with the seed of light is to awaken to the essence of our inner being.

SEED OF LIGHT

Divine universal energy exists within me.

Spiritual Quest

Shadow

The shadow is cast by the aspects of self that are suppressed or denied

 *It is up to us to guide shadow aspects towards the light.* Within the shadow lives aspects that are unable to find the light. This is experienced as emotion that creates disharmony. These emotions are linked to aspects that lurk in the shadows of our being.

Emotions are linked to aspects that formed during the early developmental years and during times where the experience outweighed the coping ability.

Shadow aspects hide in the recesses of our subconscious. Shadow aspects contribute to the "I" we identify self with, it gets in the way of self love and with sharing love with others.

When triggered the shadow will present itself, sometimes to our dismay. When the shadow goes back into hiding we are often left wondering what happened. We can either choose to ignore or find out more about the emergence of a shadow aspect. To find out more is to be welcomed into the world of emotional development.

Some emotions will be more prominent than others or there may be a key emotion that seems to always get in the way. This emotion is the key to the formation of the shadow and gives clues to where to focus healing.

Aspects of ourselves that we try to conceal or deny take up residence in the shadow. The shadow is made up of aspects that are attached to unpleasant emotion.

Lurking in the shadow is suppressed anger, guilt, shame, resentment, hostility and any other less than pleasant emotion or emotions deemed unacceptable. Shadow aspects are not our enemies, they are misguided, misunderstood and require assistance.

Being aware of shadow aspects and when they are active is essential as the shadow can blind us to our behaviour and our emotions.

Being aware of when the shadow is active gives the opportunity to utilize tools that prevent being absorbed by the memories and emotions of shadow aspects. Additionally, the utilization of appropriate techniques aids shadow aspects and helps them to develop in positive ways.

As undesirable as we may deem shadow aspects they are part of us. Everyone has shadow aspects and although we would prefer not to, as we would prefer to see to see ourselves as kind, loving and doing the "right" thing, shadow aspects help us grow. This requires vigilance and courage to see when a shadow aspect is triggered and while we may be mystified by the associated thoughts, feelings and behaviour, it is important to become an observer of such.

This is to acknowledge what is happening without getting caught up in it. Taking this approach makes it easier to identify with what triggers a particular aspect and what the underlying need is.

Sometimes shadow aspects can overwhelm our emotions and make it difficult to find the clarity needed to identify the aspect for what it is, and instead start identifying with the aspect.

The longer we stay in the emotion of a shadow aspect the more power it gains and the less empowered we become.

To deny or further suppress what emerges can result in emotional, physical and mental disharmony. This can cause a downward spiral of shadow emotion and possible self-destructive behaviour. Preventing the spiraling of shadow emotions requires conscious awareness.

Awareness shines the light and exposes the

shadow for what it is, a fearful aspect that has never learned how to express itself in helpful ways. It is a child trying to hide from overwhelmingly scary feelings it has no idea how to handle. But we can learn how to coach ourselves and appropriately express and regulate our 'scary' shadow emotions.

As confronting as it may be to acknowledge a shadow aspect, doing so provides an opportunity to transform a limitation into a strength.

Anger is an example of an emotion that can be severely limiting and destructive when in shadow. However when the light aspect of anger is expressed it becomes a powerful motivator. It can spark the energy needed to endure the most arduous tasks. Anger's intensity has fuelled the fires needed to break down imposed barriers, combat wrongdoings and challenge injustice.

Shadow aspects of self are dis-empowered, ashamed and feel rejected. These aspects present as emotions that cause inner conflict of some sort.

Different aspects have different mantras for example the inner-victim says "poor me", the inner intimidator says "shame on you" and the inner belittler says "foolish you". It takes conscious effort not to be pulled into the negative thoughts and the unpleasant emotions created by this inner monologue, which serves only to denigrate and dis-empower.

Whenever we are feeling dis-empowered we are experiencing a shadow aspect of self. If we step into the shadow our thoughts and feelings become clouded. So much so that we fail to see what we are doing to ourselves. We may be blind to our thoughts and behaviours.

Being blind to our own behaviour can have the effect of making us acutely aware of the behaviour of others. This is to see shadow projections. Which is seeing unrecognized aspects of self in others.

This may be seen as a flaw in character, unacceptable behaviour or something we deem unacceptable. Everyone we come in contact with is there for a reason and sometimes that reason is to show us what we do not see or want to see within ourselves.

It is an interesting exercise to reflect on the behaviour of someone close and relate it back to ourselves. Even if we don't like what we see, it is important to identify how what is being reflected relates to self. There are people who unconsciously take on shadow aspects for others. This is especially so for empaths, who are people that naturally feel what others are feelings and have a natural tendency to want to ease the burden for others.

Unknowingly, they accept the projection of another as their own. Empaths are particularly sensitive to energy, hence why they are susceptible to shadow projection. However, this does not assist either party, as we all need to own what is ours.

We must retain healthy boundaries to ensure that we are able do what it is we are here to do. Having empathy for another is essential, being pulled into their story is detrimental. Provide the shoulder, be a listening ear, but retain your own space.

Our inner-landscape is ours to own, integrate and where necessary transform. The burden of shadow projections must be released and the projecting of shadow aspects must be acknowledged.

Some things to remember is to try not to take the behaviour of others personally, behaviour is a reaction to what is going on within oneself. If the actions of others trigger a significant response within oneself then it is necessary to reflect to ascertain meaning of what is projected in relation to you. Please note shadow projections work on an energetic level, the person projecting a shadow does not do so with ill-intent.

What is presented by a projection and what is projected will depend on the individual, but underlying that will be belief that has its roots buried in a non-truth. For example feelings of rejection can trigger a shadow of unworthiness? But does rejection mean you are unworthy? Of course not, the perceived rejection is based upon the false perceptions of the ego and are there for a reason.

Being consciously aware of our inner feelings enables us to hear the warning bells and investigate why these feelings exist, here within lies the conduit to a priceless discovery.

Feelings of rejection and unworthiness are associated with feeling disconnected to our source, thus these feelings are a projection of what we feel within. This projection enables us to look in the mirror and see that we are not being rejected by others or that we are unworthy, but instead that we lack connection with what is our grandest treasure, our soul.

The solution is to get soul-connected and in doing so feelings of rejection and unworthiness dissolve. Through connection with soul principles we exchange the lowly perception the ego has of us and begin to see ourselves through the eyes of love, kindness and gratitude.

We can thank our feelings as they make us consciously aware of what is going on at a subconscious level.

I have personally experienced shadow projections that I have accepted as my own and have done the work needed to clear this.

It is a difficult task as I was pulling myself apart trying to find the core of what was being felt. Through meditation I was able to identify that I had energetically relieved the burden of another and in doing so placed this upon myself.

Using the techniques described later I was able to free myself. I then worked from a place of love to transmute the projection.

When connected with our soul and operating through soul principles it is understood that we are all worthy. Anything that opposes this comes from identifying to closely with a shadow aspect that is dulling the inner-light.

If we keep our vibration high and observe rather than become involved with our own story and the stories of others we gain insight without the associated discomfort.

If someone stumbles in the dark, it is pointless to stumble alongside them; it is far more beneficial to provide the support needed to guide them towards the light.

When strong emotion stirs sit with it and allow it to surface. Breathe in and when you exhale imagine the emotion dispersing. When it does look for what it is attached too. It may just be that it needs to come up to be set free. Allow, acknowledge and accept.

If the emotion doesn't shift after a few minutes then further investigation is needed. It could be that a shadow aspect is calling for your attention, but is too fearful to present itself. This is unprocessed emotion.

Unprocessed emotions are those that have not been dealt with in ways that allow positive expression. The emotion gets stuck and when triggered, reacts. The emotion and reaction are associated to an aspect of self. If the emotion is connected to the inner seven year old, then the behaviour displayed will be of a seven year old. If it belongs to the frustrated inner adolescent, then the behaviour will reflect that.

Back-biting or degrading another may be done by an adolescent or pre-adolescent as an attempt to boost wavering self-esteem during an uncertain stage of life.

Belittling and degrading others does little to boost self-esteem, but it does shift the focus onto someone else and can give feelings of superiority. These feelings are craved for by less evolved aspects of self.

As the behaviour (back-biting) received positive feedback e.g. superior in exchange for insecurity, the behaviour is reinforced and may continue into adulthood unless challenged and amended.

Getting a rise out of or degrading another is shadow aspect behaviour. Reasons for inner-teen behaviour are evident when viewed from adult perspective.

During those years there are many storms to weather and the perspective derived is aligned to that stage of development, which is often the easiest and fastest way to achieve an outcome that is better than the current way of being. However if certain perspectives and behaviours aren't remedied the inner-teen will be reflected throughout the lifetime.

The inner-teen needs to learn what was not learned during that stage of development and any unexpressed emotion needs to be processed or it will continue to lurk in the shadow.

The higher-self will attempt to bring awareness to the emotion and the associated behaviour, but as the behaviour has been reinforced it will take conscious effort to construct healthier thought patterns that enable the inner-teen to construct positive methods of overcoming insecurity and feel secure within.

We learn how to express our emotions through feedback received from our own internal interpretations and from the feedback received from others, especially significant and influential others.

The feedback received combined with inherent nature blends to become the way an individual expresses themselves. Positive feedback and guidance helps develop an emotionally aware individual. Emotional awareness is the conduit to emotional responsibility. Being responsible for our emotions prevents us from giving our power away by blaming external influences, such as people or circumstances for the way we feel, thus making us emotions puppets controlled by whatever is going on around us.

Like a flower in the breeze our emotions go in whichever direction the wind blows. Taking control of our emotions (which is different from controlling them) is empowering as we can choose how to respond to our emotions and regulate our reactions from within rather than being regulated by and reactive to external influences.

Understand that although external influences may trigger certain reactions, the response is dependent on the internal perspectives of the individual.

This knowledge can inspire a significant shift that brings awareness within. Thus begins the formation of a beautiful relationship with the inner self, which is the most important and fulfilling relationship shared. Imagine sharing kindness, consideration and tenderness with yourself. Imagine loving yourself, shadow aspects and all. Imagine being able to clearly define and express your qualities. Imagine acknowledging your emotions as key communicators that give depth to your experiences; through them you interpret the world and interact with others.

Emotions have many layers all of which help us to learn, develop and grow. Transcending the layers of less developed aspects of our being enhances our connection with more evolved aspects of self which are aligned with feelings of compassion, empathy, joy and gratitude. Inner evolution creates the foundations of inner peace.

Developing a positive relationship with our emotions is more likely a process that takes conscious effort than something that occurs naturally.

As children we expressed ourselves in its raw form, as we develop we learn how to understand and regulate our emotions and express them in ways that allow others to know how we feel.

This is being self-empowered whereby we can attend to our own needs and understand the needs of others. However creating such a relationship with our inner self doesn't always develop so easily or in positive ways and instead we find ourselves faced with aspects that cause inner conflict and disharmony. These aspects seem to present themselves at the most inappropriate times and/or at significant times of our life.

These aspects have been hiding in the shadow and are yet to develop the tools needed to process what dis-empowers them. Uncovering vulnerabilities facilitates the awareness needed to attend and broaden the perspective of vulnerable aspects.

However vulnerable aspects often go undetected or are not on our radar until triggered and it is when we are under the influence of these aspects that they reduce our capacity to attend in positive ways, hence we see a lapse into the shadow. It is during the storm that the aspect needs attention or it will go back into the shadow until next time it is triggered.

Going into the storm is taking the vulnerable aspect by the hand and providing the tools it needs to shift. Once it has the tools it will be equipped to handle situations that trigger it in the future.

This begins by acknowledging and staying with the feelings associated with the emotion the aspect presents rather than trying to avoid or escape them. Although this may cause discomfort it is essential, as avoidance and escape will result in the continuation of the trigger-reaction cycle.

In the scenario that an aspect has been triggered it is important to stop. If the emotions are overwhelming breathe deeply and count slowly to 10; if slowly is not possible just count as best you can.

The purpose of counting is that it helps bring the left (rational) hemisphere of the brain into the picture so the right (emotional) hemisphere has a chance to take a break from the emotion being experienced.

Counting helps short circuits the emotions from spiraling in a negative direction. This is a simple yet powerful technique that bridges the hemispheres of the brain so they can work in unison to balance one another. If this was taught to children to assist their emotional development there would be less conflict with shadow aspects.

When a child gets angry they most likely will receive negativity towards such an expression. This does nothing to help the child to understand their anger, but instead develops a shadow aspect as the child's interpretation of angry is bad and bad is unacceptable. As they have displayed anger it is bad and hence they are bad and unacceptable. They want to be good and accepted so anger (bad and unacceptable) is suppressed. This is a child-like evaluation of angry and one that sticks unless provided with a different point of view.

Often the only awareness we have of shadow aspects is a niggle that lingers in our waking hours, we usually can't put our finger on it and we unconsciously try to avoid the emotion associated.

We try to avoid, dull or deny the existence of what is being felt, but this is impossible because it is an aspect of us and it will be expressed. Out of sight out of mind, until the aspect that has been confined to the shadow is triggered. Although it can be masked, maybe as another more 'acceptable' emotion, eventually it will come out in one form or another. Be it related to the mind (conflict and inner turmoil) or body (illness and/or physical incapacitation) or soul (deep ache and disassociation).

Anger is the example, but any emotion housing itself in the recesses of the shadow can present itself. Be it passively or actively expressed, a shadow aspect will not remain dormant forever.

Shadow aspects can be projected towards

others in the form of violence, deceit and abuse or towards self such as self-defeat, self-punishment and self-sabotage.

There may be an internal tug of war as we wrestle with the shadow while aspiring to live in the light. However higher-aspects of self can help guide shadow aspects.

We can become our own best friend by listening to our inner self. This includes listening to the woes of the shadow aspects of our nature and providing solution-focused support that enable positive expression.

This will help shadow aspects assimilate and thus become non-reactive to previous triggers. The choice becomes to deny emotion and be cast in shadow or acknowledge and accept our emotions and be touched by the light.

All shadow aspects require healing so they can surrender and be embraced by the light.

 Settle into a comfortable position. Take some nice deep breaths. In through the nose and out through the mouth.
Breathe in the beautiful white light energy.
Draw the white light through your body.
See this beautiful white light flow through your body and dissolve all tension.
You are feeling very relaxed and ready to meet a shadow aspect of yourself.
You find yourself sitting at a dressing table.
All your personal trinkets sit upon the table.
You are in a safe place and are feeling comfortable and content.
You open the side drawer of your dressing table and pull out a beautiful hand mirror.
You bring the hand mirror up to your face and peer into it.
You see your physical self.
You smile at yourself with acceptance of what you see.
As you sit looking at yourself in your hand mirror you become aware of an aspect stirring within.
This aspect is emerging to show you it exists and

what emotion is attached to it.

You do not need to go into the emotion, you are just observing. Just quietly watching what comes.

The aspect keeps emerging.

You are safe and just continue to sit there and watch.

The aspect then unveils itself for you to see in full light.

You look fully into the mirror and truly see what is being shown to you.

You are seeing a shadow aspect of yourself.

You may see it as a word, an image, or as an emotion.

You do not need to feel the emotion, just witness it.

You ask your shadow some questions:

Where do you come from?

What do you wish to show me about myself?

Why do I deny this part of myself?

What can I learn from you?

What does it need?

Look and listen for what arises.

Patience is a virtue here.

When you have your questions answered see this shadow aspect surrounded by magnificent golden light.

See love, in the colours of pink and green, pour into this shadow aspect.

Thank your shadow aspect for expressing itself and for helping you to understand why it exists.

If any other shadow aspects arise repeat the same process.

Bid your shadow good-bye with the understanding that when you see it again you will offer love and light so it may heal.

Your shadow fades now and you find yourself gazing once again into your eyes in the mirror.

You are feeling calm and at ease.

You are now aware of what a shadow aspect looks like and can identify it if it emerges at any time.

This awareness empowers you to accept and work with your shadow in positive ways.

The shadow has profound teaching ability, provided we are aware that the shadow is an aspect of us and not who we are. This knowledge gives choice to either identify with and connect to the light aspects of self or to identify with and connect with those that cast shadows

PLEDGE FOR SHADOW ACKNOWLEDGMENT

I acknowledge my shadow aspects and choose to illuminate them with light.
Strength is found by being aware of vulnerabilities.
Through awareness I know when I am being influenced by a shadow aspect.
I take this aspect by the hand and coax it into the light.
It now sees from a different perspective.
I choose to step from the shadow and heed the messages received from my higher self.
This is the path of my highest good and purpose.

SUMMARY

- Emotions such as anger, guilt and shame lurk as shadow aspects.
- Shadow aspects need understanding and empathy to help them shift.
- Discovering shadow aspects helps emotional development.
- More prominent shadow aspects block progress and hinder self development.
- Facing a shadow aspect and shifting its perspective is the most liberating experience.

Acknowledging, accepting and embracing shadow aspects provides the light needed for them to transcend.

SHADOW

I embrace my shadow with love & bring it into the light.

Spiritual Quest

Transformation

*Embarking upon the journey of self-exploration
is the ultimate transformation*

 *The journey of self-exploration will see beliefs challenged, barriers dissolved and resistance resolved – this enables the ultimate transformation.*

Self expression and honesty are pivotal in the transformation process. Transforming from one state of being to another rejuvenates, regenerates and liberates.

Through transformation we shed the past, embrace the present and design the future. Transformation ignites an inner spark that drives our destiny. Destiny is not a destination; it is the progressive journey of our lives which is further defined through every choice made and every action taken.

As we transform we are faced with aspects of self, some of which have been rejected and denied. Some may resist going forth, fearing the exchange of old for new. All aspects need to assimilate so they can become part of the whole. Be courageous and confront challenges, while remaining emotionally aware of what emerges.

Being emotionally aware is the key to identifying when you are being met with resistance. By acknowledging the resistance and the associated feelings you can support, rather than deny, emotional vulnerability. To deny, ignore, suppress any emotion intensifies it as it pushes it aside.

Shoving down something that wants to be expressed is like putting the lid on the pressure cooker and thinking that will stop the pressure from building. Eventually the pressure will build and the lid will blow and that is precisely how pent-up emotion can feel when it surfaces.

We have creative ways of trying to escape the pressure caused, but eventually the only way is to allow it to rise and be set free. And with the use of appropriate tools and techniques emotions can be expressed in ways that circumvent this pressure cooker like scenario from exploding.

The release of suppressed emotion is transformational; however it is best done with care and consideration. An example of trapped emotion is a repetitive story. The story is the lid on the pressure cooker that prevents the actual emotion from being disclosed.

It may appear that someone is expressing by telling their story, but unless there is actual emotion expressed then the emotion will lurk beneath the surface and the story will continue. It is not until the emotion is acknowledged and processed that the need to tell the story will dissolve.

Why the repetitive story? The switch associated with the trapped emotion remains on. The emotion communicates through thoughts and as the issue is unresolved the thoughts about the story keep rolling through the mind.

The person delivering the story may not even be aware they repeat their story. The people around them will be aware, but unlikely to mention the repetitiveness of the story being told. However, for the story to be resolved conscious awareness is needed and sometimes that can only happen by being confronted. This of course is done with consideration, respect and with the intention to assist if requested to do so. Sometimes it is exactly what the person is looking for, but does not know how go about getting the assistance required.

Realizing how much we have clung to our stories and the impact this has had on our lives can come as a shock and at the same time a sense of liberation may be felt as no longer are we stuck in the story of the past.

Choosing to remain oblivious to the affect our emotions have on us is to miss an opportunity to learn and grow. Acknowledging our emotions, accepting them for what they are and adopting strategies that assist positive expression transforms emotional turmoil into emotional freedom.

Emotions are connected to aspects that seek understanding and acceptance. Even those that we deem unacceptable and would prefer to deny require our attention. Here lies the roots of our emotional needs and if we want to feel fulfilled and complete we must attend to these needs. Unmet emotional needs continue as vulnerabilities that taunt us.

Acknowledging aspects that are vulnerable brings them into the light, which means they no longer have to lurk in the shadows and seek our attention in negative ways.

Acknowledgment equals choice which empowers us to set about shifting self-defeating, non-serving emotion so they may assimilate and become part of the whole self and in doing so be part of the support team that helps us journey and transform into all we are capable of being. This enables us to expand into the flow of life and by doing so find ourselves in the right place and exactly the right time.

Being consciously aware of thoughts and emotions empowers us to take charge and transcend limitations and transform into anything we aspire to be.

Emotions are part of what makes us human, they give us dimension and depth and without them life would be robotic and mundane. Emotions are motivators that can affect us positively and negatively. The want to be happy keeps us seeking positive experiences.

If experiences don't stack up to our expectations and don't produce the results we are looking for then our emotions can shift and we experience emotion that opposes what we are trying to achieve e.g. frustration instead of elation; disappointment instead of excitement, discontentment instead of satisfaction. Feeling emotion is what makes us human; it spurs guidance, it incites action.

We interpret life through emotion. All our interactions stimulate emotion. However, we are not our emotions. Just because we feel sad does not mean we are sad, we may feel angry but that does not mean we are angry. To say "I am (the emotion)" is a significant statement that, if said often enough, can easily be reinforced and make our emotions spiral until we actually acquire that state of being.

Soon we start to define ourselves by the emotion, I am depressed, I am anxious, I am nervous, I am angry, I am whatever the overwhelming emotion is. Becoming aware of this is the same as the alarm bell sounding. The choice becomes ours to either respond or to ignore the emotions that call for our attention.

Either choice will come with its challenges, but the outcome of responding will be transformational, whereas the outcome of ignoring can lead to detrimental outcomes such as illness and possibly the use of substances to escape the unidentified lingering feeling of discomfort.

Sinking into a state of ignorance comes with associated complications. This is a significantly unpleasant path to travel especially when secondary issues compound and worsen the primary issue.

To respond is to embark on the journey of self-exploration during which you will come face to face with light and shadow aspects of self. This balance will deliver beautiful reflections of the shades that make you who you are.

From the shadow emerges light which enables us to see why shadowy aspects exist. At times there will be a battle of wills where certain shadow aspects feel threatened and cause inner turmoil.

Clashing with or ignoring these aspects will only serve to further alienate and reinforce what the aspect represents.

Instead we need to look at and reflect upon the emotion connected to the aspect; by doing this we gain insight into an underlying need. This enables us to attend to the need and in doing so the emotion transforms.

Each aspect that presents itself has needs that require attention, although the technique used may differ. For example one aspect may need a kind, gentle approach whereas another will require a more direct, firm approach.

If presented with an aspect that is trying to intimidate and pull you in a direction that is uncomfortable then a firm approach may be required. The inner-critic is an aspect that requires firm reassurance to combat the tendency to intimidate and dis-empower.

If given too much power the inner-critic can paralyze positivity with negative thoughts that can rapidly spiral into feelings of despair. If your inner-critic is intimidating then some bluff courage and confidence is called for. Silencing the inner critic in itself is transformational.

Listen to what your inner state of being is telling you. If you feel this is a difficult thing to do then rest assured there are mirror images everywhere that will reflect an inner image of self. Look at those closest to you, what do they reflect back?

Do you like what is being reflected?

Is there something in them that you would like to change?

How does this relate to you?

It may not be in the same area as what you see, but in other areas of your life. Looking at what is being presented, turning the mirror towards ourselves and interpreting the relevant meaning is to understand how powerful we are at orchestrating experiences, events and situations that enable valuable learning. This is how to transform the mundane into the magnificent.

PLEDGE FOR THE JOURNEY OF TRANSFORMATION

As I embark on the ultimate journey of self exploration I open my mind to discover all I can about myself, my journey and the life I am here to live. The barriers I have created fall and enable me to access untapped inner resources and personal power. I transcend linear thinking and expand into a lateral view of myself and the world. This transforms beliefs into those that empower and enable me to expand my vision of self. I know I can accomplish whatever it is I decide and dedicate myself to. I transform and evolve into the self I am capable of being.

SUMMARY

- Beliefs are challenged, barriers are dissolved and resistance is resolved.
- Naturally you will expand into the flow of life to become all you wish to be.
- Expanding into all you can be is to encompass the intimate connection of the mind, body, spirit trio.
- Hiding beyond the façade of who we think we are is the essence of who we really are.
- Transformation is a work in progress which will see you travel through many transitions.
- Embrace all that you are and all your experiences.
- Your perseverance will be greatly rewarded as you transform into your magnificence.

Spiritual Quest

TRANSFORMATION

*I grow and develop
into all I can be.*

> *Embracing the intimate connection of the mind, body, spirit trio is the foundation of expanding into all you can be.*

Spiritual Quest

Transition

When letting go of old in exchange for new you undergo a transitional period

Clearing of that which no longer aligns with who you are and what you want undergoes a period of transition.

Acknowledge and accept that you are going through a transition and that through this you are aligning more closely with your highest good. Growth and clarity lay beyond this point. Riding the wave of discomfort is imperative. Avoidance causes stagnation, making it difficult to expand into the future.

Reflect kindness and positivity towards yourself. If you come to an impasse, reflect on your feelings, re-evaluate your position, adjust your approach, and when you have re-established your footing-move forward.

Emergence from a transition will be immensely rewarding. There may be feelings of restlessness, dissatisfaction and maybe even chaos during a transitional period.

Acknowledge when this is happening and accept that transitions are necessary as they are what one endures during the process of exchanging the old for new. This is essential for our growth and development.

Whether planned or unexpected a transition

means that change is imminent. Whatever the reason for the transitional period it represents venturing into the unknown. Even if excited about the prospect of a new relationship, a career change or any other life-changing event, feelings of apprehension and uncertainty may emerge.

A shift in the comfort zone can have a physical, emotional and/or psychological effect. This may cause barriers to fly up, stress to flare and frustration to set in.

Struggling with a transition or refusing to endure the challenge can hinder personal growth. Accepting the challenge with the intention of doing the best you can is going with the flow.

This can be assisted by keeping the bigger picture in mind, while coaching and nurturing resistance aspects of self towards success. Journey with grace and know that beyond resistance is expansion

If you become stuck, reflect on your feelings, re-evaluate your position, adjust your approach and move forward.

ALWAYS MOVE FORWARD....

Sometimes the only indication that an aspect has shifted is that certain thoughts and feelings are no longer present and the associated discomfort that was caused no longer exists. For example, being overly sensitive to what other people think no longer has the same effect.

The mantra "I can't do that because someone might think such and such" changes to "I am doing it and don't need approval from anyone." This in itself is transformational.

What may not be realized is that there may have been years of transitions involved before the aspect holding on to this point of view was finally able to let go of the need for approval. Never give up because sometimes, often when you least expect it, there is a shift that transforms your life for the better.

Transitions enable growth. Arriving at the crossroads in life signals a shift in direction and the decision process begins. The choice will depend on numerous factors, but once made the transition commences.

During the transitional period there may be times when we want to retreat to our comfort zone, especially if shadow aspects surface and challenge the choice made. This is to meet with a limitation.

Persevering beyond limitations will see barriers and objections fade and a renewed image of self emerge.

Stepping into a transition with courage and persevering through the challenges that that entails will give rise to significant personal transformation. This is the shedding of the old to embrace the new which is to birth another dimension of your being.

TECHNIQUE

Addressing Shadow Aspects and Clearing the Way for a Smoother Transition

Transitions have the tendency to stir shadow aspects. Often the sole purpose of a transition is to uncover the aspects of self that block the way and stifle potential.

So we unconsciously attract an event, a situation or an experience that draws our attention to an aspect so we can help shift it and move forward. The battle begins when more aware aspects are ready to take the leap and the less aware aspects struggle with the proposed change.

A multitude of feelings are associated with this, all of which cause various degrees of discomfort.

Mild discomfort is relatively easy to work through, however severe discomfort causes a fight or flight response and takes considerable effort to work through.

A challenging transition indicates that there is an aspect of self, struggling with what is being proposed.

Some examples of transitions that may trigger shadow aspects include leaving or starting a relationship, leaving or starting a career, moving house or shifting to another town or country, closing down or starting a new business, pursuing a goal, challenging an addiction.

Identifying the aspect standing in your way

Holding the mirror - what qualities do you see in yourself? What qualities do you see in someone you admire?
Do you see this in yourself?
If you see it in another then it is present within you, however if you don't see it within yourself then there is an aspect blocking your view.

For example, generosity is a quality, but if you cannot see it in yourself or if you see that being generous leads to negative outcome such as being taken advantage of or if it is difficult to give to others, then not only does this hinder the ability to give but also to receive.

Detecting the aspect that is blocking the ability to be generous requires some detective work. Imagine yourself being generous with time or gifts.

While indulging this image notice what thoughts and feelings arise.

Are you enjoying being generous or is there associated discomfort?

What is the discomfort telling you?

Where does it come from?

Was there a time you wanted to be generous or was being giving and was rejected?

Was giving and receiving balanced in the home you grew up in?

If the ability to give or to receive is difficult then there will be a give/receive imbalance.

As this is not aligned with higher self qualities the time will come when something will challenge you to awaken and attend to the aspect needing to learn the quality of generosity.

The clue to aspects needing attention are in the prominent flaws you see in others, especially those that irritate the most.

The qualities you recognize in others, but do not recognize in yourself, are the ones begging your attention as they wish to be acknowledged so they can fulfill their potential.

Walking the path

 Take a deep breath in through the nose and then exhale out through the mouth.

Repeat breathing this way until you are feeling centered and relaxed. Imagine you are walking down a country lane. You are feeling comfortable and relaxed.

The sun is out and warming your body, your heart and your mind.

As you walk you notice that there is a sign up ahead, but before you reach the sign you see that someone is walking towards you.

As this person gets closer you realize that you know them.

Your eyes are drawn to the sign and you understand that to continue your transition you need to interpret the message on the sign. There is a clue that relates to the person standing in front of you. By interpreting the message you will shift what hinders your transition. As you stand on the lane you close your eyes to gain clarity. The pieces of the puzzle fit together and you receive a vision, a message, a sign or a symbol that provides the insight you need. When you open your eyes you see that the person that was standing in front of you has moved to your side.

Together you walk to the crossroads and are able to go with the flow in the direction aligned with what is in your best interest at this stage in your life.

You walk with grace and ease upon your chosen path.

PLEDGE TO AID TRANSITIONS

As I enter into a transitional period I do so with an open mind and know that I am clearing what I no longer need.

I release the baggage from the past and transition into the next cycle free from burden.

I will remain aware of my thoughts and emotions and ensure to express in ways that facilitate my growth.

Through transition, I shed what is old and outdated and emerge a wiser, stronger empowered me.

SUMMARY

- During transition thoughts, feelings and perceptions begin to align with the next stage of the journey.
- The wave of discomfort that accompanies a transition will lead to calmer shores.
- Go with the flow of a transition.
- Resistance or avoidance will lead to stagnation.
- Allow the light to guide the way through the shadows.
- On the other side of a transition emerges a stronger, wiser, happier self.
- Beyond transition lies transformation.

Spiritual Quest

TRANSITION

*I see the light guiding me through this transition.
I am wiser and stronger as I emerge and embrace
the new phase of my life.*

Spiritual Quest

Trust

Trust inner guidance and intuitive insight

Trusting in your inner guidance and the flow of the Universe is to live a wonder-filled existence.

Honour yourself and trust the initial inklings felt before rationalization.

With practice, and a decent amount of patience, self trust with extraordinary dependability develops.

Let go of doubt and have enough faith in yourself to trust your intuition. Having trust and faith in yourself forms the basis from which a phenomenal connection to your own truth can evolve.

Become centered within your truth, and know that decisions, ideas, principles and beliefs will be your own and thus perfectly aligned with your purpose.

Trusting inner guidance and the flow of the Universe is to discover your divine destiny. Inner guidance is felt as initial inklings and dissolves when rationalized.

While rationalization assists us in making grounded decisions, balance is essential or intuitive insight will be drowned out. When this happens we are robbed of the opportunity to connect with deeper understanding and meaning. When intuition and rationalization are balanced the approach is grounded and holistic.

It is important that the hemispheres of our brain communicate and co-ordinate so together they can transform our ideas, goals and desires into reality.

Dismissing or distrusting intuitive insights is to miss valuable opportunities. Shutting off our intuitive inspirations causes imbalance and the risk of becoming too 'left brained' which is process driven and stifles creativity.

Diminished creative flow produces inferior results to those inspired by imagination and intuitive incentive.

Many a brilliant idea has been diminished in its capacity due to being pulled down by logic and reasoned out of existence.

Rationalization can deflate the inspired inner drive by overshadowing it with thoughts that deem a proposed idea as too hard, not possible, illogical, dubious etc, etc.

When this occurs intuitive vision weakens, spirit is dampened and we reinforce a lack of trust in ourselves and our ability. If intuitive inspirations raise us to a level of excitement and this excitement is brought down time and time again then eventually the ability to get excited will dwindle into non-existence leaving behind a sorrowful nagging feeling of disappointment.

Hoping for something and receiving the opposite and feeling like we have received incorrect guidance or been lead up the garden path is not the fault of intuition, but due to thoughts and feelings that douse the inspired spirit.

Detrimental thoughts are not intuitively inspired. They are seeded by doubt and if given enough attention will become the garden to which we will tend. Such gardens sprout tendrils that suffocate the flowers of happiness, hope and optimism.

Weed out negative thoughts and enjoy being in a garden flourishing with positivity.

The most successful people did not become so by using logic alone, but rather blended intuition and logic to receive favourable outcomes. This is trust.

The ability to trust oneself is to trust those inner promptings which urge you to go somewhere or do something without logical contemplation of why and what for. Doing this somehow puts you in the right place at the right time or finds you doing or saying something at the right moment. What transpires from here is an amazing unraveling of events.

Although logic is used in the process, a logical explanation of the process would be intuitively inspired, for example: "I just knew", "I had a feeling", "felt it in my gut", "I don't know how it happened I just knew it would", "I trusted myself to put one foot in front of the other and somehow it all fell into place."

There will be milestones and setbacks along the way, but trust and faith in oneself will see you through to results that may have initially been deemed impossible.

The vital ingredients needed to nurture an idea to fruition are trust, focus and action. There are many formulas and models of how to achieve goals. The most effective one is the DO IT!! model. Don't sit around pondering away your inspiration. Take action.

Deep down you know what it is that makes your heart sing, trust that this is your calling, plan it, get in flow with it and trust that you will be presented with opportunities that are aligned. Proceed with an open mind and an open heart. You are on the way to exactly where you need to be.

The path leading to achieving a goal is rarely straight, inevitably there will be obstacles that deter, distract and disrupt the course. This occurs for various reasons including working out what aspects of self require attention so they can move beyond supposed barriers and to see that by confronting challenging we learn a great deal about our capabilities.

Life is a continuous journey of learning, part of which is to see that obstacles are signposts that direct our attention to elements to do with the inner self or the need to redirect as we are out of alignment in some area.

If attempts to control, manipulate or maneuver an obstacle leave you feeling powerless and frustrated, rather than wrestling with the obstacle, surrender, wait and watch to see what unravels.

Until then get on with your everyday life and be prepared to act, as something will come to show you the next steps towards your goal.

It may be that your goal needs reassessment or that adjustment is required, there may be other areas in life that need attention, other factors may have entered the picture which alters the goal.

Trust yourself to keep afloat and be flexible enough to adapt and accommodate where necessary. Take action and follow through with faith.

Trust develops from feeling safe, capable and confident to try even if there is a risk of failing because failing is not perceived as failure but rather a learning experience that helps growth and development. Within this is a feeling of security within oneself and this is what forms a strong basis of self-trust.

Part of developing self-trust is to be aware of its opposing force, self-doubt. Self-doubt festers from feelings of not being good enough, not feeling secure within self, feeling insufficient and unable to rely upon self. These feelings may be mirroring the messages received in childhood and are reinforced by false perceptions about self.

Believing false impressions about who you are and what you are capable of negates the ability to trust. If what you want for yourself opposes how you perceive yourself or what you think you are capable of then there is a discrepancy that needs to be bridged. Identifying false truths held about self is to watch for the associated aspect/s holding onto falsities.

The inner-critic and the inner-victim represent two of these doubtful aspects. Unmasking where the messages behind the doubtful voices come from will show how easy it is to be bound to beliefs and perceptions that are not a true representation of who you are and what you are capable of.

Note the aspects spoken of are part of the psyche. They are inner perceptions based on interpretations created at various stages of development. They affect how we feel.

These aspects are limited, have unmet needs and false belief about self. Their primary intention is to protect from hurt, humiliation, failure, disappointment or rejection because they do not trust that you will know how to deal with this. This is linked to a time when there was vulnerability and that vulnerability will remain until the associated doubt is exchanged for trust.

Developing self-trust takes practice, patience and empathy. Being empathetic to the insecure aspects of self establishes a stable foundation to build trust on.

The process begins by evaluating thoughts to find where the roots of self-doubt reside and creating new thought patterns with the aim of building trust in self.

What drives the thoughts in the head are the connections made to the energy centres. When balanced the energy centres provide a solid foundation upon which all else can balance.

Thoughts and feelings communicate whether the energy houses are open, closed or blocked and if energy has been processed, is being processed or needs processing.

Think of a time when you went with your inner feeling gut instinct. How did this feel? What was the outcome of trusting your instinct? Think of a time when you chose to ignore your instincts. What was the outcome?

Intuition is like a news flash. It interrupts our regular thought patterns with an important broadcast. We can choose to listen to the broadcast, dismiss it as a minor interruption or, if we are completely tuned out, miss it altogether. Intuitive 'news flashes' are delivered visually, auditorily or kinaesthetically.

Capturing the essence of our intuition in its

raw form, which is before it is filtered through personal perceptions, judgments or beliefs, is to receive a precious gift.

Appreciating the sound guidance received by your intuition and acting on it enhances the connection and the ability to interpret what is being communicated. However if there is a lack of trust in your intuition the messages may be confused, ignored or misinterpreted.

Establishing trust in your intuition is to learn what it feels like to receive intuitive insight and then test for reliability.

Think of something you would like guidance on. When doing this notice the method used to configure your request. Was it visual, a feeling or posed as a verbal question?

Noting how you communicate with your inner self will reflect how your inner self will communicate with you. After making your request notice any thoughts (those not consciously constructed), feelings and/or images that may emerge.

This is intuitive communication; it has depth, has no agenda and is not attached to an outcome. Intuitive guidance is clear and concise. If there is confusion associated then this is not intuition.

When the mind is preoccupied with thought that has no real purpose it significantly reduces the ability to hear intuitive messages.

To trust intuition is to go beyond what is thought to be true and get the truth. This instills trust within self and even if the voice of doubt does chime in its ability to negate self-trust is significantly reduced.

Each day take a thought-free moment. This is a time where thoughts are put on hold and you tune into the silent place within. It is in this space that intuitive awareness evolves.

Becoming familiar with and having trust in your intuition keeps the communication channels open. Nurturing the connection with your intuition binds a relationship that you can trust.

Compile a strengths list that reflects what you believe to be your strengths. Include in this list successes and achievements. No matter how grand or small put them on your list. For example, put down a fear you overcame, helping someone in need, being recognized in some way, standing up for someone.

If you look you will find strengths and times of

success and achievement. The purpose of the list is to remind doubtful insecure aspects that you have proven that you are capable.

If the inner-critic jumps in and starts nagging about perceived failure, remind yourself that there is no such thing as failure and that through every experience we gain skills that we add to our life tool box.

Allowing the inner-critic to howl you down can be crippling. Whatever we tell ourselves we will believe. Equipped with a strengths list you can remind yourself how capable you are.

Want to be on the path of your destiny? Then embody the essence of trust and proceed with an open mind and an open heart.

 Take a deep breath in through your nose then exhale out through your mouth. See all tension leave your body.
Take another deep breath in and then exhale. Take another deep breath in and as you do see beautiful gold light enter your body. As it flows through every cell you can see it dissolve beliefs that hold you back.

These beliefs move to the surface and move out from your energy field. Focus on one of these beliefs and as you do you see it dissolve. As it dissolves you can feel a sense of freedom.

You look within yourself and see a vacant space where the belief once stored itself.

You instinctively know that you must fill this space with new truths about yourself. The first truth is that you are a magnificent being capable of great things.

You allow yourself to feel this truth and as you do you feel the emergence of a feeling of trust in your own magnificence.

You now find yourself going into your thoughts to create a thought pattern that embeds this self-trust.

You know that you can have absolute trust in yourself.

You now find yourself in a space within that knows this truth.

You are totally absorbed in your ability to trust yourself without reservation. You fill this space with beauty and good wishes for yourself. Only that which will uphold your self-esteem and self-belief is allowed in this space.

You continue to fill this space with positivity. Positivity may be seen as light, images, messages or positive thoughts.

You can always trust that your intuition will guide you in alignment with your highest good.

Step away from limitation by creating thoughts that nourish, enrich and boost your sense of self-worth.

Spiritual Quest

PLEDGE TO ENHANCE TRUST

Within my experiences I learn the lessons that aid the evolution of my soul.

I trust that challenges provide me with the means to develop perseverance, persistence and patience.

There is always help available, I only need to ask.

I am equipped with intuition and cognitive ability to assist my journey and provide me with higher perspective of all past, present and future experiences.

My journey is enhanced with the exchange of love, laughter, empathy and compassion I share with fellow beings partaking in this life quest.

SUMMARY

- Honour the inner inklings felt before rationalization.
- Trust that what is needed will be supplied.
- Look....listen....acknowledge...act.
- Develop trust by dissolving doubt.
- Trust the ability to align choices and decisions with highest good.
- Be patient as sometimes it takes time for the right answer to resonate.
- Trust the flow of the Universe.
- Trusting that things will work out as they are meant to lessen concern over what happens in the process.

If thoughts and the resulting feelings override visions of a goal or a dream then action needs to be taken and fast. Take the steering wheel of life into your hands and turn those thoughts around so they align with your goals and dreams.

Spiritual Quest

TRUST

Faith and trust are constant companions.

I trust that my intuition will guide me wisely.

Spiritual Quest

Wisdom

I awaken to the presence of the wisdom I hold within

Oh wise one that you are ...

Access the expansive wisdom that resides within. Inner wisdom is available whenever one takes the time to access it. Knowledge plus experience equates to wisdom.

Inner-wisdom is one of the most valuable resources. Regularly connecting with the inner wise-one develops an extraordinary source of reference.

Wisdom is derived by branching concepts and perceptions laterally to encompass greater meaning. Enhanced conscious awareness recognizes that every experience is divinely orchestrated and within each experience is a pearl of wisdom. Discovering this is to see life's the complexities simplified.

Everybody has the ability to tap into inner-wisdom. To do so is to move beyond the limits and boundaries of the mind and absorb the concept of inner-wisdom.

Drawing upon inner wisdom provides deeper understanding of life, humanity, the universe and all of existence.

On a personal level accessing inner-wisdom is to explore the depth of the psyche to uncover who you are, what you are here to do and how you can achieve it.

Connecting with the inner wise-one opens the mind to an expanded frame of reference which enhances conscious awareness. Superficiality dissolves when the mind opens and accesses the inner realms of self. Thence comes the reason behind every thought, feeling and deed.

You will not look at yourself or others the same once this level of awareness is reached. Perceptions will continue to expand, complex concepts will be grasped and understanding will be derived. This is the deliverance of wisdom.

Wisdom is simplistic and complex at the same time. Choosing to skim upon the superficial aspects of life is to avoid the merit of wisdom. Delving beneath the surface makes available wisdom beyond what is currently comprehensible.

The mission of the soul is to evolve. It does so through the diverse experiences life provides. Through diversity comes challenge, from challenge arises opportunity which adds new dimension that further inspires the opening mind.

An open mind seeks knowledge which nourishes the seed from which wisdom sprouts.

This is where knowledge and experience merge and potential is fulfilled. As is the nature of evolution the reaching of potential strikes forth a new challenge from which the experience-learn-derive wisdom cycle continues.

To remain in the confines of what is known, retaining unchallenged and unsubstantiated beliefs (which are beliefs that have been imposed not discovered) and holding onto out-dated perspectives is to deprive oneself of personal evolution.

Finding what resonates is based upon individual preference and no one thing provides all the answers. The seekers' path is an expedition of great magnitude during which a multitude of tools, techniques, viewpoints, teachings and lessons are explored and if deemed worthy will be added to the ever expanding life navigation tool kit.

This kit is a valuable resource used every day. If the tool needed is not there the seekers' journey continues to find what is necessary to address the presenting issue.

Utilization of the tools and techniques within assists the natural progression of self-awareness and development. Other resources include books, workshops, courses and assistance from earth guides.

Earth guides can come in different guises including someone who has dedicated their life to helping others, a random person or someone known who delivers an insightful message through their actions or words or it may be an animal that touches your heart or provides and insight or understanding.

Messengers manifest in numerous guises and for numerous reasons. It may be to teach a valuable lesson, pass on a message, to facilitate an awakening or to provide support. They will present at precisely the right time, maybe in unexpected ways, and will stay for as long as needed.

Whatever the reason an earth guide appears they will bring with them something of significance. It is important to keep an open mind, to ponder and seek answers to things not understood and to trust what resonates.

Wisdom is a continuous journey of learning and discovery. An open mind, an open heart, intuitive guidance and sound rationale sees the manifestation of true wisdom. With this arises new awareness of the symbolic nature of life.

Interpreting the meaning of what is represented helps guide decisions, confirm intuitive hunches and derive deeper meaning of experiences.

Embracing this alternative point of view adds dimension and wonder to all that life presents. A butterfly fluttering nearby can be dismissed as just that or the symbolic meaning can be sought. Is it a butterfly or a representation of transformation?

If you open your mind and seek meaning it is likely that an 'aha' moment will emerge and the symbolic meaning of the butterfly relevant to your life will be revealed. With practice the accuracy obtained through symbolic interpretation sparks certain awe.

Reminder: If doubt creeps in before inner-knowing can be fully expressed, remember that by remaining aligned with good intention and right practice trust will develop and doubt will be dispelled.

Uniting with the inner wise-one is to align with the higher-self. This aspect functions through the soul qualities, it stimulates inner knowing. Regular communication with this aspect of self develops deeper connection. You would have felt the presence of this aspect many times, but may not have recognized it as such.

> *Those journeying the seekers' path are gathering and consolidating the knowledge and experience that is translated into wisdom.*

> *A closed mind slows the evolving soul and brings forth the need to revisit the same lessons until properly learned. Falling is inevitable, so is getting up, provided the mind is trained to encourage and support, not berate and denigrate from which it is difficult to emerge unscathed. The best remedy for a fall is to start digging to uncover the gem contained in the guise of adversity. Do not kick yourself while down, for the only one injured shall be you. Embrace yourself, hold tight the frightened aspect which cannot find its way and is unsure of how to proceed forward from a mistake. Assure yourself that mistakes are not life sentences but provide the learning needed to succeed.*

TECHNIQUE
Recognizing Higher-Self communication

Reflect upon a time when you knew something with certainty.

Remember what it was like to feel something resonate with your inner knowing.

This is knowing without doubt.

How did you experience your inner knowing? Was it through a feeling, a vision, a message delivered verbally or a concept? Being aware of how you receive insights and messages helps to acknowledge when you are receiving higher-self insight and guidance. Making choices that align with highest good and purpose can be challenging, however the utilization of inner-wisdom advises a course of action that navigates towards best possible outcome. Trust intuitive guidance here. If something doesn't feel right then chances are it is not the best choice. Tuning in to your higher-self on a regular basis is to capitalize on your inner-wisdom.

SUMMARY

- Moving beyond the limits and boundaries to expand into the vastness of intelligence available to you.
- Balancing the rationale of the mind with inner knowing and insight connects you to your most reliable counsel. That of your inner wise-one.
- Connection with this aspect develops a greater frame of reference from which your interpretations are derived.
- Concepts and perceptions branch laterally to encompass greater meaning.
- Enhanced conscious awareness allows you to acknowledge the divinely orchestrated perplexities of life.

Spiritual Quest

WISDOM

*I tune into my own inner wisdom.
I am fully aligned with my higher purpose.*

When unsure or lost call forth the panel of intuitive advisors. They can be accessed by using your breath and focusing the mind on the quiet place within.

Energy Centres

The 7 Centres of Spiritual Power

Energy centres align with aspects of the mind, the body and the soul. To understand the function of these centres we need to acquaint ourselves with their language. These centres communicate through energy which manifests itself as vibration.

How do we understand the subtle language of centres when we live in a physical world focused on physicality?

Upon pondering the question above I thought about how to best present the energy centres in a way that brings them to life and gives them character. I felt it was about getting a feeling of their resonance, which can really only be sensed and while we can read about them this is interpreted through logic, which somehow robs them of their essence.

Realising guidance was necessary I put on some relaxing music. I settled into a comfortable position, closed my eyes, brought my focus to my breath and asked to be shown how I can best represent these fascinating wheels of light. I received a vision of seven colours vibrating in harmony, I felt immense peace and as I opened my heart to receive further insight each healing center presented an associated musical instrument and that is how I knew that presenting them in this way would 'strike a note' and thus their essence would be captured.

Music enables us to understand the nature of vibration and the affect it has on us emotionally, mentally and physically. For example, when we listen to a musical instrument that is in tune it is vibrating harmoniously it delights our senses. However if we are listening to something that is out of tune the vibration is distorted and there is disharmony and discomfort.

Everything carries a vibration ranging from high to low depending on what it is. This includes thoughts and feelings which vibrate according to what they are. Those that are positive have higher vibration and those that are negative have low vibration and our energy centres respond accordingly. When something resonates or doesn't resonate this is energetic communication. When we get a vibe, we are picking up on energy. As individuals with unique perceptions and experiences we have different vibrations. By tuning into our thoughts and feelings we gain insight into the vibration we are generating and this will be reflected in our mental, emotional and physical wellbeing.

This is my personal interpretation of the musical instruments that resonate with the major energy centres:

Base - Drum
Sacral - Flute
Solar Plexus - Cello
Heart - Harp
Throat - Pan pipes
Third Eye - Wind Chimes
Crown - Harmonious Symphony

Spiritual Quest

BASE

Attunement to inner-self, Safety, Security, Longevity

Tribal beat, Grounded, Rhythmic Breathing

With feet firmly placed on the ground I walk with steadfast certainty along the path that I am destined. I will not surrender to doubt as I know that through all my endeavours I am safe, I am secure and I am supported.

Feel the power building in your base, the area at the base of your spine. Breathe into this area: you are safe and protected. You are building a strong foundation on which to grow.

Base Healing Energy is security - the ability to feel safe - the protector.

When Embraced : Grounded ◇ Assertive ◇ Loyal ◇ Motivated ◇ Determined ◇ Abundant ◇ Physical Vitality

When Denied: Lack of will or desire ◇ Disconnected ◇ Financial hardship ◇ Insecurity

◇ Fear ◇ Depression

When connected to the earth there is a feeling of belonging, security and of being protected. Feeling fearful, insecure and unsure signal balance in this area is needed. Base energy needs to be connected to the earth to ensure one feels secure enough to seek and discover their potential. Base Healing Energy is the protector. It provides a stable foundation needed to maintain the flow of energy to the rest of the Healing Energy system.

Areas: Lower back, legs, feet, hips, adrenals, kidneys

Positive Action: Earth connection. Enjoy an abundance of nature, keep a plant near your workspace or in a prominent place in the home to remind you of your connection to nature and the earth. Listen to a Drum beat while colouring a Mandala, Dancing, Deep rhythmic breaths that flow into this area.

Affirm: I am supported

Base Healing Energy grounding

Imagine gold light in your base area - breathe into this area, which is to feel your breath flowing from your nose through your body going downwards into this area.

Imagine your breath flowing further down through your legs and exiting out through your feet and into Earth.

The Earth responds to your connection and sends brilliant red and gold energy back up through your feet.

This energy flows through your legs and settles in the base areas which is at the base of the spine.

A positive connection between the base Healing Energy and the breath is made.

If there are times when you are feeling ungrounded, unsafe or disconnected do the above breathing exercise to re-establish your connection. In addition, follow on by imagining your breath and the golden light flowing down your legs and into the earth. Upon connecting to the earth the golden light penetrates the earth and divides to become strong roots, like that of a large tree. The deeper your golden light roots go into the earth the more grounded you feel. Keep this going for a minute or so and then bring awareness back into your base area and know that you are safe, grounded and protected.

Allow yourself to be with nature as often as possible. Sit with a tree and feel its essence. Take time to go for a walk, it doesn't have to be for long a few minutes in nature is enough to revitalize. Start the day by going outside and taking some deep breaths of fresh air, draw it into the lungs and feel it revitalizing you.

If feeling ungrounded or unbalanced during the day visualize roots extending from your feet into the earth and take some deep breaths and affirm: *I am grounded*

Spiritual Quest

SACRAL

Passion, Soul-Seeking, Relationships

Inspiration, Creativity, Desire

My creative expression is as unique as I am. As I tune into my inner flame I connect with my unique strengths, talents and gifts. I am never alone for I am one with all.

Sacral is the centre of inspiration and creativity. The relationship we have with self and others relates to this centre.

When Embraced :

Creativity ◇ Inspiration ◇ Ability to relate well with others

When Denied :

Stifled Creativity ◇ Restlessness ◇ Frustration ◇ Difficulty relating to others ◇ Jealousy ◇ Control

When balanced, one hones the ability to be one's self while being securely connected to others. Successful individualization that inspires the desire and will to be creatively expressive. Doubt, disconnection and sabotage indicate balance is needed.

Area: Bladder, Bowel & Lower Intestine, Reproductive organs

Positive Action: Draw, Dance, Colour, Paint, Scrapbook. Write down inspirational ideas or any ideas that pop into your mind. Do a relationship stock-take to ascertain which relationships are healthy, these are the ones which have a give and receive flow and are the ones worthy of your attention. Take, take relationships are draining and unhealthy for all involved.

Light a candle and focus on the flame while thinking about the inner flame igniting in your sacral area. Breathe.......

The Sacral Energy Centre is the centre of creativity.

When creativity is stifled this is the centre that needs attention. Stifled creativity in this area can manifest as physical ailments affecting the female or male reproductive organs. These organs create life, which is the ultimate creation.

Through the creation of life we form a connection to self as another being is produced from us and that being is now connected to us physically, emotionally and energetically. Hence the affect this centre has on our relationship to others and with ourselves.

Ailments of the female and male reproductive organs are related to an imbalance in this area. This is seen when either our masculine or feminine energy is suppressed or denied. A female possesses masculine attributes and a male possesses feminine attributes. Balance is the key to harmony.

Equal opportunity, on a large scale, created the opportunity to free the feminine essence, the outcome of which has seen significant role changes and possibly the emergence of female related health issues as suppressed aspects were released and surfaced for healing.

The same is true for male health related issues as the roles reverse and, lines get blurry. Often the pendulum will swing completely one way and then the other before it balances. Balance proceeds peace. Harmonious alignment of the masculine and feminine energy within is to acknowledge that we are whole due to the combined energy of both. Acknowledging that our existence is a magnificent creation of the feminine and the masculine energy increases the vibration of this centre. Our presence as male or female relates to the lessons we have come here to learn.

There is an extensive list of ways creativity can be expressed. Playing, dancing, singing, drawing, painting, writing, poetry, sculpturing and the list goes on. Within each of us there is a desire to do something of a creative nature, ask yourself what this is. The answer will arrive and when it does act upon it, as doing so will liberate in ways unknown to you now.

Feelings of inspiration arise from this centre, when combined with the third eye intuition creations of a magnificent kind emerge. To create it we must see it, to see it we need to inspire it.

Note: Although portrayed as separate the energy centres are intimately connected. If there is an imbalance in one others will compensate for it.

Nurturing the Sacral Energy Centre

Begin to write in a journal; jot down any creative ideas and inspirations.

Allow your pen to go free.

Enjoy the beauty that surrounds you.

See the vibrancy of life and colour in all things.

Appreciate natural harmony.

Tune into the sound of nature.

Bees buzzing around flower and bushes as they busily collect nectar.

The birds singing and chirping can sound like a symphony.

Watch the ants work as a perfectly orchestrated team with nurse ants carefully carrying the babies from one location to the next.

Wonderful things are occurring all the time, we just need to take a moment to notice.

Appreciating life as a wonder-filled creation resonates with sacral centre energy.

Example of Sacral Energy Centre Awakening Personal Story

In search of my inner creativity and the birth of the images.

I believed I had no ability to create the images for the reflections contained in this book and so I sought the assistance of an artist. As the Universe would have it, this did not eventuate. I was faced with a problem that begged me to seek a solution.

It made my heart ache to think that I may have to abandon something I felt guided to do. This dilemma whirled through my head.

Then it dawned on me that the method I was using to find a solution opposed everything I had written. After some positive self talk, I was able to stop the cyclone of thoughts invading my mind and see myself clear to put on some relaxing music and take a moment of quiet contemplation.

I sat in silence and used my breath to connect with the sacred space within. I was presented with a vision of me purchasing a sketchbook and pencils. I scoffed a bit, but followed my intuitive guidance. It seemed quiet ridiculous when I actually made the purchase, but

I was intrigued where this was going.

When I arrived home I mocked myself for perhaps being deluded by some notion that perhaps it was going to be me that did the artwork, I couldn't help but laugh at myself at this point, but alas I had given my word that I would not doubt my intuition, even though it felt ridiculous at the time. And so I sat with the sketchpad on my knee and pencil in hand waiting for some amazing thing to happen.

Nothing did and after some time I believed my original deluded impression and then seconds before packing up and giving up, I noticed that sitting next to me was a statue of the goddess Quan Yin – I had seen this statue every day, but until that moment had never really seen it.

I started to really see this statue, the contours, the shades. I was captivated by how the light reflected on her and how this added dimension and gave her shapes and contours.

I put my pencil on the paper and starting following the shapes and contours I saw. After a while I had an outline of Quan Yin. Then I followed the light and shade variations as I saw them emerge.

When I had finished I was stunned that I was able to draw what I had. In artists terms it was amateur at best, but to me, the drawer of stick figures, it was remarkable. Something within me transformed, which was the beginning of a love affair with drawing. Every spare moment I had I drew and coloured.

There were many throw-outs along the way but I was actually getting somewhere. My husband was hugely encouraging of what I was doing and one day came home with a set of quality pencils, with a broad spectrum of beautiful colours. It brought tears to my eyes.

Through my love of this new found hobby a new world was born. I was noticing people in different ways, I was really seeing their features; I saw the colours of their eyes, the way the light reflected on their skin, the shape of their lips, it was a wonder-filled experience.

The world is full of the most amazing shapes, colours and reflections when one takes the time to notice. Something within me was awakening and I was loving it.

Sketch by sketch the drawings took shape. They are not the work of an artist, but each has their own story and have been created with love. Through adversity I was faced with a choice to focus on the problem or dig deep and seek a solution.

By choosing to dig deep and answer the challenge, I connected with an aspect of myself that I did not know existed and for that I am forever grateful. The Universe works in mysterious ways, but always in favour of helping us to discover more about who we are and what we are capable of.

Note: The inner critic was very active during this time, which made me feel that I should abandon the idea of doing the drawings. I listened to the criticism but did not take it on. Instead I chose to listen to the inner voice of encouragement.

Eventually the booming voice of the inner critic softened and when it did I embraced the images with new light and hope. They have been pivotal to my growth and contributed to the purpose of my writings.

Just like me, every single one of you is capable of doing whatever it is you desire. Sometimes you just have to dig deeper than you thought possible and when you do you will uncover something you never knew existed and when you do you will be rewarded with one of the most amazing experiences imaginable.

SOLAR PLEXUS

Emotional Awareness, Empowerment, Assertion

Centred, Confident, Content

Through emotional awareness, empathy and deeper understanding of myself and others I am enriched with a sense of inner peace and harmony. I empathise, I understand and I attend to my needs in positive and fulfilling ways.

Solar Plexus Healing Energy is the emotional centre, related to relationship with self and emotional awareness.

When balanced we feel empowered, are emotionally aware and self confident. Disharmony, dis-empowerment and lack of confidence indicates balance in this energy centre is needed. Identity crisis stems from the solar plexus and sacral centre energies. The emergence from such a crisis is empowering and contributes to the growth and discovery of the true self.

Areas: Adrenal glands, pancreas, liver, stomach,

nervous system and bladder, stomach, upper intestines, back

Positive Action: Make regular entries into a personal journal. Take note of the sensations in this area. Breathe deeply into this area often. Be present with emotions when felt to gain insight into what they are trying to communicate. Connect with your inner child.

Attending to your Solar Plexus: Gardening- Tune into your Solar Plexus area and see what image is presented to you. Is the garden flourishing or is there attention needed? Proceed to attend to your inner garden by taking out the weeds and replacing them with flowers of your choice. Feeding your garden with positive thoughts will help keep your garden vibrant and healthy

When Embraced

Self empowered ◇ Positive self esteem ◇ Emotional awareness ◇ Confident ◇ Courage

When Denied

Lack of power ◇ Emotional disturbance ◇ Lack of self-esteem and/or self-worth ◇ Insecurity ◇ Fear of rejection

◇ Dis-empowerment

Through self exploration we gain insight into the power of this centre. Stimulation of this centre arouses the ego. All that has been harboured as beliefs begin to surface. This is the layer effect that protects us from revealing the true essence of our being for fear that to reveal will make us vulnerable to attack. This could not be further from the truth as it is through our essence that we find courage, resilience and the undeniable power of love.

The beginning point is to understand thought awareness as this gives insight into how thoughts stir the emotions and how emotions trigger behaviour. Through thought and emotional awareness we can dig a little deeper and identify how underlying beliefs also provokes thoughts, feelings and emotions.

While one may not be aware of exactly what the belief is there is awareness that something deep within has been triggered. When this happens we may find ourselves at the mercy of an automatic reaction as our defence mechanisms kick in.

Sometimes, depending on what has been triggered, the reaction is likened to "seeing red" (which also relates to the base centre as somewhere here our security or safety feels threatened and shows how interlinked the centres are).

Often the person is almost blinded to what is occurring, feeling more like the witness of their actions or losing themselves altogether. However there is an awareness within that is silently acknowledging the reaction.

Although we may be remotely aware of this, when the ego is in the driver's seat we are merely puppets until we take back our power and the steer things in a positive direction.

This is done by observing thoughts, being curious about our emotional responses and consciously changing our behaviours. Once the emotional needs of the aspects residing in this area are met great freedom is found.

Examples of some of the beliefs that can cause an emotional reaction:

- fear of rejection
- lack of self-worth
- feeling disempowered

Please Note: If trauma or abuse has been experienced it is not advised to do these practices alone and one should seek the assistance of a professional.

Solar Plexus Healing

Loosen clothes around the abdomen area.
Breathe in through your nose, take the breath deep into the abdomen and exhale slowly through your mouth.
See tension dissolve on your out breathe.
Do this a few times or until you are feeling relaxed and attuned to this area.
Connect with your inner emotions.
Ask **"*what am I feeling now?*"**
Be aware of movement, tightness, stirring, or any other feeling in this area.
When experiencing strong emotion tell yourself that you are safe, but if too intense simply open your eyes and reconnect with your physical surroundings.
If you feel you can proceed gently ask yourself if the emotion experienced belongs to you or if it has been transferred.
We can sometime tune into other's emotions and take them on as our own.
We need to own what is ours and release what is not.
Bring your aware into your heart area and imagine it filling with pink light.

When full and radiant imagine this pink energy flowing into your solar plexus area and healing the emotion.

If the emotion does not belong to you see ask that it returns to where it came from for healing.

When freedom if felt from the release of this emotion imagine the area filling up the the loving pink energy again.

When ready bring your focus back to where you are and return to your day feeling lighter and better than before.

Spiritual Quest

HEART

Love, Joy, Compassion, Harmony

Giving & Receiving, Empathy, Elation

Through love I see my true self and the true essence of others. Through love I acknowledge, through love I grow, through love I live a purpose filled life of abundance.

Heart is love, self love, care and compassion, the nurturer that heals all.

Love infuses the mind, the body and the soul with a radiant glow.

Distrust, despair and depression signals that the heart energy centre is in need of attention.

When Embraced: Self Love ◇ Acceptance ◇ Forgiveness ◇ Compassion ◇ Empathy ◇ Love

When Denied: Lack of love ◇ Reduced empathy ◇ Lack of compassion ◇ Love with expectations, conditional love ◇ Distant, unable to connect with self and others ◇ Sadness ◇ Hatred

Areas : Heart, middle back, thymus gland, immune system), blood circulatory system, the endocrine system, lungs

Positive Action: Acknowledge this area every day by breathing into it while focusing on something that brings joy. Really feel and embrace the loving energy that flows from this centre. Cross your hands over your heart area, breathe in and affirm: "Love is my essence" repeat it several times while focusing only on those words.

Persevere through objections or resistance and you will gain access to your inner knowing that will confirm that what you are saying is true. Think kind thoughts about self and others, if you catch yourself being self loathing, judgemental, angry, upset or any of the emotions that interfere with your connection to your heart.
Slather these feelings with compassion and see how the intensity reduces. Visualise pink and green while taking a deep breath and imagining those colours flowing into your heart centre.

Love is the true nature of who we are, it is our essence (it is interesting that we spend a good proportion of our lives trying to return to what is naturally ours). Societal conditioning douses the essence of unconditional love. We begin to reject our true selves, which is love, as conditions are laid upon us.

Certain human emotions are deemed unacceptable and this is what leads to suppression or negative association. Suppressed human traits may lay dormant, but will continue to exist and there will come a time when denying them will no longer align with who you want to be and thus begins the journey towards self realisation, which includes the unravelling of the bound aspects of self. This begins with acceptance of all aspects of self and it is through this acceptance that self love spawns.

Through love we connect with our true self, our loving essence which dissolves judgment and criticism and enables us to embrace, rather than reject, denied and misaligned aspects.

When we see through the eyes of love our perceptions shifts and we see that whatever human emotion is presented is an expression that signals whether one is fulfilled or unfilled. And if the later is true, we can feel compassion. It is through love and compassion that we transform our lives.

Forgive yourself, forgive others and know that what happens is part of the bigger picture of life.

Before acting or reacting remember to ask:
What Would Love Do?
Heart-Centred Healing

Effective for:

- Lingering emotional memories.
- Feelings of sadness.
- Bitterness and Resentment.
- Healing of past or current relationships
- Forgiveness of self and others

Take some deep breaths inhaling in through the nose and exhaling out through the mouth.
Do this until feeling calm and relaxed.
Bring your awareness into your chest.
Just observe this area, without analysing or judging.
Notice any thoughts or feelings that emerge, but do not go into them.
Gently breathe through any discomfort and notice if what happens.
Does the discomfort disappear or is it felt elsewhere?

If it is felt elsewhere imagine this aspect is a frightened little child who needs to be made feel safe and loved.

Now imagine your heart centre is filled with beautiful pink light cross your arms over your chest to embrace yourself and feel the pink energy flow from your heart into your arms and into your palms.

Place your hands on or imagine placing your hands on the discomfort felt.

As the discomfort absorbs the pink light it receives the love needed.

THROAT

Expression, Communication, Consideration

Truth, Justice, Peace

My expressions are pure, clear and concise delivered with compassion and in consideration to myself and others. I express myself in positive ways that deliver messages as intended with ease.

Throat is expression, openness and honesty - communication.

Be honest with yourself about feelings and express with openness and honesty in a way that is received as intended. Getting choked up, feeling one thing and saying another indicates that the throat energy centre needs attention

When Embraced: Ability to express the truth ◇ Open expression of feelings ◇ Redirecting gossip ◇ Honesty

When Denied: Dishonesty ◇ Ambiguity ◇ Misaligning words with emotions ◇ Gossiping ◇

Fear of expressing inner feelings and emotions ◇ Sore throat ◇ Neck pain

Areas: Skull, Eyes, Brain, Nervous system, Nose, Sinuses

Positive Action:
Have meaningful conversations and avoid those which are negative. Speak your truth, with honesty and integrity and what you say it will be received as intended.
Avoid manipulation of yourself and of others. Speak with clarity and if this is difficult ask yourself what clouds your speech. It could be fear of what others will think, which is irrelevant as everyone interprets through their own point of reference which is configured into an opinion, which is purely subjective. Caring too much about what others think is one of greatest immobilizers.
Fear of rejection? Those who reject you are not meant to be in your life, which makes room for those who are.
Uncertainty? if unsure of what to say - try running it through your heart centre, this will enable you to speak with consideration for yourself and for

others.

Think and speak rather than say and think - because once said - it stays.

Sing, even if you think you can't.

Wear the crystal Lapis Lazuli.

Be bold, be brave and speak up. Notice the tone and rate of your voice as your speak, what does it tell you?

Self-expression - where messages are communicated from the heart with clarity, honesty and integrity - is delightful. Open, honest communication between two or more people nourishes the soul and lays the foundation of truth and trust. This type of communication allows all parties to express and be heard. Voicing ourselves in positive ways revitalizes our well-being. A refreshed sense of self emerges where we are connecting with emotions and aligning with our thoughts and feelings knowing that we do not need to betray ourselves by saying one thing and thinking or meaning another. Lighten the load with free expression of self.

Journal your voice by giving an honest account of what is being felt. If what is true for you is suppressed, then the throat energy centre will become blocked. Not allowing others to express their truth carries equally detrimental consequences. Allow others to express without taking what is said personally, if your words and actions have caused discomfort or another has caused discomfort to you communicate this reasonably and with respect for the feelings of the parties involved. Generally it is egos that bump up against each other, if we put down our ego derived defenses we would be viewing through the eyes of understanding and empathy. Which would make it impossible to be anything other than kind to one another?

When expressing an irritation take responsibility for the irritation, what we feel is based upon our own perception. Frame sentences using I rather than you e.g. "I feel annoyed" rather than "you made me feel annoyed" this is for two reasons one is that we need to take responsibility for how we feel without blaming or shaming and secondly when we allow our feelings to be hijacked by others we are give our power away.

A smoother transaction will occur if we allow time for others to process what is being said and gather their thoughts and feelings so they can respond accordingly. This will achieve more beneficial communication outcomes than what is seen when defense mechanisms are raised.

Throat Energy Centre Clearing

Take some deep breaths inhaling in through the nose and exhaling out through the mouth.

Become of the breath as it enters your body and fills your lungs.

Feel your lungs expand to receive the life source energy.

Breath in again and imagine a blue light energy come in on the breath a move into your throat energy centre.

This energy swirls gently in your throat centre and as it does it clears any debris that has collected there.

This debris gets cleansed by the blue energy that you now blow into a balloon.

When finished you tie the balloon. Imagine yourself shaking the balloon and as you do the debris dissolves.

When completely gone the balloon shrinks to nothing and disappears.

Bring your focus back into your throat area, you have a renewed sense of self and are free to express yourself openly and honestly knowing that what you say will be received as intended.

With this you notice that your ability to express your creative self is also enhanced. Creative expression is what motivates and inspires in new and enlightening ways. You find yourself getting curious about new endeavours and adventures.

THIRD EYE

Intuition, Imagination, Intention

Vision, Ideas, Wonder

Through my eyes I see what is here, through my eyes I see what I want to see, but through my third eye I gain visions of what is perfectly aligned with me.

Third eye is intuitive insight, wisdom and clarity.
Having trust and faith in your intuitive ability forms the foundation of self-trust.

When Embraced : Open mindedness ◇ Imaginative exploration ◇ Clarity ◇ Visual Imaging ◇ Intuitive Insight

When Denied: Closed mindedness ◇ Lack of clarity ◇ Lack of vision ◇ Overly logical ◇ Headaches ◇ Hazy Vision

Areas: Skull, Eyes, Brain, Nervous system, Nose,

Sinuses.

Positive Action: Get daily doses of daylight. Feel the sun revitalizing the area between your eyes. Take leave from thought for a couple of minutes a day, which is to clear the mind and let it go blank, if thoughts intrude just observe them without hooking into them. Release tension in this area by consciously relaxing the forehead, the temples, the eyes, the cheeks and mouth, the chin, then bring your focus back to your forehead just observe. Listen to music that is calming. Hang a set of wind chimes and tune into them when they are chiming.

Float the aromas of Frankincense and Sandalwood essential oils throughout your home. Dab Sandalwood essential oil on the wrists and enjoy the aroma as it wafts around you.

Upon entering this earth you were granted a special gift. That of your intuition. The third eye provides insight. It is linked with our imagination, which is used extensively by most children in their play and creative imaginary. Children are extremely adept to using this powerful tool. However often the child's use of their imagination is considered just that 'child's play'.

The powerhouse of our creation is belittled and may even be thought of as silly. This false perception suppresses the magnificence of the imagination, it become the sleeping prophet waiting to be awakened. Visions, messages, feelings, and inner knowing is your intuition at work, it shows you possible scenarios, visions and gives profound insight. The more often we exercise our intuitive ability the more aware we become of its immense power and capacity to achieve as we imagine.

Imagination versus Intuition

How do we know if we are imagining or receiving intuitive insight. Intuition has a feeling of inner knowing attached to it, it resonates. Imagination is contrived and lacks inner knowing. Intuition is passive-it comes to you. Imagination is created by you. Imagination can be used to create the images of our desires. It all begins as an idea and when an idea is infused with positivity it evolves to become a tangible thing. We must also know when to let go and allow our desires to find the energy needed to bring back to us what we have asked for. If we hold on and become attached we stifle the process and keep ourselves in a state of wanting rather than being open to receive. Being open to receive and trusting that we will be delivered what is aligned with our highest good opens enhances the connection with our intuition.

The following technique will help strengthen the connection with your intuitive insight and inner wisdom.

Third Eye Technique

Remove the blindfold so you may see.

Settle yourself a comfortable position.
Take a few deep breaths until you are feeling comfortable and relaxed.
Bring your focus to the area between your eyes.
Tune into the feeling in this area.
Pretend there is a blindfold over this area. Imagine reaching up and untying the blind fold.
As the blindfold falls you can see a radiant eye the colour of indigo (deep purple) peering out.
This is your third eye, the seat of your intuition.
Breathe deeply and as you do imagine the breath

going into this area filling it with large doses of oxygen which refreshes and revitalises it with new vigour and strength.

Making this connection will enable you to recognise intuitive insight and to utilise the tools of your imagination more effectively.

Create and manifest as you imagine.

As you imagine, it shall be.

CROWN

Spiritual Awakening, Connection, Freedom

Expansion, Elevation, Ecstasy, Enlightenment

As my awareness grows I realise that I am on my path and will follow it with faith that everything I have done and everything I do is aligned with what is needed to fulfil the contract I have with my soul. I see, I hear, I feel, I know.

The "crown" energy centre is spirituality, connection, wisdom and awareness.

When Embraced: Awakened spirituality ◇ Feelings of connectedness ◇ Realizations ◇ Deeper understanding and awareness ◇ Humanitarianism

When Denied: Feelings of isolation ◇ Disconnection ◇ Loneliness ◇ Lack of awareness ◇ Reduced zest for life

Areas: Nervous system, brain, top section of the head.

Positive Action: Meditation-where there is point of focus or a mantra to tune into, this only needs to be for a short period of time, which can be built upon. Bringing the golden ray through the crown ccentre and uniting it with the all the energy centres and then allowing it to infuse through into the physical body. Be consciously aware, which is to be present.

Gain deeper understanding and insight by looking seeking symbolic meaning to all that is presented in the physical world. Open your mind and your heart and see your perception shift in profound ways.

Connecting with the energy of the crown centre is to align with ones spiritual wisdom, which makes one aware that spirituality is not a set of beliefs, but the way one lives their life. Living with a heart filled with love and an open mind is to live spiritually.

One who treats themselves and others with kindness and compassion is living a spiritual life. What matters is how we choose to live our lives, be it through our spiritual or ego selves. It is also important to remember that past ways of being are in the past what matters is our present choices.

Identifying with the Ego : The ego will judge. The ego will cheat. The ego will emote negativity. It is destructive, it disempowers and harnesses greed. It will try to control. It does all of this, not out of malice, but because it has created a false identity that it believes is protecting us from perceived harm.

When perceived in this way we can better see how the go operates and see that ego is nothing more than aspects of self with unfulfilled needs and that those aspects have strengthened within the human psyche because they remain in the shadow when really what is needed is the light of love to shine through. This is to align with our true self and in doing so the false identify, self-image (which is just an image) become less pronounced.

Aligning with Spirit : Our spirit will honour, will empathize and hold the light so we may see which aspects of self are attached to ego-perspectives. Our spirit knows the truth of who we are. Spirit is like a ray of sunshine that penetrates all else and lights us up with its brilliance. Inspiration, intuition, positive intention and purpose all arise from our spiritual selves. Connecting with the essence of our spirit dissolves the illusion so we may see everything in its true light. This knowledge empowers us to transcend the clutches of the ego and start living a soul-filled life.

When we see the ego for what it is and attune to the virtues of spirit we open to the source energy, our life essence. This awakening brings profound shifts. We begin to see that we are more than physical bodies. We are energetic beings.

Connecting to our energetic selves helps to transcend our earth bound bodies and see from higher perspective. From this perspective we gain an overview of life and what it entails. We can become so caught in our physical lives that we are blind to the world of energy. We need only take the time to deepen our vision to discover the symbolic meaning of all we see. The universe is communicating with us on all levels at every given moment. A flower, an animal, a sign, a feather, a tree - all have symbolic association. There are messages to guide us, to give us hope, to inspire. Don't just look, Observe and See!! Every day will instil magic into your life. Believing is seeing and when we see we cannot deny. If we are consumed by the details of our lives, we miss seeing the higher purpose life provides. We have been given a grand opportunity to discover our magnificence. This can infuse us with power enough to transcend our burdens and turn them into blessings. Remember we see the flaws when seeing through physical eyes, when we look through the eyes of our spirit the picture transforms. Ask yourself: Which perspective do you choose to align with.

Crown Centre Awakening

Focus on your breath.
Take a couple of deep breaths in through your nose, draw it down into your belly and then exhale out through your mouth.
When you exhale ... imagine tension releasing from your body.
When you are feeling relaxed ... imagine yourself being surrounded by beautiful white light energy. This energy has a feeling of safety, you feel protected and secure in your white-light cocoon. Imagine the top of your head opening and a golden light flowing down from above.

This light is your soul-source energy.

It flows down and cascades through your entire body, filling you with love and light. Imagine it going to any area where you feel tension ... and dissolving it.

In place of the tension is a radiant golden glow. You are healing at cell level.

When you have done this throughout your body, imagine the golden light withdrawing from your body - and as it leaves the top of your head, your crown area closes.

The golden energy sits above your crown centre, ready to infuse you with its brilliance whenever you need it.

Take some deep breaths to finish off and return your focus to where you are so you can continue on with your day or evening ... feeling comfortable, relaxed and rejuvenated.

SPIRITUAL FIRST AID

GROUNDING TECHNIQUE

Grounding is vital. As we enhance our conscious awareness it is imperative to remain grounded and connected to Earth and our physicality. This enables us to explore outside of our limitations, while remaining firmly planted on the ground.

Here is a grounding technique to use as part of a daily routine or if feeling scattered, lightheaded, dizzy, flighty, fidgety or a general feeling of not being centered.

Note: If any of these symptoms persist please seek medical advice.

Before starting the grounding exercise try to stand on the Earth near a tree or look out at nature. If not just close your eyes and conjure up a vision of the earth and a tree in your mind.

Take a deep breath in through the nose and then exhale out through the mouth.

Take another deep breath in through the nose and then exhale out through the mouth.

Take another deep breath in through the nose and then exhale out through the mouth this time you breath in beautiful golden light, this golden light moves slowly through your body bathing every cell with its healing energy.

You feel the golden light move down into your legs, your legs feel heavier as the golden light extends out of the bottom of your feet and connects you with the rich, warm, Earth.

You continue to sink your golden light energy into the earth. And like tree roots it goes deeper and deeper connecting you with Mother Earth.

You feel safe, secure and grounded.

You stand connected to Earth until you feel you are completely grounded.

When you are ready you may open your eyes and when you do you know that you are grounded and whenever you feel like you need grounding you only need look at a tree and see its trunk and know that the tree, like you is safely secured to the ground by strong, sturdy roots.

Wear earth tone colours such as brown, yellow, red and deep orange in dark hues for if additional grounding needed.

BREATHING TECHNIQUE

Using the correct breathing technique is important as the breath provides every cell with life sustaining oxygen. Our nose works like a filter that cleanses the air and delivers it in perfect measurement to the lungs. When we breathe through our nose our body uses the diaphragm and belly which draw the breath deep into the lungs. Whereas breathing through the mouth does not provide a filter for the air, does not use the same muscle groups as when air is breathed through the nose which means that we shallow breathe.

Breathe in through your nose as you feel the stomach expand you can feel beautiful fresh, clean air filling your lung.
Now exhale out through your mouth and when you do you feel all the stale air leave you body taking with it all tension.

Breathe in through your nose as you feel the stomach expand you can feel beautiful fresh, clean air filling your lung.
Now exhale out through your mouth and when you do you feel all the stale air leave you body taking with it all tension.

You take another breath this time you breathe in beautiful white light this white light flows down through your body and down through your feet connecting you with the Earth. You white light roots go all the way down. You are feeling very grounded, safe and protected now.

You keep your focus on your feet. Breathe deeply in through your nose, you can feel the breath go right down into your feet. You feel your feet tingle as they become invigorated with the fresh, clean oxygen. When you exhale out through your mouth your feet relax as they release any tension they are holding.

You now bring your focus to your lower leg. You breathe deeply in through your nose, the air flows into your legs they tingle as they fill with the fresh, clean oxygen. As you exhale out through your mouth they relax and release pent up tension.

Your focus now comes into your thighs. Breathe deeply in through your nose, your thighs receive the clean, fresh air. You can feel the oxygen improve the circulation in this area. When you exhale out through your mouth your thighs feel relaxed, yet firm and sturdy.

Your focus moves into your pelvic region. You take a deep breath into your nose the air flows into your pelvic area and provides it renewed vigor. When you exhale out through your mouth you know that your pelvic area gives strong support to your torso the home of your internal organs.

Focusing now on your lower abdomen. Breathe in through your nose and down into the lower abdomen as this area expands you feel it fill with calming, soothing energy. As you exhale you feel any tension in this area leave your body out through the mouth.

Breathing now in through your nose and down into your lungs, you can feel your lungs filling with life sustaining energy. The clean, fresh air fills the entire lung. Exhaling now out through your mouth and as you do you release all tension and any built up carbon dioxide. You can breathe freely and know that your lungs will maintain a pure flow of life sustaining oxygen to every cell in your body.

Taking your awareness into your chest now. Take a deep breath in through the nose and as you feel your chest expand you feel it fill up with air that brings warmth and comfort to this area. When you exhale out of through your mouth your chest falls gently into a comfortable position. You can feel your shoulders also drop and rest free of tension.

Your focus now fixes on your face and head. You take a deep breath in through your nose, the air moves into your face and head and nourishes it with clean, fresh air. When you exhale out through your mouth you feel the right and left hemispheres of your brain come into balance.

Your awareness moves into the back of your neck and down into your spine. You take a deep breath in through nose and as you do you can feel the air glide down your neck and spine it reaches out and covers your entire back. As you exhale out through your mouth you feel the muscles in your neck and back relax and you say good-bye to any pent up tension.

You are aware of the importance of your breath and breathing patterns and remember to use your breath when feeling stressed, tired, overwhelmed, frustrated or at any time when you want to feel the benefits of life sustaining oxygen flow through your body.

TOOLS FOR YOUR JOURNEY

CREATE

To have it, is to create it. There is profound potential locked in every idea. One only needs to imagine its creation and then summon the courage to bring this image to life. You are stepping onto the path of infinite potential. Do not deviate from this path. Snatch up inspiration as it arises. Add determination to your recipe and aim for whatever it is you desire. Trust your intuition, it is your faithful guide. Have confidence that you will succeed. Be clear on what it is you want, see it, feel it. Listen with a quiet mind as this is where our creative inspirations come from. Be guided by the flow that is moving you in the direction of your dreams.

REFLECT

Reflecting is to capture an overview of events current or past or a combination of both. The past affects the present which, if allowed, will affect the future. Until awareness is applied to the present then mistakes of the past will repeat. Reflection offers the opportunity to make the connection of what is, what has been and what will be. Contemplation comes into the picture when you allow yourself to deeper levels of your psyche and find more complex answers.

EXPRESS

Our creative expression is forever in motion. The presentation of self is an expression of our inner being. The way in which we talk, walk, dress are all a reflections of our internal world. We express our thoughts and feelings through the words we speak and the way we act or react. Evaluating your thoughts, feelings and beliefs begins the process of peeling away the layers, the masks that have allowed you to hide behind a facade of false truth. Have the courage to acknowledge your vulnerabilities, and what role they have played. Accept that they no longer serve the truth of who you are and let them go. You are transitioning and transforming. You are awaking to the true expression of who you are.

DISCOVER

Life is the journey of discovery, the more we experience the more we learn and develop. Each stage of our development brings with it new realisations about ourselves. Our concepts and perceptions expand as our knowing and awareness evolves. This is a lifelong process; we are always learning and expanding. Clarity in one area may bring forth new challenges for us to explore, but with each new realisation we uncover and reveal different dimensions of our own existence and we re-create and replace old with new. As we resolve and renew we continue to discover.

PATHWAYS

Each step we take upon our life path gives us the opportunity to be the best we can be. While upon the path of life one must be cognizant of all the components that make us whole: that is matters of the Mind, Body and the Soul. Life, however is not linear in its process it is more likened to a spiral of cycles. As we enter each new cycle we take with us the wisdom received from the past experience. If there is imbalance then the natural flow of the cycle is disturbed and we receive the call to seek our balance. One must refocus and ascertain what is being neglected: be it the Mind, the Body or the Spirit. Making the necessary adjustments may see a period of transition. However harmonisation of one with the other is transformational.

EVOLVE

At soul level we are all one, there is no separation. As a collective the concept of individual souls is void as there is no separation. Your soul/My soul is purely an ego based perspective that belongs to this dimension, whereupon the soul has fragmented and imagining a reality based upon the learning it seeks. When the soul fragments it is offered choices to assist its journey back home. This is to awaken and remember the essence of its being and that it belongs within the collective consciousness. Feelings of disconnectedness and loneliness are not because we are disconnected and alone, but rather that we have forgotten who we are. We are never alone, there is guidance every step of the way. The complication is that we have denied our spiritual-selves and identified with the ego. This is a case of stolen identity, whereby we believe what is false to be real and what is real to be imagined. To evolve we must reverse this perception and embrace the essence of the soul.

MANIFEST

Drive your imagination positively so you may see the manifestation of your desires. Be strong in your belief and determined that you will create. Your reality can be moulded to any design you want. The key ingredients of positive manifestation are based in your intention. Belief minus doubt will see you reap the rewards. Always remember to give thanks for what you have; gratitude is a powerful ingredient of abundance.

PURPOSE

Purpose enriches your life. Having purpose is to be doing something that you find meaningful and fulfilling. Finding purpose may need some the assessment of where you currently find yourself. Evaluation of where you have been and where you are gives insight into why you are where you are right now. Explore your motivations and opportunities, past and present. What are your strengths? If you could change one thing in the immediate world around you what would it be? What would you do differently if you could? Tracing the course of your life leads to answers. By evaluating your experiences and learning you will see that nothing has been in vain. Ask yourself "Do you have an inner yearning? Do you desire to take a another direction? Or are you content to continue along the path you are currently travelling?

Letter of Commitment to Self

Print this letter out as a declaration of your commitment to getting in touch with your inner self.

Letter of Commitment

I , ………………………………………… solemnly declare to drive my destiny in the direction of my dreams.

I take the steps necessary to ensure I receive what it is I desire.

I open my mind and my heart to receive the insights and understanding that guide me to where I need to go.

Being in the flow of life enables me to be in the right place at the right time that aligns with my purpose.

I have gratitude for what is in my life currently as this has contributed to my learning.

It is my intention to let go of what is no longer needed so I may receive what I need to reach my potential.

I prioritise to ensure I dedicate time to the tools and techniques available so I may receive the benefits they offer.

Place this letter in a place you can see it every day or put it in your journal and read every day.

About

As a seeker of truth, an unquenchable thirst for knowledge and my belief that there is so much more to life and the world than meets the eye has put me on a path of relentless exploration and discovery.

The quest to satisfy the deep yearning to discover and expand my understanding of who we are, why we are here and how we can find our purpose has resulted in extensive study across many areas such as Naturopathy, Counselling, Psychology, Reiki and many other modalities.

I have made many discoveries throughout my journey and stand in awe of what one can manifest within this life. There is no end to the possibilities.

There have also been many profound realizations. One such realization is that whilst there is much knowledge to be gained from external sources, *we already hold amazing natural wisdom within ourselves.* By tapping into this rich resource we can discover beyond what we think – and delve into what we know. It is through this connection with our inner-selves that we are able to find the key to living an enriched and enlightened life.

Upon reflection of this I put pen to paper. As I wrote, the pages began to spring to life bringing forth the creation of Spiritual Quest. Writing Spiritual Quest has assisted me in accessing my own inner source of inspiration and wisdom which has allowed me to discover much about the diverse beings that we are. This awareness has helped me achieve a deep level of satisfaction, which is the foundation upon which one builds their own personal state of enlightenment. It is my wish to share these discoveries with you.

May we be guided by the love in our hearts and the light of our soul, Sandy.

GLOSSARY

Affirmation- Is a positive expression which assists the mind to be positively focused. Affirmations can be used to exchange unhelpful, outdated thought patterns for ones that inspire and assist the co-creation of possibilities that were previously thought unobtainable.

Aspect-We are all composed of aspects that have been created during different stages of development based upon the interpretation of our experiences. These aspects contribute to our perceptions, thoughts, feelings and beliefs.

Ego-is composed of the shadow aspects of the inner self. Basically these aspects have disassociated from the higher self and although we are not consciously aware of these aspects, they have significant impact on our lives. The interesting thing is that although the impression of the ego is negative, as with everything, it also serves in positive ways. One of which is that when we become aware that we are operating through ego aspects, or aligning with ego-perspectives, then we receive some of our most profound learning. By becoming aware of ego-perspectives we are empowered to use the tools and techniques that will assist that aspect. Ego aspects present in multiple guises and can be difficult to detect as they are accepted as part of our identity. This is an illusion because the truth is that everything that opposes love, joy and peace is derived from ego. Hence the true essence of our nature is also love, joy and peace and anything else is merely part of a falsely constructed identity.

Energy Centres-are portals that provide access to the energetic realm of our being. It is here where mind-body-soul merge and enable us to see how they interlink. It is here that one becomes all and where all divides and becomes one. It is here that we find the answers to many of our questions such as reasons for feeling as we do, the reason for physical ailments and why we think in certain ways – even when misaligned with what we want for ourselves. It is through these portals that we exchange what we think for what we know. This is to gain access to our inner wisdom, gain meaning of our experiences, where we can attune to the collective consciousness and access divine guidance. It is all within you. You only need to tune in, listen and observe. You will be delighted and amazed at what will be revealed. Entering the energetic realm of our existence is to embark on an awe-inspiring journey.

Failure- Failure is a constructed concept that has us cowering in the corner while our dreams walk out the door. If failure is viewed as failure it damages our self-esteem and confidence. However, if failure is viewed as feedback it provides valuable information and could be the stepping stone to success. The measure of success is purely subjective and quantifiable only by the person experiencing it.

***Grounding*-**Being grounded is to be firmly planted in the body. This increases awareness as there is something to anchor ourselves to, which provides the balance needed to gain insight and clarity. If we are ungrounded we are affected by energies that can make us feel like windflowers dancing in the air. Ideas remain just that. Grounding helps us to focus and get the job done.

***Guided Journey*-**Gallop on a black stallion across the sands of the Arabian Desert. Drink from the Fountain of rejuvenation and longevity. Meet your Guardian Angel. Tap into your creative centre and recognise the immense potential available to you. Open a treasure chest filled with abundance. This is the gateway to your intuitive insights and the awakening of a profound aspect of self. Close your eyes, settle into a comfortable position, take a deep breath in through your nose and gently exhale out through your mouth. You are relaxed, calm and ready to enter your guided journey where you will go on an adventure to the inner realms of self. It is here that you will uncover the essence of your being.

***Inner Child*-**This is the Child aspect of our inner self. This aspects holds memories, has its own thoughts, feelings and perspectives on life. It is immature and wise at the same time. It is closely connected to the true essence of who we are, which is why is can be somewhat disillusioned by the loss of innocence it underwent as a child. This being said, it is through our inner child that we return to our innocence and in doing so release ourselves from the clutches of the ego and rekindle our connection to source. It is worthwhile taking the time to establish a positive relationship with the inner child as anything other than this may see us at the mercy of child-like behaviour. Eg. tantrums, sulking, withdrawal, irrational fears.

Inner Self / *Self*-is all the aspects that we identify with being who we are. The inner self is composed of aspects that are aware and aligned with our purpose and those that exist in the shadow. These are unaware aspects and can be defined as our limitations. However, they are only limitations while in the shadow, when we bring them to the light they provide significant insight and learning.

Mantra-Thoughts are mantras – they can be constructed positively or negatively. Constructing positive mantras is a process that requires conscious awareness.

Mistakes-are learning tools and can be what helps guide us onto the path we are here to walk. Repeated mistakes signal that a certain lesson is yet to be learnt. To understand what the lesson is look at what the mistake relates to e.g. relationship, finances, career, lifestyle choices and ask what it is you need to see. Wait, listen and learn.

Pledge-Powerful expression of a commitment to self. Regular use of a pledge, especially when paired with an image and feeling of positivity, is a potent motivator that speaks directly to the subconscious.

Soul Perspective-Our perspectives form the lens in which we view ourselves, others and the world. Our lens determines whether we view life through the eyes of the ego or the eyes of the soul. The good news is the lens we see through can be altered. If we are discontented with the reality we see we can shift focus and create a new reality for ourselves. When our focus shifts our physical reality will also shift to align with the visions emerging from our new perspectives. Clues we are aligning with ego-perspectives can be found in feeling stuck, uninspired, unfocused, unbalanced, discontented, restless, doubtful, disillusioned. Basically it is a feeling of being misaligned with what you know is inherently yours. It may be difficult to explain this feeling, but you know that it is there. The solution is one that is profoundly simple and yet challenging at the same time. It is the exchange of ego-based perspectives for spiritually aligned ones, which is to become soul-driven. Being soul focused is to align with the principles of love, joy, peace and acceptance. These qualities lie at the core of our being and when we align with them we connect with who we really are. The heart will sing and as it does one by one our ego-perspectives transform and we see ourselves becoming more loving, joyful, calm and accepting individuals. Where is the challenge in this you may ask? The challenge is in the emergence of the aspects attached to ego-perspectives; this is where we need to be soul-focused so we can attend to the needs of what emerges. This is how to hold our own hand and guide ourselves gently towards the light. Having soul-based perspectives does not mean that we will be forever positive and our experiences will always be enlightening, but our perception of life in general will be.

Spirituality-is not a belief system, it is the principles and practices one chooses to align themselves with. It is not a belief in karma, god and angels that makes a person spiritual – it is the practice of kindness, compassion and acceptance of others that does. We are all on a Spiritual Quest that is the purpose of life; if you are here right now you are part of spirit. We are all spirit, hence we are all on a Spiritual Quest, that is the purpose of LIFE.

- **L**essons
- **I**ntended
- **F**or
- **E**volution

Third Eye-is our intuitive centre and provides deep insight. When balances we are focused and have clear thought and clarity of mind. Whereas, an imbalance can cause thoughts to be scattered, intuition to be jaded and vision to be hazy. The third eye provides the screen upon which we view our internal visual images. The picture that is conjured up in your mind, when asked to imagine a red rose, is seen upon your third eye screen.

If we harness the essence of our soul we would see that our core virtues are love, trust, gratitude, integrity and respect. By sharing these core virtues with each other humanity would unite and peace would be ours.

With a heart full of gratitude and an abundance of love and blessings for your journey and may the divine be your guide and inner-peace be your rock. Sandy Lee.

www.souldrivenlife.net

www.ingramcontent.com/pod-product-compliance
Lightning Source LLC
Chambersburg PA
CBHW071148230426
43668CB00009B/874